An Easy Guide
to Korean History

Published on November 3, 2009

Publisher Lee Ki-taek

Published by Association for Overseas Korean Education Development

   604-3 Daewoo Bldg, Sejongno, 167 Naesu-dong, Jongno-gu, Seoul

   TEL 82-2-782-5121-2   FAX 82-2-782-5123

   www.aoked.or.kr

Written by Shin Hyong Sik

Printed by GWANGJANG Printing Co.

ISBN 978-89-962593-0-5 (Set)

발행일	2009년 11월 3일
발행인	이기택
발행처	사단법인 해외한민족교육진흥회
	서울시 종로구 내수동 167 세종로 대우빌딩 604-3
	TEL 02-782-5121-2 FAX 02-782-5123
	www.aoked.or.kr
지은이	신형식
인쇄처	광장인쇄(주) TEL 02-2277-3993

ISBN 978-89-962593-0-5 (세트)

An Easy Guide
to Korean History

•

알기쉬운 한국사

Shin Hyong Sik | 신형식 지음

사단법인 해외한민족교육진흥회

The Association for Overseas Korean Education Development (KED) is proud to present *An Easy Guide to Korean History*, published in English, Japanese and Russian, as a part of 'Korean National Heritage Awareness Movement for Foreign-living Countrymen' , in celebrating the 60th anniversary of the national foundation day of the Republic of Korea.

Chairman Lee Ki-taek
이사장 이 기 택

We hope to give an opportunity for foreign-born, non-Korean speaking fellow countrymen to learn the abstract of Korean history. Thus, we have asked Professor Shin Hyong Sik to write this book, texts written both in Korean and in local languages, currently published in English, Japanese and Russian.

In the future, KED will continuously publish *An Easy Guide to Korean History* in more languages such as German, French and Spanish so that Koreans around the globe can easily access the learning material of the Korean history.

The Korean people have succeeded to build a great nation, overcoming a number of challenges and adversities in recent history: countless cases of foreign occupation including recent Japanese occupation of Korean peninsula, a division of our country followed by the tragic Korean War, unimaginable pain and suffering that the Korean people faced in forming an industrialized country and in achieving democracy. In spite of such challenges, Korea is now among the leading countries of the world. It may not be an overstatement to say that such a dramatic achievement is truly a miracle in the world history that cannot happen elsewhere.

The Korean People have continuously emigrated throughout the world in the course of modernization. Today, there are approximately seven million Koreans abroad. Though the history of Korean migration to other part of the world has started with forceful requisitions during Japanese occupation and the exile of Koreans to central Asia by Soviets, Koreans are recognized as one of the most successful immigrants throughout the world. The seven million Korean living abroad are now the spiritual foundation and a great representation of the people of the Republic of Korea who will lead the global era.

President **Park Kye-dong**

회 장 **박 계 동**

본 (사)해외한민족교육진흥회가 대한민국 건국 60주년 기념 '해외한민족 우리역사 알리기 운동'의 일환으로 오랜 시간 정성을 들여 준비해온 〈알기 쉬운 한국사〉 영어판, 일본어판, 러시아어판이 드디어 동시 출간되었다.

우리글을 읽지 못하는 상당수의 해외한민족 동포들에게 최소한 우리역사의 개요나마 알게 해주자는 뜻에서, 저자인 신형식 교수에게 〈알기 쉬운 한국사〉의 집필을 의뢰한 뒤 한국어와 현지어를 병기하여 이번에 영어판, 일본어판, 러시아어판을 출간한 것이다.

앞으로 본 (사)해외한민족교육진흥회는 〈알기 쉬운 한국사〉의 독일어판, 불어판, 스페인어판 등을 계속 출간함으로써 전 세계 각지에 살고 있는 해외한민족 동포들이 모두 우리역사를 쉽게 접할 수 있도록 노력할 것이다.

우리민족은 근현대사의 온갖 고난과 역경을 극복하고 오늘날의 자랑스러운 대한민국을 이루어내었다. 일제 감점을 비롯한 수많은 외세의 침탈, 남북 분단과 민족상잔의 비극, 산업화와 민주화 과정에서 치른 엄청난 고통 등을 이겨내고 당당하게 선진국 대열에 들어섰다. 우리민족이 아니면 결코 이뤄낼 수 없는 세계사적 기적이라 해도 지나치지 않을 것이다.

그리고 이러한 근현대사의 과정에서 우리 한민족의 해외 이주는 끊임없이 이뤄져 오늘날 '해외한민족 700만 시대'를 맞이하고 있다. 고려인의 중앙아시아 강제이주, 일제의 야만적 징용 등 우리 한민족의 해외이주사는 영원히 지워질 수 없는 피와 눈물로 시작되었지만, 오늘날 우리 해외한민족은 전 세계 방방곡곡에서 가장 성공적인 해외진출 사례로 기록되고 있다. 이제 700만의 우리 해외한민족은 글로벌시대를 이끌어갈 대한민국의 정신적 토대이자 위대한 표상인 것이다.

우리 해외한민족은 한민족 특유의 끈기와 지혜로 현지화에 성공하여 오늘날 대체로 현지 주류사회에 편입되고 있다. 그러나 이러한 과정에서 현재 해외한민족의 젊은 세대들이 상당수 우리말, 우리글, 우리문화, 우리역사를 접하지 못해 민족정체

Our fellow countrymen around the world have successfully become a part of mainstream in countries where they live, using our unique tenacity and wisdom. Through the course of this assimilation, however, today's younger generation Koreans of the world tend to forget their national heritage for lack of opportunity to learn our language, literature, culture and history. It is indeed a regretful phenomenon.

Since its establishment, KED have continuously offered programs that are designed for the seven million Koreans of the world in order to promote national heritage awareness and pride. In particular, there are two main programs that KED focuses on, "Overseas Korean ethnic education promotion Award" that provide support and encouragement to those who teach Korean culture all over the world, and "Korean National Heritage Awareness Movement for Foreign-living Countrymen" which is intended to help Koreans of the world to learn our history and philosophy.

We sincerely hope that this publication of *An Easy Guide to Korean History* in English, Japanese and Russian editions help our fellow Koreans of the world to build a firm ground of their ethnic heritage and to discover the pride of our people. Furthermore, we wish to provide an opportunity to build a strong allegiance to their motherland so that we, together as one, may add new chapters to the great history of the Korean people.

We would like to express our sincere gratitude to Kookmin Bank for their selfless support and to Dr. Shin Hyong Sik who wholeheartedly undertook the task of authoring this book.

November 2009

Association for Overseas Korean Education Development

Chairman **Lee Ki-taek**

President **Park Kye-dong**

성을 점차 잃어 가고 있어 참으로 안타까운 일이 아닐 수 없다.

　이런 점에서 우리 (사)해외한민족교육진흥회는 창립 이래 우리 700만 해외한민족에게 민족정체성과 자긍심을 불어넣기 위한 사업들을 시행해 왔다. 특히 2대 중점 사업으로 전 세계 민족교사들의 사기를 북돋우고 지원하기 위한 '해외한민족교육진흥상 시상'과 해외한민족에게 우리역사의 개요와 기본정신을 알려 주기 위한 '해외한민족 우리역사 알리기 운동'을 꾸준하게 시행해 왔다.

　이번 〈알기 쉬운 한국사〉의 영어판, 일본어판, 러시아어판의 출간을 통해 우리 해외한민족이 자랑스러운 민족으로서의 민족정체성을 확립하고 나아가 모국과 하나가 되어 한민족의 위대한 역사를 함께 일궈나가는 계기가 되길 바라는 마음 간절하다.

　끝으로 이번 〈알기 쉬운 한국사〉 외국어판 시리즈 발간을 전적으로 후원해 주신 국민은행과 기꺼이 집필해 주신 신형식 박사께 깊이 감사드린다.

2009년 11월

(사)해외한민족교육진흥회　이사장 이 기 택
　　　　　　　　　　　　　　회 장 박 계 동

Korea is a major country in East Asia with a long history and time-honored traditions. After going through the Paleolithic Age, which began 700,000 years ago, the Neolithic Age, and the Bronze Age, the Korean people founded a nation on the Korean Peninsula and in Manchuria (northeast China), and their unique culture has been flourishing flourished.

Since Dangun Joseon (the first Korean state founded by Dangun), the Korean people has preserved their own language and custom and proudly maintained their nation in Manchuria and the Korean Peninsula while fighting off several invasions from China. Korea simultaneously embraced and further refined Chinese culture and passed it on to Japan. It fostered a splendid Buddhist culture, represented by Bulguksa Temple and Seokguram Grotto, and developed the world's first printing woodblocks (the Tripitaka Koreana) and moveable metal type (Jikjisimgyeong) as well as a unique writing system (hangeul), maintaining the people's strong pride in their culture.

Korea failed to effectively respond to incursions by foreign powers in the late 19th century and suffered occupation by the Japanese from 1910 to 1945. The Korean people finally regained independence after ceaseless struggle against Japan. Korea was liberated in 1945 but it was immediately divided into South Korea and North Korea. A path of confrontation and conflicts began as South Korea adopted an open, free democratic society (capitalism), while North Korea established a closed communist society (socialism). Nonetheless, the pioneering spirit and diligence of the Korean people about seven million Korean abroad, who underwent numerous hardships, are well reflected in the lives of self-supporting overseas Koreans. In particular, Koreans who migrated to Manchuria to evade oppression by Japan led the resistance against Japan, while those dragged to Central Asia by Stalin overcame a challenging environment and are maintaining the spirit of the Korean people with dignity.

In the recent past, the Koreans underwent the painful experiences of the Japanese occupation and national division into south and north after liberation, but the Republic of Korea weathered these challenges and developed into a leading country both culturally and economically. Sadly, however, many overseas Koreans are not aware of the proud history of their motherland.

This book was written for overseas Koreans who do not know the history of Korea and foreigners who have a skewed view of Korean history. Korea's history is not presented by dynastic period but according to a high-level framework of ancient, middle, modern, and contemporary times in a perspective of world history. Joseon is defined as a pre-modern society. This book will serve as a guide to understand the magnificent history of Korea. The Korean people have tremendous pride in the history of Goguryeo, a great empire in the fifth century, and the splendid Buddhist culture of Unified Silla in the eighth century.

The Koreans thrived under King Sejong (1418~1450) in the 15th century and King Yeongjo (1724~1776) and King Jeongjo (1776~1800) in the 18th century, and they are prospering yet again in the 21st century. The Koreans should recall their proud history and reach for new glory. No matter where we are, when we maintain our dignity as Koreans, and keep the "northward history" deep in our minds, the third take-off will come near like a beacon shining over Asia.

2009. 11　Shin Hyong Sik

우리나라는 유구한 역사와 전통을 지닌 동아시아의 대표적인 나라이다. 우리민족은 70만전의 구석기시대로 부터 신석기시대와 청동기시대를 거치면서 한반도와 만주(중국의 동북지방) 일대에 일찍부터 국가를 이루면서 독자적인 문화를 이룩하여 오늘에 이르고 있다.

최초의 단군조선 이래 우리나라는 하나의 언어와 풍속을 지켜왔으며, 수많은 중국의 침략을 막으면서 만주(중국의 동북방)와 한반도에서 당당한 국가를 건설하였다. 동시에 중국문화를 받아들여 이를 더욱 발전시켜 일본에 전해줌으로서 동아시아 세계의 교량자 역할을 하였으며, 찬란한 불교문화(불국사와 석굴암)를 비롯하여 세계최초의 목판인쇄문화(팔만대장경과 직지심경)와 독창적인 언어문화(한글)를 개발하여 문화민족의 긍지를 지켜왔다.

우리는 비록 19세기말 제국주의 침략을 효과적으로 대처하지 못하고 일본의 지배(1910-1945)라는 수모를 당했으나 꾸준한 항일투쟁으로 독립을 되찾을 수 있었다. 더구나 1945년 해방을 맞았으나 남·북의 분단으로 남한은 개방된 자유민주사회(자본주의)를, 북한은 폐쇄적인 공산사회(사회주의)로 대립과 갈등의 길을 걷게 되었다. 그러나 수많은 시련을 극복하였던 우리 국민들의 진취적이며 부지런한 습성은 700여만의 해외교포들의 자활의 삶 속에서 잘 나타나 있다. 특히 일제의 폭정을 피해 만주로 이주한 동포들은 항일운동을 주도하였으며, 스탈린에 의해 중앙아시아로 끌려간 동포들은 어려운 환경을 이기며 민족의 얼을 당당하게 지키고 있다.

다만 우리는 현대에 이르러 일제의 지배라는 쓰라린 역사를 경험하였고, 해방 후 민족분단이라는 비극을 맞기도 하였으나, 대한민국은 이러한 시련을 극복하면서 당당한 문화·경제 대국으로 발전되었다. 그러나 많은 동포들이 이러한 자랑스러운 모국의 역사를 모르고 있다는 사실을 생각할 때, 가슴 아프게 생각된다,

이 책은 우리의 과거를 모르고 있는 해외동포들을 위해, 그리고 우리역사를 왜곡되게 알고 있는 외국인을 위해 만들었다. 특히 시대구분은 종래의 왕조별 구분이 아니라 세계사적인 고대·중세·근대·현대라는 큰 틀 속에서 정리하였다. 다만 근대 앞에 전근대사회로서 근세시대(조선)를 설정하였다. 따라서 이 책은 당당했던 우리역사 이해를 위한 안내서가 될 것이다. 5세기 대제국이었던 고구려의 강렬한 역사와 8세기 통일신라의 찬란한 불교문화는 우리민족의 자랑이었다.

무엇보다도 15세기의 세종(1418~1450)과 18세기의 영조(1724~1776)·정조(1776~1800)의 민족번영기를 경험했던 우리는 이제 21세기의 제3의 중흥기를 맞을 때가 되었다. 이러한 희망 속에서 우리는 당당했던 과거를 되새기며 다가올 번영을 찾기위해 함께 노력하여야할 것이다. 우리는 어느곳에 있더라도 민족의 긍지를 잃지말고 당당했던 '북상의 역사'를 마음 속 깊히 간직할 때 아시아의 등불로서 제3의 도약이 다가 올 것이다.

2009년 11월 신 형 식

An Easy Guide to Korean History

Contents

[Photo] Dokdo
[사진] 독도

A Proposition to Understand Korean History

한국사 이해를 위한 전제

1. Nature of Korean History

[1] Geographical Environment of Korean History

Just as every person has a unique personality, So Korean history have a unique character. In today's era of globalization, highlighting one's own unique personality is not recommended, but each country has unique features because it has a different political, social, and cultural environment.

Korea is on peninsula covering 220,000 km^2 (South Korea: 100,000, North Korea :120,000) in the Far East at 33~43° latitude north. It belongs to the temperate zone; therefore, it has four distinctive seasons, clear air, and a mild climate. Its people are warm-hearted, and its various food culture (fermented foods such as kimchi and bean paste) has been developed due to the significant seasonal changes. About 70% of the country's landmass is mountainous, but the Korean people overcame this challenges according to their diligent habit in all that they could develop their various arts in accordance with the appreciation of the beautiful scenery of mountains and rivers.

Korea is surrounded by Japan over the East Sea, China over the Yellow Sea to the west, and Manchuria (three northeastern provinces of China) and the Maritime Provinces of Siberia (Russia) over the Amnok River and Duman River to the north. These countries have all been threats to Korea at different times in the past. The Koreans many times stood together and defended their country against invasion and

1. 한국사의 성격

[1] 한국사의 지리적 환경

모든 인간이 자신의 특성을 지닌 것처럼 우리 역사도 다른 나라와 구별되는 독특한 성격을 갖고 있다. 오늘날 세계화 시대에서 지나치게 자기나라의 고유한 성격만을 강조하는 것은 바람직한 사실은 아니지만 나라마다 각국의 정치 · 사회 · 문화적 조건이 다르기 때문에 독자적인 특성을 갖기 마련이다.

한국은 극동아시아의 반도국가(22만km^2, 남한 10만 · 북한 12만)로서 위도상 33~43° 사이에 위치한 북반구 온대에 속한다. 따라서 4계절의 변화가 뚜렷하여 맑은 날씨와 살기 좋은 기후를 갖고 있다. 그러므로 국민성이 온순하고 계절의 변화에 따라 다양한 음식문화(김치, 된장 등 발효식품)가 발달하였다. 또한 국토의 대부분(70%)이 산악으로 되어있어 부지런한 생활습성으로 이를 극복하였으며, 아름다운 강산에 따른 심미적 취향으로 다양한 예술이 발

were able to rise as a center of East Asian culture based on Buddhism and Confucianism. Korea was also able to convey this culture to Japan and hasten the development of ancient Japanese culture.

The Koreans improved poor farmland by their diligence and patience. As explained on the international front, they repulsed military threats from neighboring countries with an unyielding spirit and upheld their national integrity and unique culture. Unlike China obsessed with supremacy and Japan obsessed with shrewd dualism, the Koreans were able to feel proud as a county of courteous people in the East.

[Photo] Cheonji Lake

[사진] 백두산 천지

달 할 수 있었다.

한국은 동쪽으로 동해를 건너 일본, 서쪽으로 서해를 건너 중국이 있으며, 북쪽으로는 압록강・두만강을 건너 만주(중국의 동북3성)와 연해주(러시아)가 접해있어 과거에는 이들 나라들이 위협적인 존재였다. 그러므로 이들의 군사적 위협을 벗어나려는 국민적 단합으로 나라를 지켜왔으며, 그러한 어려움 속에서도 불교와 유교를 중심으로 동아시아 문화의 중심국가로 우뚝 설 수 있었다. 더구나 이러한 문화를 일본에 전수하여 고대 일본문화를 개발하는 여유를 보이기까지 했다.

이와 같이 한국은 지리적으로 부족한 농토를 부지런한 인내와 끈기로 개간하였고, 국제적으로 주변국가들(중국・일본・러시아)의 군사적 위협을 불굴의 정신으로 물리치면서 민족의 정통성과 문화의 독자성을 지켜왔다. 여기서 우리는 패권주의에 사로잡힌 중국과 약삭빠른 일본과는 다른 동방예의지국으로서의 긍지를 지킬 수 있었다.

특히 대한민국은 남・북 분단의 시련 속에서도 민주주의와 경제발전을 이룩하여 선진국으로 발돋움함으로써 후진국들의 모범이 될 수 있었다. 이제 우리는 정치・경제의 발전을 바탕으로 남북의 갈등을 넘어 통일한국의 건설을 위해 노력하고 있다.

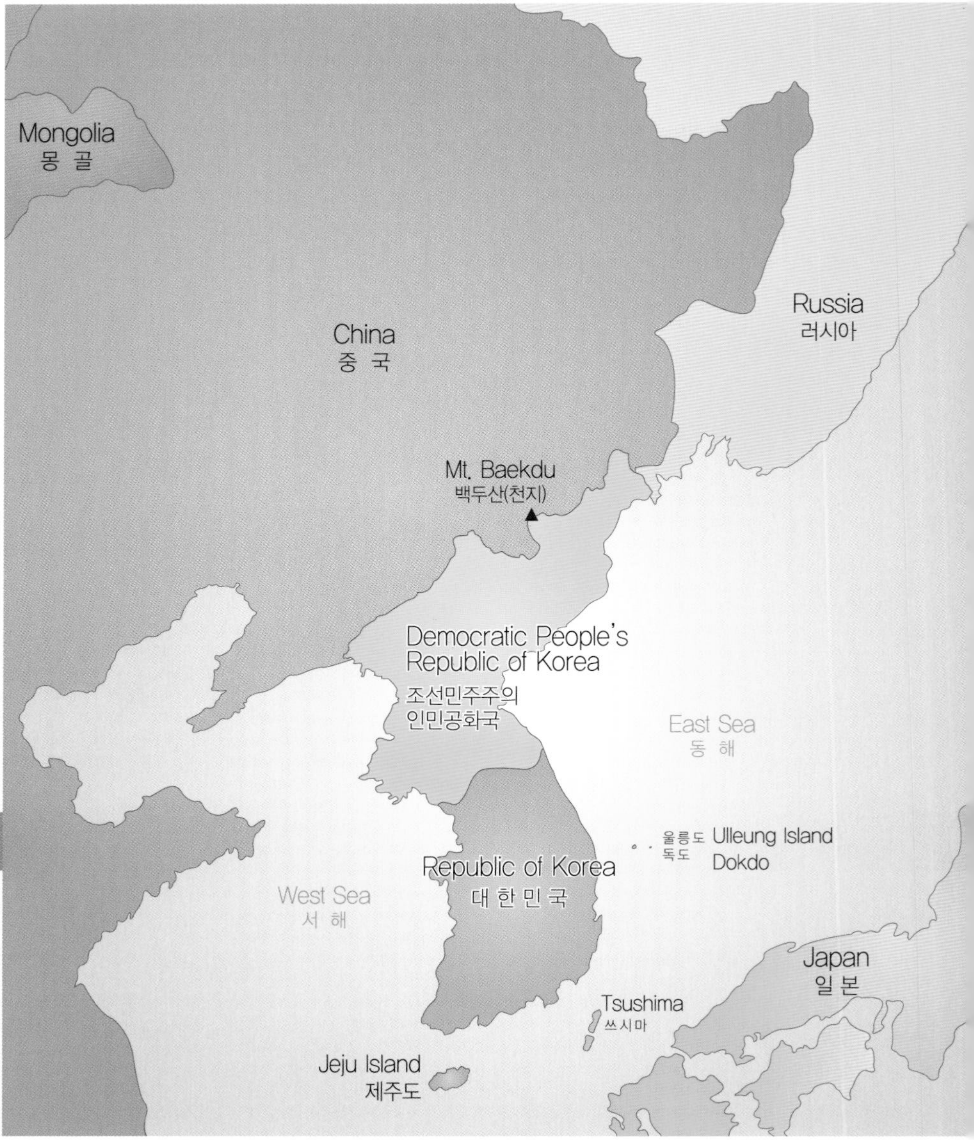

[Map] The Republic of Korea and neighboring countriesis

Korea is on a peninsula covering 220,000㎢ (South Korea: 100,000, North Korea: 120,000) in the Far East at 33~43° latitude north. Its population is 71 million (South Korea: 47 million, North Korea: 24 million). It borders both China (three northeastern provinces of China: Manchuria) along the Amnok River and Duman River and Russia (the Maritime Provinces of Siberia) along the lower Duman River to the north. Over the East Sea (Ulleung Island & Dokdo) are the Japanese Islands, and to the south, across the Korea Strait, lie the Tsushima Islands.

[지도] 우리나라와 그 주변국가

우리나라는 22만㎢(남한 10, 북한 12)으로 인구는 7100만(남한 4700만, 북한 2400만)으로 북위 43~33° 사이의 반도이다. 압록강·두만강으로 중국(동북3성 : 만주)와 접해있고, 두만강 하류에 러시아(연해주)와 접경하고 있다. 동해(울릉도·독도)를 건너 일본열도가 있으며, 남쪽으로 대한해협을 지나 쓰시마가 있다.

The Republic of Korea has set a good example to developing countries by achieving democracy and economic development despite the ordeal of being a divided country. Based on its political and economic development, Korea is now striving hard to resolve the inter-Korean confrontation and build a unified Korea.

[2] Features of Korean History

Even in its earliest days, Korea was a conservative, agrarian society that considered the extended family of utmost importance. Showing respect to the elderly and practicing filial piety were considered natural duties, and parents typically made great sacrifices to give their children the best education they possibly could. Korea was long a closed agrarian society and was slow to recognize the importance of commerce and industry. It was late in its pursuit of modernity.

Korean society in the past was very hierarchical and was ruled by the *yangban* (noblemen). The *yangban* dominated politics, education, and the economy; the majority of Koreans were not able to partake in the political process. The ruling class was accustomed to Chinese culture and had long been criticized for extolling powerful China. Despite Chinese influence, however, Korea managed to maintain flexible foreign relations and preserve its identity.

Korea established Dongyi culture, which is different from Chinese culture. In Dongyi (meaning "*yi* of the east"), the character "*yi* (夷)" means "a source of kind-

[2] 한국사의 특성

한국은 일찍부터 농업을 중심으로 하던 나라였음으로 대가족 제도를 바탕으로 보수적인 공동체 사회를 이루고 있었다. 따라서 윗사람을 공경하고 부모에게 효도하는 것을 인간의 도리로 여겼으며, 부모의 희생 속에서 높은 교육열을 가진 나라였다. 무엇보다도 폐쇄적인 농업사회에서 상공업의 중요성을 인식하지 못하여 근대사회로의 이행에 늦을 수밖에 없었다.

한편 과거의 우리나라는 정치적으로는 지배층과 양반위주의 계급사회를 이루어 정치·교육·경제를 그들이 독점함으로서 대다수 국민들은 정치참여의 길을 갖지 못했다. 특히 지배계급들은 중국의 문화에 익숙해짐으로서 중국에 사대주의 굴레를 벗어나지 못한다고 오랫동안 비판을 받았으나, 중국의 영향속에서도 탄력적인 대외관계를 유지하면서 우리 주체성을 지켜왔다.

더욱이 문화적으로 한국은 중국문화와는 다른 동이문화권을 이룩하였다. 이때 동방의 이(夷)란 '어질고 생명을 중시하는 만물의 근본' 이라는 뜻으로 올바른 자세로 인간의 도덕

hearted creatures respecting life." It refers to a country with a culture that values human morals and ethics with proper attitudes. Korea embraced Buddhism and Confucianism and laid the foundation for the national culture. As a result, Korea today has a number of globally recognized properties of world heritage, including Goguryeo tomb murals (Jian and Pyeongyang), the royal court culture of the Joseon Dynasty (Jongmyo Shrine and Changdeokgung Palace Complex), Hwaseong Fortress, splendid properties of Buddhist culture (Bulguksa Temple and Seokguram Grotto), Goryeo celadon, and over 40 Royal Tombs of the Joseon Dynasty. They all reflect Korea's tradition of nature, religion, and arts.

Despite a surfeit of Chinese culture, the Korean people have effectively protected their cultural tradition. In fact, Goguryeo, which ruled Manchuria, stopped China (Tang Dynasty) from expanding eastward and protected the Korean Peninsula. However, in the 20th century, Korea succumbed to Japanese interference and suffered 36 years of Japanese occupation. The Koreans eventually managed to regain independence as a result of ceaseless resistance against Japan.

Even after liberation from Japan, the Republic of Korea faced a number of challenges: invasion from North Korea (the Korean War), inter-Korean confrontation, and struggle toward democratization. The country nevertheless succeeded in achieving remarkable economic growth to become one of the world's top 10 economies today. Such a meteoric rise enabled Korea to host the 1988 Summer Olympics in Seoul and the election of Ban Ki-moon as UN Secretary-General.

과 윤리를 중시하는 문화를 이룩한 나라라는 것이다. 따라서 불교와 유교를 받아들여 민족 문화의 바탕을 마련하였으며, 고구려 고분벽화(집안 · 평양)를 비롯하여 조선시대의 궁중문 화(창덕궁 · 종묘)와 수원화성, 그리고 찬란한 불교문화(불국사와 석굴암), 고려청자 그리고 자연 · 종교 · 예술의 전통을 간직한 40기의 조선시대 왕릉 등 세계의 대표적인 문화유산을 남기게 되었다.

이와 같이 우리민족은 중국문화의 범람 속에서도 한국의 문화전통을 지켰고, 특히 만주 를 지배한 고구려는 중국(당)의 동방진출을 막고 한반도를 보호하기까지 하였다. 그러나 20 세기에 이르러 일제의 침략에 굴복하여 36년간의 암흑생활을 하였으나 우리민족은 줄기찬 항일 · 독립운동으로 민족의 광복을 되찾을 수 있었다.

더욱이 광복 이후 대한민국은 북한의 침입(6.25전쟁), 남북의 갈등, 그리고 민주화를 위 한 많은 시련이 있었으나, 눈부신 경제성장으로 세계10대 경제대국으로 성장할 수 있었다. 이러한 한국의 국제적 지위향상은 1988년에 제 24회 올림픽을 개최하였으며, 아시아를 대표 하여 UN사무총장을 배출할 수 있었다.

19

[Photo] A Complete View of Seoul
[사진] 서울시 전경

2. The Past and Present

[1] Progress of Korean History

Like China and India, Korea also has a very long history and glorious ancient culture.

Human ancestors first inhabited the Korean Peninsula about 700,000 years ago. The Neolithic Age dawned about 10,000 years ago, and the Bronze Age began about 3,000 years ago. Early forms of a state emerged around then, and Dangun founded Gojoseon, the first nation of the Korean people.

Later, Goguryeo (B.C. 37~668) dominated the northern half of the Korean Peninsula and Manchuria, and Silla (B.C. 57~935) and Baekje (B.C. 18~660) controlled the southern half. This was the Three Kingdoms Period, which marked the development of ancient nations in Korea. During this period, Goguryeo repulsed invasions from the Sui Dynasty (581~618) and the Tang Dynasty (618~907). Silla later unified three nations into one and established a brilliant Korean culture. Later, in Manchuria, Goguryeo was succeeded by Balhae (698~926). Balhae extended into Manchuria and the Maritime Provinces of Siberia and represented the Korean people in East Asia. All these ancient societies created a vibrant culture. Baekje conveyed its culture to Japan and contributed substantially to the establishment of East Asian culture.

The tumultuous late period of Silla (Later Three Kingdoms period: 892-918) came to

2. 한국사의 어제와 오늘

[1] 한국사의 전개과정

우리나라는 중국이나 인도와 같이 오랜 역사와 우수한 고대 문화를 갖고 있다.

이미 70만년 전에 한반도에는 사람이 살고 있었으며, 1만 년경부터 신석기시대가 시작된 후, 3천년전에 청동기시대가 이룩되었다. 이때부터 초기국가가 나타나 단군이 고조선을 세워 최초로 국가가 나타나게 되었다.

그 후 한반도의 북방과 만주(중국의 동북부)에는 고구려(B.C.37~668)가, 남방에는 신라 (B.C.57~935)와 백제(B.C. 18~660)가 나타나 삼국시대가 시작되어 한국의 고대국가가 발전 하기 시작하였다. 이때 고구려는 수(581~618)와 당(618~907)의 침략을 막아냈으며, 신라는 3 국을 통일하여 찬란한 민족문화를 이룩하였다. 그후 만주에는 고구려를 계승한 발해 (698~926)가 세워져 만주와 연해주까지 지배하여 우리민족이 동아시아를 대표하는 나라가

an end with the establishment of the Goryeo Dynasty (918-1392). It reunified the Korean people and ushered in the Middle Age. However, the Goryeo aristocracy eventually suffered a serious rift between the civil officials and military officers, which led to a military coup by Jeong Jung-bu in 1170. After the military dictatorship (1196-1257) and a war with Mongolia (1231-1356), the Goryeo Dynasty fell apart and the Joseon Dynasty (1392-1910), a modern society, was established in its place. Although the territory of the Goryeo Dynasty did not extend beyond the Korean Peninsula, it left behind a great deal of important world cultural heritage such as Goryeo celadon and movable metal printing type.

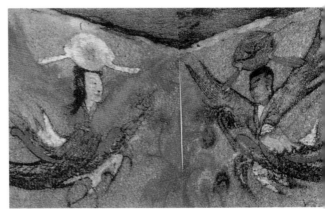

[Photo] Goguryeo Tomb mural (Ji' an, China, Tomb NO.5-4)
Images of male deity holding(carring) a toad(moon), and a fale deity holding a crow(sun). This appears the beauty, religion and flavor of Goguryeo's mural.

[사진] 고구려고분벽화 (지안 5회분 4호묘)

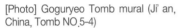

되었다. 이러한 고대사회는 찬란한 민족 문화를 이룩하였으며 삼국 특히 백제는 그 문화를 일본에 전해주어 동아시아문화권 형성에 기여하였다.

　　이어 신라 말의 혼란(후삼국시대:892-918)을 수습하고 고려왕조(918-1392)가 민족을 재통일하여 중세사회를 열게 되었다. 그러나 고려귀족사회는 문·무신간의 갈등으로 무신란(1170년 정중부의 난)이후 무신집권시기(1196-1257)와 몽고와의 항쟁(1231-1356)을 끝으로 근세사회로서의 조선왕조(1392-1910)가 성립되었다. 비록 고려왕조는 그 영토가 한반도로 축소되었으나 고려청자나 금속활자등 세계적인 문화유산을 남겨주었다.

　　조선왕조 세종(1418-1452)은 한글창제(우리문자)와 국토확장 등 새로운 민족국가를 건설하였으나 그 후 지배층의 갈등으로 사회가 동요되어 일본의 침략(임진왜란:1592-1598)과 청의 호란(1627-1636)을 받게되었다. 그러나 18세기에 이르러 정치·경제제도의 개편에 따른 산업의 발달과 실학이 대두되면서 영조(1724~1776),정조(1776~1800)의 중흥이 있었으나 19세기 이후 조선왕조의 모순은 극복될 수가 없었다.

　　이어 대원군(1864~1873)의 개혁 이후 근대화의 추진은 계속되었으나 개화·보수파의 갈등과 일본·청·러시아 세력의 침투로 대한제국(1897~1910)을 끝으로 일본의 지배

King Sejong (1418-1452) of the Joseon Dynasty transformed an anew nation by inventing hangeul (the Korean alphabet) and expanding the realm of the kingdom. This was one of the glorious periods of the Joseon Dynasty. Later, conflicts within the ruling class led to disturbances in society and Joseon suffered two major invasions from Japan (1592-1598) and an invasion by the Qing Dynasty (1627-1636). But drove away invasion and chaos in the 18th century, national prosperity revived during the reigns of King Yeongjo (1724-1776) and King Jeongjo (1776-1800) as a result of industrial development enabled by political and economic reforms and the emergence of the *silhak* (practical study) movement. Sadly, the Joseon Dynasty was greatly weakened in the 19th century by widespread internal strife.

Initiatives for modernization gained renewed momentum as a result of reform efforts by Daewongun (1864~1873), but Korea's fortunes continued to wane due to conflicts between the liberals and the conservatives and increasing domestic interference by Japan, Qing, and Russia. In 1897, Joseon renamed itself the Great Han Empire (1897-1910) but was annexed by Japan in 1910 and occupied until the end of World War II in 1945. During this period, the Korean people resisted Japan, and some migrated to Manchuria (China), Siberia (Russia), and Hawaii (the U.S.) to support themselves.

Shortly after the liberation from Japanese rule in 1945, Korea was divided due to conflicts and ideological confrontation between the U.S. and Soviet Union. Notwithstanding, the Republic of Korea overcame the tragic Korean War, achieved democratization and economic development, and eventually joined the ranks of advanced countries. North Korea, on the other hand, has been experiencing political and economic

(1910~1945)를 받게 되었다. 이 시기에 우리민족은 항일투쟁은 물론 자활의 길을 찾아 만주 (중국) · 연해주(러시아) · 하와이(미국)로 이주하기까지 하였다.

1945년 광복 이후 미 · 소의 갈등과 이념적 대립으로 민족이 분단되었으나, 대한민국은 6.25의 비극과 같은 시련을 극복하고 민주화와 경제개발로 선진국 대열에 들어서게 되었다. 그러나 북한은 소위 폐쇄사회로 정치 · 경제적 어려움에 시달리고 있으면서도 핵 개발에 착 수하여 더욱 고립에 빠지고 있다. 그러나 남북 간의 화해를 위해 6.15선언(2000년) 이후 이산 가족상봉과 개성공단의 조성 등 남북교류를 추진하고 있으나 북한의 돌출행위로 어려움을 겪고 있다.

Comparison / Dynasty	South Korea — Period	South Korea — Description	North Korea — Period	North Korea — Description
Pre-historic Period	Primitive Period	Stone Age	Primitive Period	Primitive group & matrilineal community
		Bronze Age · Tribe Period		Patrilineal clan community
Tribe State	Ancient period	Early State Period	Slavery Period	Slavery society
Three Kingdoms		Ancient State Period		Establishment of Feudal System
Unified Silla		South-North Period		Development of Feudal System
Goryeo [918]	Middle Age	Aristocracy	[B.C 277] Feudal Society	Strengthening of feudal subordination 〈Regime controlled by military officers〉
		Military dictatorship & Mongolian invasions		
		Influence of incumbent aristocrats & emergence of new noblemen		
[1391] [1392] Joseon	Pre-modern society	Noble bureaucratic society		Reorganization of Feudal System 〈Establishment of Rijo Feudal state〉
		Confucian scholar politics		
		Social upheaval in late Joseon		Formation of Capitalistic Relations
		Collapse of yangban (noblemen) society		Crisis of Feudal System
	[Late 19th century] Modern Society	Conflict between liberals and conservatives	[Late 19th century] Modern Society	Beginning of Bourgeois Movement
		Donghak Revolution, Modern Reform		Bourgeois Reform
[1910]		Great Han Empire · Protection of sovereignty		End of Bourgeois Movement
Japanese rule		Japanese rule & sovereignty restoration movement	[1926] 26~45	Anti-Japanese military struggle
US military administration	[1945] Contemporary Society	45~48 U.S. military administration	[1948] Contemporary Society / Democratic People's Republic of Korea — Kim Il-sung Period — 45~50	Establishment of democracy
[1948] Republic of Korea		48~60 Rhee Syngman Administration	50~53	War of Liberation
		60~61 Chang Myon Administration	1953 ~ 1968	Construction of socialism Establishment of Juche ideology
		61~63 Military Administration		
		63~81 Park Chung-hee Administration		
		81~88 Chun Doo-hwan Administration	1994	Death of Kim Il-sung
		88~93 Rho Tae-woo Administration		
		93~98 Civilian Government	Kim Jong-il — 1994	Succession by Kim Jong-il 〈Seongun (military-first) Politics〉 ↓
		98~03 Government of the People		
		03~08 Participatory Government		
		08~ Lee Myung-bak Administration		

[Table 1] Comparison of Historical Periods of South and North Korea

남북한비교 / 왕조명	남 한		북 한	
	시대구분	주요항목	시대구분	주요항목
선사시대	원시시대	석기시대	원시시대	원시무리 · 모계공동체
		청동기시대 · 군장시대		부계씨족 공동체
부족국가	고대시대	초기국가시대	노예제시대	노예소유자사회
삼국시대		고대국가시대	[B.C 277] 봉건사회	봉건제도의 성립기
통일신라시대		남북극시대		봉건제도의 발전기
고려시대	[918] 중세사회	귀족문벌사회		봉건적 예속강화기 〈무신관료배의 정권장악〉
		무신정권 · 몽고간섭기		
		권문세족 · 신흥사대부		
[1391] 조선시대	[1392] 근세사회	양반관료사회		봉건체제의 재편성 〈리조봉건국가의 성립〉
		사림정치		
		조선후기사회변동		자본주의적 관계의 발생
		양반사회파탄		봉건제도의 위기
	[19세기말] 근대사회	개화 · 보수의 갈등	[19세기말] 근대사회	부르죠아운동의 시작
		동학혁명 · 근대개혁		부르죠아 개혁
[1910]		대한제국 · 국권수호		부르죠아 운동의 종말
일제시대	[1945] 현대사회	일제시대 · 국권회복운동	[1926] 조선민주주의인민공화국 [1948] 현대사회	26~45 항일무장투쟁시대
미군정		45~48 미군정시대	김일성시대	45~50 민주건설
[1948]		48~60 이승만정부		50~53 조국해방전쟁
대한민국		60~61 장면정권		53이후 1968 사회주의건설 주체사상확립
		61~63 군정시대		
		63~81 박정희정부		
		81~88 전두환정부		1994 김일성사망
		88~93 노태우정부		
		93~98 문민정부	김정일	1994 김정일 승계 〈선군정치〉 ↓
		98~03 국민의정부		
		03~08 참여정부		
		08~ 이명박정부		

[표 1] 남북한 시대구분의 비교

24

difficulties because of its so-called "closed society" and has been attempting to develop nuclear weapons, further isolating itself from the rest of the world. For reconciliation between the two Koreas, South Korea has been promoting inter-Korean exchange since the Declaration on June 15, 2000, including the reunions of separated families and the construction of Gaeseong Industrial Complex. Unpredictable behavior of North Korea is rendering difficult, South Korea's efforts toward reconciliation.

As Table 1 shows, South and North Korea interpret Korean history or the periods differently because of political and ideological differences. South Korea seeks inductive description based on objective facts; North Korea focuses on individual deductive interpretation based on its *juche* ideology and struggles by the people. Clearly, the reinterpretation of Korea's history has to be restored according to a correct viewpoint.

[2] Overseas Koreans Upholding the Spirit of the Korean People

Korea has the fourth largest contingent of overseas residents, with about seven million Koreans living in other countries. There are about two million in China (mostly three northeastern provinces), roughly 2.2 million in the U.S., some 800,000 in Japan, about 140,000 in Canada, and another 110,000 in Latin America. In 1937, Stalin forced some 500,000 Koreans to migrate to the former Soviet Union. They live in Uzbekistan (230,000), Kazakhstan (180,000), Russia (150,000), and in several Eastern European countries.

[표1]에서 보듯이 남북한에는 정치와 이념의 차이로 역사의 해석이나 시대구분에서 차이가 보인다. 남한은 객관적인 사실 위주의 귀납적인(Inductive)인 서술이지만 북한은 주체사학에 입각한 개인 위주의 연역적인(Deductive)인 해석과 인민들의 투쟁에 초점을 두고 있어 올바른 역사복원이 필요하다.

[2] 민족의 얼을 지켜가는 교포

한국은 700만 명의 동포를 가진 세계 4대 해외동포국가이다. 중국(주로 동북3성)에 200만, 미국에 220만, 일본에 80만, 캐나다에 14만, 그리고 중남미에 11만이 살고 있다. 특히 1937년에 스탈린에 의해서 강제로 구소련에 이주된 50여만의 동포는 현재 우즈베키스탄에 23만, 카자흐스탄에 18만, 그리고 기타 동유럽 각지에 흩어져 살고 있으며 러시아에도 15만이나 살고 있다.

특히 구러시아(특히 중앙아시아)지역의 동포(고려인)들은 전혀 다른 환경 속에서 온갖

Goryeoin (people of Goryeo), Koreans in the former Soviet Union (especially Central Asia), were put through all kinds of hardships in a completely different environment, but they persevered with patience and diligence being like a phoenix. About 170,000 Goryeoin were forced to migrate from Siberia on the pretext of being "Japanese spies." They contributed greatly to the advancement of farming technology and productivity. Nonetheless, the different culture was a great challenge to Goryeoin. They were banned from engaging in political and social activities, and forced into production activities. Their miserable reality of life became worse and worse the situation was exacerbated by the Soviet's variable policy, as Soviet administration was changed according to the times.

This region was under the rule of Russia and familiar with the situation and systems of North Korea, so the Goryeoins were not aware of the free environment and actual situation in South Korea. When the Soviet Union collapsed in 1991, Goryeoin society was thrown into confusion. Fortunately, since the establishment of the CIS, the Goryeoin finally became aware of the true changes in the outside world and the reality of South Korea. Their situation is now improving as a result of the recent emergence of the Global Korean Network.

Other Koreans had been forced to engage in wars or hard labor in Japan or other regions (Siberia or Southeast Asia) until the end of World War II. They lived hopeless lives as powerless mineworkers in coal mines or as victims of misguided Japanese ambitions on the battlefield. Numerous young Korean women were impressed into service during the war as "comfort women," leading miserable existences. After the

시련을 겪으면서 인내와 성실로 역경을 극복한 불사조와 같은 존재들이었다. 당시 17만의 고려인들은 '일본의 스파이'라는 구실로 연해주로부터 강제 이주되었지만 이들은 선진의 농업기술과 식량확보에 큰 기여를 한 것은 사실이다. 그러나 현지에서는 문화상 차이는 고려인들에게 너무나 커다란 장벽이었다. 더구나 고려인들은 정치·사회활동이 금지되었고 오직 생산활동에만 강요당하는 비참한 현실과 함께 변화되는 러시아 정권에 따라 정책의 변동은 더 많은 어려움으로 나타났다.

더구나 이 지역이 계속 러시아의 통치권이 미치는 곳이었기 때문에 북한실정과 성격에 익숙해져서 남한의 자유스러운 환경과 현실을 알지 못하였다. 따라서 1991년의 소비에트 붕계과정에 나타난 고려인 사회변화는 의식의 혼란이 수반되었다.

다행히 CIS(독립국가연합)체제의 출범 이후 늦게나마 외부세계의 변화와 한국의 실정을 이해하게 되었다. 근래 글로벌 코리언 네트워크가 본격화되어 고려인들의 위상이 높아지고 있다.

또한 징병·징용으로 일본과 기타 지역(사할린·동남아시아)으로 끌려간 동포들은 일본의 전쟁도구로 인간 이하의 대접을 받고 살았다. 탄광에서는 힘없는 광부로, 전쟁터에서는

war, the ordeal for Koreans living in Japan continued. The Japanese government discriminated against them and held them in contempt, calling them "Josenjin". The Jochongryeon (General Association of Koreans Living in Japan) and Mindan (People of the Republic of Korea in Japan) were antagonistic to each other. Fortunately, with recent reports on the circumstances in North Korea, the awareness of Koreans in Japan has begun to change, and the Japanese government is expected to pursue flexible and reasonable polices.

The Korean people who migrated to Manchuria after the 17th century deeply rooted the spirit of the Koreans as pioneers there by providing new farming technology to the local people and restoring the fertility of the farmland in Jiandao. While observing the Sino-Japanese war, the Joseonjok (ethnic Korean-Chinese) quietly restored the deserted land and protected Jiandao as a base for the independence movement against Japan. Koreans who settled down there while witnessing victories of the independence movement against Japan in Jilin Province (Bongo-dong and Cheongsan-ri) were hard workers and had a strong desire to pursue education. As a result, they maintained the most outstanding identity among all 55 minority groups in China.

The Joseonjok in China (mostly three northeastern provinces) experienced difficulties and conflicts between their status as Chinese citizens and their patriotism toward Korea as Korean Chinese. Because of a mandate to join the Chinese mainstream, the second generation of Joseonjok is very different from the first generation. Thankfully, since the establishment of diplomatic ties between the ROK and

일본제국주의 야욕의 희생자로서 희망없는 삶을 살게 되었다, 더욱이 젊은 여성들은 '종군위안부'로 처참한 생활을 견뎌 나갔던 것이다. 종전 후 일본정부의 차별정책은 '조센징'으로서의 멸시를 받으면서도 조총련과 민단의 갈등이 겹쳐 재일동포의 시련은 계속되었다. 다행히 근래에 이르러 북한실정이 알려지면서 동포들의 의식전환이 증가되고 있으니만치 일본정부의 융통성과 합리적인 정책이 기대된다.

그리고 17세기 이후 만주(동북3성)지역에 진출한 우리민족은 그곳에 새로운 영농기술을 보급하고 공지에 가까운 간도를 개척하면서 한민족의 얼을 뿌리내리게 한 선구자였다. 청일간의 갈등을 목도하면서도 조선족은 묵묵히 버림받은 땅을 개척하였으며 일제에 항거하면서 독립운동의 기지로서 간도를 당당히 지켜왔다. 봉오동과 청산리의 승리를 지켜보면서 그곳에 정착한 동포들은 높은 교육열과 부지런한 노력으로 중국의 55개 소수민족 중에 가장 훌륭한 자기정체성을 지켜왔다.

그러나 중국(주로 동북3성)속의 조선족은 중국 공민으로서의 위상과 조선족으로서 조국관(祖國觀) 사이에서 어려움과 갈등을 겪었으나, 중국의 주류사회에 진입해야 할 명제 때문에 2세대 이후는 1세대와 큰 차이를 보게 된다. 다행히 1993년 한·중 수교 이후 북한의 현실

China in 1993 and the increasing awareness of the Joseonjok of the true situation in North Korea, they have taken a more proactive approach toward South Korea. Korean Chinese should remember their identity as Koreans while fulfilling their duties as Chinese citizens.

The homogeneity of these overseas Koreans and their determination to overcome the bitter reality are seen as indispensible for putting an end to the national division and ideological differences.

3. Truth About the Northeast Project by China

China recently started to conduct the Northeast Project (2002~2007) as her national policy. It had a set of political objectives for governing minorities (the Uyghur in the west and the Tibetans in the south) in the Chinese borderlands. As a post-unification measure for Korean Chinese living in Manchuria, the Northeast Project is aimed to weave historical issues between Korea and China, ranging from the history of Goguryeo to the Jiandao they think it is unsettled issue, in the Chinese history.

China is distorting history in order to reclassify Korean Chinese according to its unified multi-ethnic state policy by applying the ideology of China in Chinese world order mentioned in their ancient books. China names Goguryeo as "Chinese Goguryeo." In an official historical map book (People's Education Publishing, 2008),

을 확인한 이후 한국에 대한 적극적인 접근으로 교포들의 인식이 변하고 있다. 따라서 중국의 조선족(동포)은 중국의 공민으로서의 임무속에서 우리민족의 정체성은 잃지 말아야 할 것이다.

이들 해외동포들의 동질성과 꿋꿋한 현실 극복의 자세는 민족분단과 이념의 벽을 헐고 민족통합의 매개체나 교량자가 될 수 있으리라 믿는다.

3. 중국의 동북공정을 바로 보자

중국은 최근에 동북공정(2002~2007)이라는 국책연구과제를 추진하였다. 이 계획은 중국 변방의 소수민족(서쪽은 위글족, 남쪽은 티베트족 등)의 통치를 위한 일련의 정치적 목적을 갖고 추진된 것이다. 특히 동북공정은 동북3성(만주)에 살고 있는 조선족에 대한 통일 후의 대책으로서 고구려사로부터 간도문제의 완결에 이르는 한·중간의 미결문제의 중국사 편입

Goguryeo, which had existed during the Sui Dynasty, is not indicated on a map showing the Tang Dynasty at its height. Goguryeo is a typical example of historical denial. It is described as a local regime set up by a Chinese minority living in the northeastern region. The main details of the Northeast Project are as follows.

① From its inception to downfall, Goguryeo was a Chinese regime established by a minority group living on Chinese territory.
② Goguryeo was a vassal state paid tribute to China.
③ The wars with the Sui Dynasty and the Tang Dynasty were civil wars to punish Goguryeo because it challenged China.
④ When Goguryeo collapsed, it had a population of 700,000~800,000. However, excluding those who were killed during the war, taken prisoner, captured, or fled, only about 100,000 remained. Therefore, most people of Goguryeo were assimilated into China.
⑤ Goguryeo and Goryeo are not related to each other, in that their royal families (political leaders), eras of survival, and territories were different.

These claims by China are based on its distortions of Goguryeo history according to its Chinese ideology. It is known that the story of Joseon was already written in *Shiji*, China's first history book. China had recorded Goguryeo as one of its eastern neighbors that existed along with Baekje and Silla, even stating that Goguryeo had distinctive cuisine, clothing, rituals, and folklore.

을 목적으로 한 것이다.

이러한 중국의 역사왜곡은 그들이 자신들의 고전에 나타난 중국적 세계질서(Chinese World Order)라는 중화사상을 현재에 적용하여 조선족을 그들의 통일적 다민족국가론에 편입시키려는 것이다. 그러므로 중국은 고구려를 「중국고구려」라 표기하고 있으며, 공식적인 역사부도(인민교육출판사, 2008)에는 수나라 시대에는 있었던 고구려가 당나라 전성기 지도에는 없어지고 있다. 따라서 고구려를 중국 동북방에 살던 중국의 소수민족이 세운 지방정권이라는 역사말살의 대표적 사례가 된 것이다. 동북공정의 핵심적인 내용은 아래와 같다.

① 고구려는 출발부터 멸망까지 중국 영토 안에 존재한 소수민족이 세운 중국의 지방정권이다.
② 고구려는 중국에 신하의 나라로서 조공을 통해 중국에 예속된 나라이다.
③ 수, 당과의 전쟁은 고구려가 중국에 도전하였음으로 토벌(응징)한 국내전쟁이다.
④ 고구려가 멸망 당시 70~80만 정도의 인구가 있었으나, 전사 · 포로 · 납치 · 도망자를 제하면 10만 정도에 불과하였음으로 고구려인들은 대부분 중국인으로 동화되

The claims by China are easily shown to be the distortions from the truth. First, Manchuria, where Goguryeo existed, was not under the control of ancient China. Second, paying tribute to China was an ancient diplomatic practice, which had no bearing on the independence or integrity of a country. Third, Goguryeo built the Great Wall of Korea over a period of 16 years (631~646) to prevent invasions from the Tang Dynasty, but Tang never opposed the construction. Moreover, China had mobilized one million soldiers in order to punish her subordinate country. The fact that this was not a war does not make sense logically. In addition, a state letter sent to Goguryeo shortly before the war stressed China's hope for peace between the two countries.

Fourth, the population at the time of Goguryeo's downfall was not 700,000~800,000 but 2.1 million. About 800,000 had been killed or displaced because of the war (forced migration: 400,000, war casualties 100,000, prisoners of war: 85,000, refugees to Silla or Baekje: 200,000). Some 1.3~1.4 million lived on the land of Goguryeo. Along with Silla, they were leading struggles against the Tang Dynasty. Lastly, Goryeo succeeded Goguryeo as a nation and was so named. Xu Jing, an envoy from the Song Dynasty, confirmed that Goryeo was the successor to Goguryeo in the *Illustrated Accounts of Goryeo*. Then, in 993 (12th year of King Seongjong), Seo Hee clarified this fact in a meeting with the enemy's general, Xiao Sunning.

As explained, Goguryeo was not founded by a Chinese minority group. China's distortion of history is the outcome of contradictions and mistakes in applying the ancient Chinese ideology to the present. History is all about disclosing the truth. Denying the fact that the Tang Dynasty was defeated by Goguryeo does not change

었다.
⑤ 고구려와 고려는 그 왕족(정치주인공(政治主人公)), 존속기간, 그리고 지배지역이 달랐음으로 서로 관계가 없다.

이러한 중국 측 주장은 고구려사를 중화사상에 입각하여 중국식으로 왜곡하여 설명한 것이다. 이미 중국 최초의 역사책인 「사기」에 '조선전'을 둔 이래 동방의 이웃나라(East Neighbours)로 고구려는 백제와 신라와 함께 존속된 나라로 그 음식 · 의복 · 예절 · 풍속이 다르다고 기록하고 있다.

중국의 주장에 대해서 첫째로 고구려가 존속한 만주지역은 고대중국의 통치권이 미치지 않는 곳이었다. 둘째로 조공이라는 것은 의례적인 고대외교의 형식으로 국가의 독립성과 정통성과는 관계가 없다. 셋째로 고구려는 당나라의 침략을 막기 위해 16년간(631~646) 천리장성을 쌓았는데 당나라는 이에 대해 반대를 하지 않았다. 더구나 중국이 자신의 속국을 징벌하는데 100만 대군을 동원하였는데 그것이 전쟁이 아니라는 논리는 성립할 수 없다. 그리고 전쟁 직전에 고구려에 보낸 국서에 두 나라의 평화를 강조하고 있었다.

[Photo] Kyong-chol-wha's History of China Goguryeo

[사진] 경철화의 「중국고구려사」

[Photo] Shin Hyong Sik's History of Goguryeo (Korea)

[사진] 신형식의 「고구려사」

history. At that time, Goguryeo which repulsed invasions by both Sui and Tang had the Asia's strongest power and was Asia's strongest power and was a powerful empire. Therefore, eliminating Goguryeo does not highlight Chinese history, and distorting history does not change the truth. The Northeast Project is an invasion of Korean history.

4. Korea's World Heritage

UNESCO protects cultural and natural heritage around the world considered to be of outstanding value to humanity by inscribing it on the World Heritage List. As of July 2008, there were 878 properties so recognized, including 679 cultural, 174 natural, and 25 mixed (natural + cultural), in 141 state parties. Of these, Korea has seven cultural heritage properties on the list: Seokguram Grotto and Bulguksa Temple; Haeinsa Temple Janggyeong Panjeon; Jongmyo Shrine; Changdeokgung Palace Complex; Hwaseong Fortress; Gyeongju Historic Areas; and Gochang, Hwasun, and Ganghwa Dolmen Sites. It also has one natural heritage property on the list: Jeju Volcanic Island and Lava Tubes. In 2009, 40 Royal Tombs of the Joseon Dynasty were also inscribed on the World Heritage List.

Seokguram Grotto and Bulguksa Temple are major properties of Buddhist art created in the heyday of Unified Silla (8th century). Inside Seokguram Grotto is a life-size statue of the Buddha with a benign and kind-hearted expression. Bulguksa Temple

그리고 넷째로 고구려 멸망 당시 70~80만의 인구가 아니라 210만이었고 전쟁으로 80만 정도가 감소(강제이주 40만, 전쟁희생 10만, 포로 8만5천, 신라·백제로의 귀화 20만)되어 130~140만 정도가 고구려 국토에 살고 있었다. 이들은 신라와 함께 대당투쟁을 주도하고 있었다. 끝으로 고려는 고구려를 계승하여 국호를 고려라 하였으며 송나라 사신으로 온 서긍(徐兢)도「고려도경」에서 고려가 고구려의 후계자임을 확인한 바 있다. 그리고 993년(성종 12)에 서희(徐熙)는 적장(소손녕)과의 대담에서 그 사실을 분명히 밝히고 있다.

이와 같이 고구려는 중국의 고대 소수민족이 세운 지방정권이 아니다. 중국의 역사왜곡은 고대의 중화사상을 현대에 적용하려는 모순과 오류의 결과로 나타난 것이다. 역사는 진실을 밝히는 것으로 당나라가 고구려에 패배한 사실을 없애버렸다고 역사가 없어지는 것이 아니다. 고구려는 수, 당나라의 침략을 당당히 격퇴시킨 당시 아시아의 최대강국이었고 대제국이었다. 그러므로 고구려를 없애버렸다고 중국사가 부각되는 것은 아니며, 역사를 속한다고 진실이 없어지는 것은 아니다. 따라서 동북공정은 한국사에 대한 역사침략인 것이다.

includes Daeungjeon in the main courtyard (the Land of Seokgamoni Buddha), which represents the present world; Geungnakjeon (the Land of Amitabha) at the west of the main courtyard, which stands for the future world; and Birojeon (Land of Birosana Buddha) at the north, which represents the past. Seokgatap and Dabotap, two stone pagodas in the main courtyard, add to the beauty of Bulguksa Temple.

Janggyeong Panjeon at Haeinsa Temple is a set of wooden buildings housing the Tripitaka Koreana, the world's oldest set of wooden printing blocks. Tripitaka refers to a Buddhist canon of scriptures, including Sutras (teachings by Buddha), Vinaya

[Photo] A View of Seokguram Grotto
〈Source: Korea Tourism Organization〉

[사진] 석굴암
〈사진제공:한국관광공사〉

4. 한국의 세계문화유산

유네스코는 인류문명과 자연유산에 있어서 세계적으로 보존가치가 있는 것을 세계문화유산으로 지정하여 보호하고 있다. 현재 세계 141개국에서 문화유산 679, 자연유산 174, 복합유산(자연+문화) 25등 총 878개(2008 7월 현재)가 지정되어 있다. 그 중에서 우리나라는 석굴암, 불국사, 해인사 장경판전, 종묘, 창덕궁, 수원화성, 경주역사유적지구, 고인돌 유적(고창 · 화순 · 강화도)등 문화유산 7건과 제주 화산섬과 용암동굴의 자연유산 1건이 현재 등재된 유산이다. 이번(2009)에 다시 조선왕릉 40기가 새로 세계문화유산으로 등록되었다.

석굴암, 불국사는 통일신라 전성기(8세기)에 만들어진 불교예술의 대표적 유적으로 석굴암은 온화하고 자비로운 석가여래상을 나타내고 있다. 불국사는 중앙의 대웅전(석가모니불)은 사바세계(현재), 서쪽의 극락전(아미타불)은 극락세계(미래), 그리고 북쪽의 비로전(비로자나불)은 연화장세계(과거)를 상징하는 불교의 이상을 나타내고 있으며, 다보탑 · 석가탑이 그 멋을 더해준다.

(Buddhist precepts), and Abhidharma (commentaries on the sutras and Vinaya). The Tripitaka Koreana woodblocks were made from 1238 (23rd year of King Gojong) through 1251 (38th year of King Gojong), which are kept safely in this depository to control the temperature, humidity, and ventilation with special means.

Jongmyo Shrine houses the ancestral tablets of the kings and queens of the Joseon Dynasty. The shrine includes Jeongjeon (main shrine hall), which houses the tablets for the kings with the most outstanding achievements and their queens, and Yeongnyeongjeon, which enshrines the tablets of other kings and queens nominated after death. Jongmyo Jeryeak (an elaborate performance of ancient court music) and the Jongmyo ritual are held regularly at Jongmyo Shrine.

Changdeok Palace was built as a secondary palace next to Gyeongbok Palace, but it served as the main palace in the late Joseon Dynasty. The palace complex includes Injeongjeon (a main hall for state affairs), Seonjeongjeon (an office for the king's daily meetings with his officials), Huijeongdang (king's workplace), Nakseonjae (residence hall of King Gojong and King Sunjong), and Daejojeon (official residence of the queen). Its main gate is called Donhwamun. In addition to other buildings, Changdeok Palace is also home to Biwon, a garden in the rear known as the Secret Garden.

Hwaseong Fortress was built by King Jeongjo over a period of about three years (Jan. 1794 ~ Sep. 1796) on a plain stretching across Suwon. It was a new town with 48 facilities, gates, roads, bridges, and shops. It has four main gates: South Gate (Paldalmun), Bukmun (Janganmun), Dongmun (Changnyongmun), and Seomun (Hwaseomun). There are also Gongsimdon (an observation tower) and Seojangdae (a

해인사 장경판전은 세계 최고의 목판인쇄물인 팔만대장경을 보관하고 있는 목조건물이다. 대장경은 부처님 말씀인 경, 불교의 교리인 율, 그리고 교리의 해설인 논인 불교경전을 말한다. 이곳에 보관된 팔만대장경은 1238년(고종23)부터 1251년(고종 38)에 만든 것으로 온도·습도·통풍이 조절되는 특수한 장치로 보관되고 있다.

종묘는 조선시대 역대 왕과 왕비의 신주(위패)를 모시는 사당이다. 여기에는 정전(공적이 많은 왕과 왕비의 신위)과 영녕전(정전에서 빠진 왕·왕비와 추존된 왕·왕비)이 있으며 정기적인 행사때 보여주는 종묘제례악과 종묘제를 지낸다.

창덕궁은 경복궁(궁궐)의 별궁으로 지어진 궁궐로 조선후기에는 정궁으로의 역할을 하였다. 여기에는 인정전(조례 거행), 선정전(왕·신하간 국정논의: 편전), 희정당(왕의 정사), 낙선재(고종·순종의 편전), 대조전(침전) 등이 있으며, 정문으로 돈화문이 있다. 창덕궁은 다양한 건물 외에도 비원과 같은 후원을 갖고 있다.

수원화성은 정조가 약 3년간(1794.1~1796.9)에 걸쳐 이룩한 평지성으로 그 안에 48개의 시설물, 대문, 도로, 다리, 상가 등을 갖춘 신도시를 말한다. 특히 남문(팔달문), 북문(장안문), 동문(창룡문), 서문(화서문)의 4대문과 공심돈(망루), 서장대(군사지휘소) 등이 있어 멋

military command office). It is a sophisticated complex and is very representative vestige of the architecture of the 18th century in terms of both style and strategic function.

The Gyeongju Historic Areas are divided into five belts: the Namsan Belt (Buddhist art monuments), the Wolseong Belt (palace sites), the Tumuli Park Belt (Silla royal tombs), Hwangnyongsa (Buddhist remains), and Sanseong Fortress (capital defense facilities). The Gyeongju Historic Areas, which epitomize Silla culture, show a complete view of the cultural heritage of a thousand-year-old city, including Buddha images carved into the rocks in the Namsan Belt, Cheomseongdae Observatory and Anapji Pond in the Wolseong Belt, Cheonmachong (Heavenly Horse Tomb) and Hwangnamdaechong in the Tumuli Park Belt, the site of Hwangneungsa Temple in Hwangnyongsa Belt, and capital defense systems of Wolseong and Myeonghwal Fortress in the Sanseong Fortress Belt.

The Dolmen Sites in Gochang, Hwasun, and Ganghwa Island are important sites of cultural heritage of the Bronze Age. Separated by the Han River, the dolmens are generally classified into the northern type and southern type, but the dissected stone type, which does not have supporting stones, is most common. Dolmens were used as tombs for the ruling class or as altars. They also bear traces of diagrams of constellations or religious symbols.

As mentioned previously, 40 royal tombs of the Joseon Dynasty were registered on the World Heritage List. Out of 42 royal tombs of the Joseon Dynasty, including those of 27 kings, queens, and kings and queens honored posthumously, only two were not

[Photo] View of Hwaseong Fortress
〈Source: Korea Tourism Organization〉

[사진] 수원화성
〈사진제공·한국관광공사〉

과 전략적 기능상으로 18세기의 멋지고도 이상적인 도시유적이다.

경주 역사유적지구는 남산지구(불교미술), 월성지구(궁궐터), 대릉원지구(신라왕궁), 황룡사지구(불교유적), 산성 지구(왕경방어시설) 등 5개 지구로 되어 있다. 신라문화를 상징하

registered - Jereung Tomb (tomb of Queen Sinui, first wife of King Taejo) and Hureung Tomb (tomb of King Jeongjong and his wife, Queen Jeongan) - because they are in Gaeseong, North Korea. Tombs are not simply graves of kings, but they reflect the style and aesthetics of Joseon architecture through unique structures (Hongsalmun - red door for entry, room for ptrparing riters, a T-shaped shrine for royal tomb rites) and landscape and sculptures (literary men, military men, a pair of stone posts in front df tomb) based on harmony with nature.

In addition to these eight sites inscribed on the World Heritage List, Korea has six old documents on the Memory of the World Register, including the *Hunmin Jeongeum Manuscript*, *The Annals of the Joseon Dynasty*, *The Diaries of the Royal Secretariat (Seungjeongwon Ilgi)*, and the second volume of the *Anthology of Great Buddhist Priests' Zen Teachings (Jikjisimcheyojeo* - Jikjisimkyung: kept at the National Library of France). Also, the Royal Ancestral Ritual in the Jongmyo Shrine and its Music, the Pansori Epic Chant, and Gangneung Danoje Festival are inscribed as World Intangible Heritage. These registractions on the World Heritage List demonstrate that Korea's brilliant ancient culture is highly acclaimed worldwide.

는 이곳에는 특히 남산지구의 마애불상, 월성지구의 첨성대와 안압지, 대릉원지구의 천마총과 황남대총, 황룡사지구의 황룡사터, 그리고 산성지구는 월성 외에 사방으로 명활산성(동), 서형산성(서), 남산성(남), 북형산성(북)등이 경주외곽을 지켜줌으로서 천년고도의 문화유산을 볼 수 있다.

고인돌 유적(고창 · 화순 · 강화도)은 전국적으로 분포되어있는 청동기시대의 대표적 문화유산이다. 한강을 중심으로 북방식 · 남방식으로 구분되지만 오히려 받침돌이 없는 개석식 고인돌이 더 많이 남아있으며 지배층의 무덤으로서 또는 제단(Altar)으로 활용되었다. 특히 고인돌에는 별자리나 종교적 의미를 나타낸 흔적이 남아있다.

최근에 조선왕릉 40기가 세계문화유산으로 등재되었다. 조선시대의 27대 왕과 왕비 및 추존된 왕 · 왕비릉 등 42기의 조선왕릉 중 북한에 있는 2기「개성에 있는 제릉(태조의 비 신의왕후릉)과 후릉(정종과 정 안왕후릉)」을 제외한 40기가 새로 지정되었다. 왕릉은 단순히 왕의 무덤이 아니라 자연과의 조화를 이룬 바탕에 독특한 건축(출입문인 홍살문, 제사 준비하는 제실, 제사지내는 정자각)과 조경양식과 조각물(문인 · 무인 · 망주석)의 멋과 미 의식이 반영되어 있다.

5. Dokdo and Jiandao Issues

[1] Dokdo

Dokdo is a group of small volcanic islets which includes two main islets of east and west, and 36 rocks in the East Sea, 92 kilometers east from Ulleung Island. It was discovered by Le Liancourt, a French whaling ship, in 1849. As part of a larger complex of Ulleung Island, Dokdo has the same geology and vegetation as Ulleung Island and has been a part of Korean territory for a very long time. However, through the Shimane Prefecture Notice No. 40 released in 1905, when Korea was deprived of its diplomatic rights, Japan named the islets Dakesima and claimed them as its territory. The issue is still a point of heated contention between the Republic of Korea and Japan.

Dokdo is indeed a part of Korea's territory and is guarded by the Korean Coast Guard. On October 25, 1900, Dokdo had become effective as a part of Gangwon-do. Along with Ulleung Island, Dokdo was made part of Silla in the 13th year of King Jijeung (512) and recorded as islets attached to Ulleung Island in Korean literature (*Sinjeungdonggugyeojiseungnam* -geology of Korea and *Mangiyoram* - materials for administrative affairs). However, Dokdo was a no-man's island group and did not attract much interest. The Japanese came to the islands for fishing, but Ahn Yong-bok drove them away in the 19th year of King Sukjong (1693) and confirmed to the Japanese government that Dokdo was Korean territory.

이와 같은 8개의 세계문화유산 외에 6개의 세계기록유산(훈민정음 · 조선왕조실록 · 승정원일기 · 직지심체절요(직지심경: 프랑스국립도서관))과 종묘제례 · 종묘제례악 · 판소리 · 강릉단오제 등 3건은 세계무형유산으로 올라있다. 이로서 한국의 찬란한 고대문화는 그 가치를 세계적으로 인정받고 있다.

5. 독도와 간도문제

[1] 독도

독도는 울릉도 동쪽 92Km 해상에 있는 동 · 서 두 개의 섬과 부근 36개의 암초로 구성된 화산도이다. 1849년 프랑스 포경선 리앙크루(Liancourt)호가 발견한 섬으로 일찍부터 울릉도의 부속도서로서 지질이나 식물분포가 울릉도와 같은 우리 영토이다. 그러나 일본은 죽도(Dakesima)라 하여 우리나라가 외교권을 빼앗긴 1905년 시네마현 고시 제40호로 이 섬을 다

Japan now claims Dokdo as its territory on the grounds of the Shimane Prefecture Notice No. 40 and requested the International Court of Justice to deliberate the issue based on the peace treaty - Japan lobbied to leave out provisions on Dokdo - signed between Japan and the allied powers in San Francisco in 1951. Nonetheless, Dokdo is clearly Korean territory, and there is no need to present the issue to the International Court of Justice. Moreover, the New Korea-Japan Fishing Agreement signed in 1999 defined the waters around Dokdo as Korea-Japan Joint Management Waters, but this does not apply in any way to Korean sovereignty. It is time for Japan to withdraw its groundless claim. The Korean government set up the Dokdo Research Center within the Northeast Asian History Foundation and is continuing to search for documents stating that Dokdo is Korean territory and communicate its findings to the international community.

[2] Jiandao Issue

Jiandao is the southern and northeastern region of Manchuria north of the Amnok River and Duman River. The area north of the Amnok River is called West Jiandao, the area north of the Duman River is East Jiandao, and the northeastern area from East Jiandao is referred to as North Jiandao. Often, North and East Jiandao are called simply Jiandao. The area has been explored by ethnic Koreans since the 17th century and served as a base for resistance against Japan. This region has been establishing Yanbian

케시마라 하여 일본영토라고 주장하여 현재까지 외교적 마찰을 빚고 있다.

그러나 독도는 우리 영토로 우리 해경이 지키고 있다. 이미 1900년 10월 25일에 이 섬을 강원도에 부속시켰으며, 신라 지증왕 13년(512)에 울릉도와 함께 신라에 편입된 이래 우리 영토로서 우리나라 문헌(「신증동국여지승람」·「만기요람」)에도 '울릉도의 부속도서'로 명시되어 있다. 다만 독도가 무인도로서 주목을 받지 못한 탓에 일본인들이 고기잡이를 위해 들어왔음으로 숙종 19년(1693)에 안용복이 이들을 추방하고 에도(일본)정부에 독도가 우리 영토임을 확인한 바 있다.

다만 일본은 시네마현 고시〈제40호〉를 내세워 일본영토임을 주장하고 1951년 샌프란시스코 대일강화조약(일본과 연합국 간의 평화조약- 독도에 관한 규정이 일본의 로비로 빠짐)을 내세워 국제사법재판소에 심의를 요구하고 있다. 그러나 독도는 엄연히 우리 땅임으로 국제사법재판소에 갈 필요가 없다. 더군다나 1999년의 「신 한일어업협정」에서 독도 주변 바다를 한일공동관리수역으로 정하였으나, 이는 영유권과는 별도로 해석된다. 일본은 이제 그 부당한 주장을 철회할 때가 되었다. 이에 정부는 「동북아역사재단」내에 「독도연구소」를 설치하고 독도가 우리영토였음을 나타낸 문헌을 계속 발굴하여 국제사회에 알리고 있다.

Korean Autonomous Prefecture.

As a land of Goguryeo and Balhae, Jian in Jilin Province was the capital city of Goguryeo. Helong was the central capital of Balhae, and Hunchun was the east capital. Ningan in Heilongjiang Province was the capital of Balhae, where ancient Korean culture flourished. Moreover, Bongodong (Hong Beom-do - Domun) and Cheongsan-ri (Kim Jwa-jin - Helong), sites of victories by independence fighters during Japanese rule, are located there. Yoon Dong-ju, a poet born in Jiandao, give us a heart-breaking story about this area.

Since the founder of the Qing Dynasty, Emperor Kangxi (1661-1722) declared the area off-limits in order to protect the area as the birthplace of Taejo (Nurhaci), the ban continued till the years of Emperor Qianlong (1735~1795). Then, farmers from Hamgyeong Province crossed the Duman River and used new farming technology to continue development.

In 1712, (38th year of King Sukjong), the border between Qing (Mokgeukdong) and Joseon (Park Kwon) was formally demarcated, but conflicts between the two countries continued due to the Tomun River issue. Joseon and Qing officials met in 1885 (Eulyu Meeting) and 1887 (Jeonghae Meeting) to resolve the dispute, but with little result. Korean officials suggested that the border should be Odobaekha (a tributary of the Songhua River), while Qing officials suggested Seoeulsu (a tributary of the Duman River). In the process, the Qing Dynasty lifted the ban and began to exercise its control over the area. When Qing was defeated in the Sino-Japanese War (1894~1895), the Joseon Government set up a border area security office (1901) and began to govern

[2] 간도문제

간도는 압록강·두만강 이북의 만주(동북3성)의 남부 및 동북부 일대를 말한다. 압록강 이북을 서간도, 두만강 이북을 동간도, 그리고 동간도의 북동지방을 북간도라 부르는데, 흔히 동·북간도를 합해서 간도라 부른다. 이곳은 17세기 이후 우리 동포가 이주하여 개척한 곳으로 항일투쟁의 거점이며 현재 연변조선족자치주가 설치되어 있다.

이곳은 고구려·발해시대의 영토로서 길림성의 집안(Ji' an)은 고구려의 수도였고 화룡은 발해의 중경, 훈춘은 동경이었다. 그리고 흑룡강성의 영안은 발해의 수도(상경)로서 우리의 고대문화가 꽃핀 곳이다. 더구나 일제 시에 독립군의 전승지인 봉오동(홍범도-도문)과 청산리(김좌진-화룡)도 여기에 있으며 윤동주의 애달픈 사연을 갖고 있는 곳도 여기이다.

그러나 청의 강희제(성조:1661-1722)는 이곳을 태조(누르하치)의 출생지로 보호하기 위해 봉금지(출입금지지역)로 설정한 이래 계속되어 건륭제(고종:1735~1795)때 강화되었다. 이때 함경도 농민들은 두만강을 건너 그곳에서 새로운 기술로 농사를 지으면서 개발을 계속

Jiandao. This exacerbated the complexity of the matter.

After the Russo-Japanese War (1904~1905), Japan transferred its rights about Manchuri to Qing, signed the Jiandao Convention (1909) by 'Dong3 Sung3 plan' to move forward to the continent and assigned Jiandao to Chaina by specifying the boarder at Sukilsu. Then, in 1952, the Sino-Japanese Peace Treaty rendered all previous treaties between China and Japan null and void, but China still ruled Jiandao. In 1962, North Korea signed a boundary treaty with the People's Republic of China setting the boundary at Hongtosu.

This is how Jiandao was stripped from Korean territory. Jiandao is a land where Korean people toiled and then shed blood during the anti-Japanese resistance movement. Our soil was lost in a dispute between other countries (Qing and Japan). The Tomun River definitely did not refer to the Duman River; it meant Odobaekha (a tributary of the Songhua River). We, therefore, need to firmly establish the grounds to recover Jiandao deprived without relating to our intention, and we should not forget our tragic history. We should also remember that the Amnok River and Duman River do not run from Cheonji Lake.

하였다.

1712년(숙종38)에 중국(목극등)과 조선(박권) 사이에 백두산정계비를 세웠으나 토문강 문제로 양국 간의 마찰이 계속되었음으로 1885년 을유회담(乙酉會談)과 1887년 정해회담(丁亥會談)을 열었으나 두만강의 강원(江原 · 시발점)은 해결되지 않았다. 조선 측은 오도백하(송화강지류)를, 청은 석을수(石乙水 · 두만강지류)를 주장하여 결국은 결렬되었다. 이러한 과정에서 청나라는 봉금정책(封禁政策)을 해제하고 이 지역에 대한 지배권을 행사하기 시작하였다. 조선정부도 청일전쟁(1894~1895)에서 청이 패하자 변계경무소(邊界警務所 · 회령:1901)를 두고 간도를 통치하게 되면서 복잡성을 띄게 되었다.

일본은 러일전쟁(1904~1905) 이후 만주에 대한 지배권을 청에게 양보하고 대륙진출을 위해 「동3성6안(東3省6案)」에 바탕으로 간도협약(1909)을 맺고 석을수를 국경선으로 하여 간도를 청나라에 넘겼다. 그 후 1952년의「중 · 일 평화조약」에서 기존의 중 · 일간에 체결된 조약을 무효화하였으나, 간도를 여전히 지배하고 있었다. 1962년 중국과 북한의 「중조변계조약(中朝邊界條約)」(주은래 · 김일성)으로 홍토수를 경계로 국경선을 확정하였다.

이로서 간도는 우리 땅에서 떨어져 나가게 되었다. 간도는 우리민족이 개척한 땀의 고장

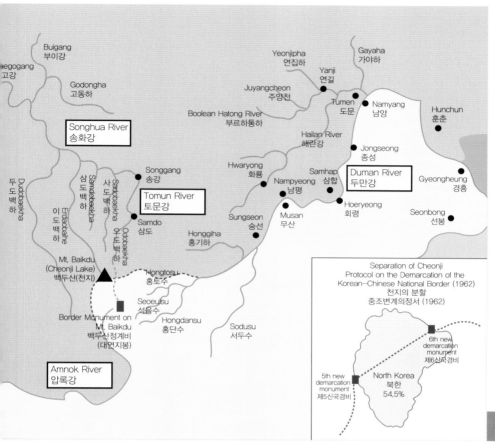

[Map] Tomun River
[지도] 토문강

이며, 항일운동(독립투쟁)의 피의 땅이다. 이렇게 우리 땅이 타국(청·일)의 이권으로 빼앗긴 것이다. 토문강은 분명히 두만강이 아니었고 오도백하(송화강 지류)이다. 따라서 우리는 우리의 의사와 관계없이 빼앗긴 간도를 되찾을 수 있는 바탕을 마련해야 할 것이며, 피맺힌 과거의 슬픈 역사를 잊어서는 안 될 것이다. 동시에 천지에서 압록강과 두만강은 흐르지 않는다는 사실을 잊지 말아야 할 것이다.

[Photo] Mural of a Procession on the Eastern Wall of Goguryeo Anak Tomb No. 3
[사진] 고구려 안악 3호분 '전실동벽' 의 행렬도 : 벽화

Evolution of Ancient Korean Society

한국고대사회의 발전과 그 문화

1. Origin of the Korean People and Prehistoric Age

[1] Origin of the Korean People

The Korean people are ethnically the yellow race and descendants of Altaic-speaking tribes who belong to the Mongolaid, and are called 'Dongyi' tribe in Chinese literature. The Dongyi people were distinct from the Chinese people and were kind-hearted and respect human life and take a serious view of human virtue. They first inhabited the Korean Peninsula and Manchuria tens of thousands of years ago and have the roots of Yemaek people and proto-Koreans. It is believed that Ye people worshiped the tiger, the Maek people adored the bear, and the proto-Koreans worshiped the sun; they joined together and became the parent of Korean people in the late Neolithic Age.

The first human ancestors settled on the Korean Peninsula about 700,000 years ago, and their traces are found across South and North Korea. They were not the direct ancestors of the Korean people, though. The Korean people as a distinct group began to come into being about 10,000 years ago, in the Neolithic Age. The process was completed in the Bronze Age about BC 3,000 years, when the Korean people embraced earlier people.

1. 민족의 기원과 선사시대

[1] 한민족의 기원

우리민족은 인종상으로 황인종이며 몽골족에 속하는 알타이어계로서 중국 문헌에는 동이족이라 불렀다. 중국인과 다른 동이족은 어질고 생명을 존중하는 인간의 덕목을 중시하는 민족으로 수만 년 전부터 한반도와 만주대륙에 걸쳐 살고 있었으며, 예맥족과 한족(韓族: proto-koreans)이 근간을 이루었다. 예족은 범, 맥족은 곰, 그리고 한족은 태양을 숭배하는 종족으로 생각되며 이들이 결합하여 신석기후기에 한민족의 모체를 이루었다.

한반도에는 약 70만년전부터 사람들이 살고 있었음으로 남·북한 여러곳에서 그 흔적이 발견되고 있다. 그러나 이들이 한민족의 직접 조상은 아니었고, 약 1만년 전의 신석기시대가 되면서 점차 우리민족의 바탕이 이룩되기 시작하였다. 그후 3천년 경에 청동기시대가 되어 앞선 사람들을 흡수하여 우리민족이 형성되었다.

[2] Prehistoric Period

About 700,000 years ago, the sea level was much lower and there was no Yellow Sea. The Korean Peninsula and Manchuria were a single cultural region during the Paleolithic period. The Neolithic Age began about 10,000 years ago, and it was only then that the Yellow Sea was created. The Neolithic Revolution took place in the warmer climate and witnessed the development of farming, fishing, and hunting. During this period, comb-patterned pottery and semi-lunar stone knives were used,

[Photo] Dwelling sito in Neolithic age
〈Source: Korea Tourism Organization〉

[사진] 신석기시대의 움집
〈사진제공:한국관광공사〉

[2] 선사시대

약 70만년전에는 황해가 없어 한반도와 민주 일대는 하나의 문화권으로 구석기를 거쳤으며, 약 1만년 전에 신석기시대를 맞게 된다. 이때 황해가 나타나고 기후가 따뜻해지면서 농경과 수렵을 통해 신석기 혁명을 맞게 되었다. 이 시기에 빗살 무늬 토기와 반달 모양의 돌칼이 사용되었고 움집을 중심으로 씨족공동체를 이루었다.

기원전 3천년 경에 청동기가 시작되어 무기 · 제기(祭器)가 변하고 무늬 없는 토기를 사용하면서 집안생활을 하게 되었다. 여기서 지배 · 피지배의 계급사회가 나타났으며, 사유재산이 나타나 초기 국가가 발생하였다. 이때의 대표적인 유적은 고인돌과 바위 그림이다.

and clan communities were formed around pit dwellings.

The Bronze Age began around BC 3,000 years. Weapons and ritual vessels were further developed, plain earthenware was used, and people began to live in houses. Around then, a hierarchical society with a ruling class and a subordinate class emerged. The concept of private property was also created, and early states were formed. Major remains from this period are dolmens and rock art.

[3] Establishment of Early States

During the Bronze Age, the emergence of classes (rulers vs. citizens) and private property brought about drastic societal change. Cities came into being as a result of collective activities and interactions, and trade and war led to chiefdom societies and, later, early states (or walled-town states).

The early states were ruled by kings, but they held little actual power, and were the religious leaders, in perspective of uniting religion and state. Power resided with the clan heads, but the kings had primitively subordinate officials and could govern their states. Laws necessary to maintain society were enacted, and various religious events were held to unite the people.

[3] 초기 국가의 성립

청동기사회는 계급(지배자와 피지배자)과 사유재산이 나타나게 되어 사회의 큰 변화가 일어났다. 집단생활을 통해 도시가 나타났으며 상호교섭, 무역. 그리고 전쟁이 일어나 군장 사회(Chiefdom)로 발전되어 초기국가(성읍국가)가 되었다.

초기 국가는 중앙에 왕이 존재하였으나 그 권력은 약하였다. 그러나 제정일치의 입장에서 종교의 지배자였다. 비록 모든 권력이 부족장회의에 있었지만, 왕은 원시적인 관료를 거느리면서 국가를 지배할 수 있었다. 그리고 그 사회를 유지하는데 필요한 법률이 있었고 국민적 단합을 위해 각종 제천행사가 있었다.

[4] Gojoseon (Old Korea)

By evolving the bronze culture, Gojoseon became the first state of the Korean people. According to *Samgukyusa*, Hwanung, the son of Hwanin (the Lord of Heaven), descended to Mount Taebaek and founded the Holy City. Then, he married the woman transformed from bear, Ungnyeo. The two soon had a son, Dangun Wanggeom, who founded Gojoseon in 2333 B.C. In China, this was the Yaoshun Period. This is not simply a myth but the beginning of Korea's long history.

[photo] Dolmen in Bronze age
⟨Source: Korea Tourism Organization⟩

[사진] 고인돌
⟨사진제공·한국관광공사⟩

[4] 고조선

청동기문화가 발전하는 과정에서 우리나라 최초 고조선이 성립되었다. 「삼국유사」에 의하면 하느님(桓仁)의 아들인 환웅이 태백산에 내려와 신시(Holy city)를 열고 곰의 변신인 웅녀와 결혼하여 태어난 단군왕검이 B.C. 2333년에 고조선을 세웠다고 하였다. 이때가 중국의 요순시대와 비슷하였는데 이것은 단순한 신화가 아니라 장구한 우리역사의 시작을 의미한다.

고조선은 곧 철기문화를 바탕으로 국가체제를 갖추었고 주변을 정복하여 요하를 넘어 만주의 서남부(요동·요서)와 한반도의 대동강 일대에 이르는 큰 국가를 이루어 B·C 5세기에는 연(燕)나라에 맞설 수 있었다.

고조선은 중국가 법속이 달라서 생명을 중히 여기고 사유재산을 보호하기위해 「8조의 법」(살인·상해·절도의 금지)이 있어 미풍양속으로 이어져 한국인의 전통이 되었다.

The Myth of Dangun: Korea's founding legend is told in the *Memorabilia of the Three Kingdoms* (*Samgukyusa*) (1285) written by Il-yeon (1206~1289) as follows. "Hwanung, the son of Hwanin (God of Heavens) descended to Mount Taebaek, accompanied by his ministers of wind, rain, and clouds, with the intention of benefitting mankind. He founded the Holy City and ruled the people by taking care of some 360 essential matters including grains, life, and punishment. One day, a bear came to him and asked to become a human. Hwanung told the bear to eat mugwort and garlic. The bear became a woman. Later, the woman married Hwanung and gave birth to a son, who was named Dangun. Dangun Wanggeom founded a nation named Joseon and designated Asadal as its capital."

As the Iron Age progressed, Gojoseon soon organized a state structure and conquered surrounding areas. It expanded beyond the Liao River, across Manchuria, and into an area around the Daedong River on the Korean Peninsula, which had a major power. By the 5th century B.C., it was able to stand up against Yen of China.

Gojoseon had laws and customs unlike those of China. It had the "Code of Eight Articles" (banning murder, assault, and theft) to uphold the value of life and protect private property. Such social morals and customs became integral to Korean tradition.

[5] Vicissitudes of Gojosoen

Gojoseon became a strong power with a vast territory stretching from southwestern Manchuria and into the northern Korean Peninsula. However, it had to relocate to the

단군 신화 우리나라의 건국 신화는 일연(1206~1289)이 쓴 「삼국유사」(1285)에 기록되어 있는 바 그 내용은 다음과 같다. "환인(하느님)의 아들 환웅이 인간을 널리 이롭게 할 목적으로 바람 · 비 · 구름을 각각 주관하는 부하들을 거느리고 태백산에 내려와 신시를 열고, 곡식 · 생명 · 형벌 등 인간에게 필요한 300여 가지를 주관하여 사람들을 다스렸다. 그러던 중에 곰이 찾아와 사람이 되기를 원하므로 환웅은 곰에게 쑥과 마늘을 먹게 한 후 여자로 변하게 하고, 그와 혼인하여 아들을 낳았다. 이가 곧 단군이다. 단군왕검은 아사달에 도읍을 정하고 나라를 세워 조선이라 하였다."

[5] 고조선의 변천

고조선은 만주의 서남부와 한반도 북방에 걸친 큰 나라가 되었으나 연나라의 침입으로 대동강 유역으로 나라를 옮겼다. 그후 중국이 전국시대의 혼란기에 주민의 이동이 심한 틈을

Daedong River region in the face of an invasion by Yen. Later, when China fell into turmoil and people were on the move, Wiman Joseon (194~108 BC) was founded, but it was very anti-Chinese and was crushed by Emperor Wu of Han.

When Wiman Joseon fell, four Chinese commanderies (108 BC~ AD313: Nangnang, Jinbeon, Imdun, Hyeondo) were set up on the former territory of Gojoseon, but the Korean people soon managed to wrest back control of Jinbeon and Imdun. Hyeondo and Nangnang were later seized by Goguryeo (313), and the legacy of Gojoseon was succeeded by Goguryeo.

[6] Other Early States in South and North

When Gojoseon prospered in Liaodong and the Daedong River region, a number of other early states emerged across Manchuria and the Korean Peninsula: Buyeo, Goguryeo, Okjeo, Easter Ye, Mahan, Jinha, and Byeonhan. These states used advanced agriculture technologies using iron tools and developed agriculture, livestock farming, and fishing. They flourished through trade with other countries.

Although kings and officials were at the center of power, regional clan chiefs ruled by their own bureaucratic organizations. In short, these states formed confederated kingdoms. The kingdoms held heaven-worshipping ceremonies (*yeonggo* in Buyeo and *dongmaeng* in Goguryeo) every spring and fall, and people held rituals for the

타서 위만조선(B·C.194~108)이 세워졌으나 반 중국정책을 고수하다가 한무제의 침입으로 멸망하였다.

위만조선이 멸망하고 고조선 옛 땅에는 한사군(B.C. 108~A.D. 313 : 낙랑·진번·임둔·현도)이 설치되었다. 그러나 우리민족의 줄기찬 저항으로 진번과 임둔이 곧 폐지되고 이어 현도와 낙랑이 고구려에 멸망하여(313) 한군현이 없어졌으며, 고조선의 전통은 고구려에 계승되었다.

[6] 남북의 여러 나라

고조선이 요동과 대동강 유역에서 발전하고 있을 때, 만주와 한반도의 여러 곳에는 부여(夫餘)·고구려(高句麗)·옥저(沃沮)·동예(東濊)·마한(馬韓)·진한(辰韓)·변한(弁韓) 등의 초기 국가가 출현하였다. 이 국가들은 발달된 철제 농기구와 연모를 이용하여 농업과 목축 및 어업을 발전시켰으며, 무역을 통해 초기 국가를 번성시켰다.

heaven and sand during which they danced and released prisoners. These events were not only modest religious ceremonies wishing for a good crop and giving thanks for the harvest but also occasions to strengthen communal spirit for the solidarity of tribes.

2. Formation of the Three Kingdoms and Development of Ancient States

[1] Characteristics of Ancient States

The Three Kingdoms of Goguryeo, Baekje and Silla are often described as ancient states. During this period, royal authority was absolute and kings were succeeded by the eldest sons. Chieftains of the early states were appointed as bureaucrats. Kings would often go on royal processions to provincial areas to show their authority and rule the areas. In this way, these states whose poewr was centralized, developed the bureaucratic system. These kingdoms were intent on expanding their territories and often engaged in wars against China.

They also embraced Buddhism, which was merged with the traditional ideology. It allowed the unity of ideology among people and served as a foundation of cultural development. On the other hand, Confucianism set political, social, and ethical principles. The Three Kingdoms expanded their lands and built states with clear

이들 초기 국가에는 중앙에 왕과 관료가 존재하였으나, 각 지역의 부족장들이 독자적인 관료 조직을 거느리고 세력을 떨치고 있었으므로 일종의 연맹국가였다. 또한, 각 나라에서는 농사를 하는 봄과 가을에 국가적인 제천(祭天)행사(부여의 영고·고구려의 동맹)를 개최하여, 하늘에 제사를 지내고 춤과 노래를 즐기며 죄수들을 풀어 주었다. 이러한 제천 행사는 풍년을 기원하고 수확에 감사를 드리는 소박한 종교 의식이였을 뿐만 아니라, 전국적인 축제를 통하여 부족의 통합을 위한 공동체 의식을 강화시키는 행사였다.

2. 삼국의 성립과 고대국가의 발전

[1] 고대국가의 성격

삼국 시대를 흔히 고대 국가라고 한다. 고대 국가는 왕권이 절대화되었고 왕은 세습(장자

borderlines. In order to protect their territories, they mobilized the people to build fortresses at strategic points. It was commonly believed that the progenitors of kings in the Three Kingdoms were all sons of gods, just as in China. This served as a source of great pride and self-respect in creating the national culture.

[2] Formation of the Three Kingdoms

The Three Kingdoms period is Korea's first ancient state period. Goguryeo, Baekje, and Silla developed competitively during this time. According to the oldest book on Korean history 'Samguk Sagi', Silla was established in 57 B.C., Goguryeo in 37 B.C. (277 B.C. according to North Korea), and Baekje in 18 B.C. However, considering the relationships with China at that time, Goguryeo was probably built first and Silla last.

Goguryeo took shape while warring against China. It laid its foundation as a state early during the reign of King Taejo (53~146) while reclaiming a Chinese commandery (Hyeondo) and serving as a bulwark of defense for the Korean Peninsula. Taking advantage of its geographical location near the Han River, Baekje absorbed Mahan and developed into a powerful state during the years of King Goi (234~286). Then, geographically isolated Silla inherited the tradition of Jinhan and built its power during the years of King Naemul (356~402). It continued to gain forces through negotiations and conflicts with Baekje and Goguryeo.

상속)으로 계승되었으며, 초기 국가의 족장들이 관료로 편제되었다. 이때의 왕은 지방을 수시로 순행(:巡幸-Royal tour)하여 자신의 권위를 나타내면서 지방을 통치하였다. 이러한 중앙 집권적인 국가는 관료제도가 발달하였고, 정복 국가로서 특성이 뚜렷하여 중국과의 전쟁이 계속 되었다.

더구나 불교가 수용되어 기존의 전통사상을 흡수하고 국민적인 사상 통일을 이룩하여 문화 발전에 바탕이 되었으며, 유교는 정치와 사회 윤리의 기준이 되었다. 삼국은 각기 영토를 확장하여 국가의 형태를 갖춤으로써 국경선이 뚜렷해졌으며, 자국의 영토를 지키기 위해 요충지에 성곽을 쌓아 국민을 부역에 동원하였다. 특히 삼국의 시조는 중국과 같이 하느님의 아들이라는 자부심과 긍지를 갖고 민족 문화를 건설하였다.

[2] 삼국의 성립

삼국 시대는 고구려 · 백제 · 신라가 경쟁적으로 발전된 우리나라 최초의 고대국가시대

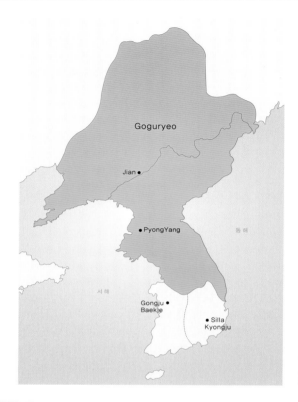

[Map] Goguryeo (5th Century)

[지도] 고구려의 강역(5세기)

이다. 한국 최고의 역사책인 「삼국사기」에는 기원전 57년에 신라, 기원전 37년에 고구려(북한은 기원전 277년), 그리고 기원전 18년에 백제가 성립된 것으로 기록하고 있다. 그러나 당시의 사회 환경이나 중국과의 관계를 고려할 때 고구려가 제일 먼저 건국되었고, 신라가 가장 늦게 성립되었을 것으로 추측된다.

　고구려는 중국과 싸우면서 성립되었다. 중국의 한군현(현도)을 축출하면서 한반도의 방파제로 일찍 태조왕 때(53~146)에 국가기반을 마련하였고, 백제는 한강 유역의 유리한 지리적 환경을 바탕으로 마한을 흡수·통합하면서 고이왕(234~286) 때 나라를 크게 발전시켰다. 그리고 지리적으로 격리된 신라는 진한의 전통을 이어받아 내물왕(356~402) 때 강력한 국가로 발전하여 제·려(濟麗: 백제와 고구려)와 교섭과 충돌을 거치면서 발전하였다.

[3] 고구려의 강성

　고구려는 태조왕(53~146) 때 국가적 체제를 갖춘 후 미천왕(300~331)때 낙랑을 축출하

[3] Power of Goguryeo

Goguryeo became a full-fledged state during the reign of King Taejo (53~146), drove out Nangnang under King Micheon (300~331), and emerged as a power in the northern region, but it faced tremendous challenges due to endless confrontation with China (Ye and Yen). Then, during the reign of King Sosurim (371~384), Goguryeo embraced Buddhism and promulgated administrative laws to lay the foundation for a strong state.

[Photo] The First Capital of Goguryeo (Wunu Fortress located in Huanren, Liaoning Province, China) In 37 B.C., Jumong traveled south from Buyeo with Jesa, Mugol, and Mukgeo and founded Goguryeo here.

[사진] 고구려 첫 도읍지(중국 라오닝성 환련시 오녀산성)
기원전 37년 고주몽이 재사 · 무골 · 묵거 등과 함께 부여에서 남하하여 이곳에 처음으로 고구려를 세웠다.

여 북방의 강자로 성장하였으나, 계속된 중국(위 · 전연)과의 전쟁으로 많은 시련을 겪게 되었다. 그러나 소수림왕(371~384) 때는 불교를 받아들이고 율령을 반포하여 강국으로서의 기반을 마련하였다.

이어 광개토왕(391~413) 때에는 만주를 거의 지배하고 백제와 가야에 와있던 왜를 정복하면서 신라까지 지배하에 두었다. 그 뒤를 이은 장수왕(413~491)은 서울을 평양으로 옮겨 동아시아 최강국이 되어 만주(중국의 동북3성)를 지배하면서 중국에 맞섰던 나라가 되었다. 현재 지안(지린성)에 남아 있는 광개토왕비가 이를 증명하고 있다.

현재 고구려에 대하여 중국에서는 그들 동북공정(2002~2007)에서 소수 민족이 세운 그들의 지방정권이라고 하면서 고구려의 국가적 독자성을 부인하고 있다. 그러나 고구려는 중국의 동아시아 지배를 허용치 않았으며, 끝까지 중국과 다른 정치체제와 사회조직을 유지하였으며, 언어와 풍속이 엄연히 다른 당당한 독립국가였다. 더구나 수 · 당이 대군을 이끌고 고구려 정벌을 꾀한 사실은 그것이 국내 전쟁이 아니라 동아시아 지배를 거부한 고구려와의 국제전쟁이었음을 증명해 준다. 결국 당나라는 신라와 연합하여 고구려를 멸망시켰다.

In the later years of the reign of King Gwanggaeto (391~413) in later years, Goguryeo dominated Manchuria and conquered Wae (Japan), which was present in Baekje and Gaya, and even put Silla under its control. King Gwanggaeto was succeeded by King Jangsu (413~491), who relocated the capital to Pyeongyang and made Goguryeo the most powerful state in East Asia, which was against China by controlling Manchuria (east and north three provinces of China). This fact is proven by a stele standing at the tomb of King Gwanggaeto in Jian (Jilin Province, China).

In its Northeast Project (2002~2007), China refuses to recognize the sovereignty of Goguryeo and claims that Goguryeo was a regime built by an ethnic minority group in China. However, Goguryeo did not allow China to rule all of East Asia and maintained unique political and social systems, language, and customs. Moreover, the fact that the Chinese dynasties of Sui and Tang mobilized large forces and attempted to conquer Goguryeo testifies to the fact that these conflicts were not civil wars but international wars against Goguryeo. In the end, Goguryeo was overrun by allied forces of Tang and Silla.

[4] Victories Against Sui and Tang

In the course of Goguryeo's rise as the greatest power in East Asia, it repeatedly engaged in wars against China to keep its leadership. The wars against Sui and Tang, which unified China in the late 6th century, were especially intense. Goguryeo intended to stop China from advancing into the Far East and defended the territory and

[4] 수 · 당 전쟁의 승리

고구려는 동북아시아 제일의 대제국으로 발전했기 때문에 그 주도권 쟁탈을 위해 중국과 치열한 전쟁을 되풀이하였다. 특히 6세기 말에 중국 대륙을 통일한 수·당과의 전쟁은 처절한 것이었다. 이 전쟁은 중국 세력이 극동 지방으로 진출하는 것을 막고 우리민족의 영토와 문화를 지키려는 싸움이었다. 수양제(煬帝)는 612년에 113만의 대군을 이끌고 고구려를 공격하였으나 을지문덕(乙支文德)이 이끄는 고구려군에게 살수싸움에서 전멸하였다. 이러한 살수대첩은 고려시대(강감찬)의 귀주대첩(1018)과 조선시대(이순신)의 한산도대첩과 (1592)과 함께 우리역사의 3대첩의 하나이다.

그후 수나라를 계승한 당나라는 치욕을 씻기 위해 고구려를 위협하기 시작하였다. 당 태종(太宗)은 645년에 수십만 대군을 이끌고 고구려를 침략했지만, 안시성 혈전에서 참패하고 말았다. 이러한 고구려의 수·당 침입 격퇴는 동아시아에서의 중국의 지배권을 저지한 것이며, 고구려 중심의 세계관을 이룩한 사실이다.

culture of the Korean people. In 612, Yang-ti of Sui attacked Goguryeo with an army of 1.13 million soldiers but was utterly defeated by a Goguryeo army led by General Uljimundeok at the Great Battle of the Salsu River. This battle, the Great Battle of Guiju (1018) in the Goryeo Dynasty (General Kang Gam-chan), and the Great Battle of Hansando (1592) in the Joseon Dynasty (General Yi Sun-sin) are the three most important victories in Korean history.

Tang later succeeded Sui and began to threaten Goguryeo in an effort to wipe away the disgrace of the defeat. In 645, Tang Emperor Tai Tsung invaded Goguryeo with an army of tens of thousands of soldiers but was defeated at the bloody battle of Ansi Fortress. Goguryeo's victories over the Sui and Tang prevented China from achieving hegemony over all of East Asia and shifted the focus of history to Goguryeo.

[5] The Rise and Fall of Baekje

Baekje had the advantage of being close to the Han River and built its power by

---

The Great Battle of the Salsu River was Korea's first victory against a foreign army. Jo Jun, a politician of late Goryeo and early Joseon, wrote a poem about the battle.

> A vast expanse of the Salsu River waves in the air and
> gulps down millions of Sui soldiers.
> Still talked about among fishermen and lumbermen,
> they cannot be even laughed at by wanderers.

살수대첩은 우리나라 역사상 최초로 외국과의 전쟁에서 이긴 역사적 사건이다. 고려말 조선초의 정치가인 조준은 다음과 같은 시를 남겼다.

> 살수는 넓고 넓어 허공에 출렁일 때
> 수나라 백만대군 물고기밥 되었구나
> 지금도 어부들과 나뭇꾼의 이야기 되어
> 나그네 웃음거리도 못되었네

---

[5] 백제의 융성과 쇠퇴

백제는 한강 유역의 유리한 환경을 바탕으로 남쪽으로 마한을 복속시키고, 북쪽으로 고구려와 항쟁하면서 발전하였다. 특히 4세기 중엽의 근초고왕(345~375)때에는 남으로 마한세

ruling Mahan to the south and competing with Goguryeo to the north. In the mid-fourth century, during the reign of King Geunchogo (345~375), Baekje absorbed Mahan and attacked Goguryeo. In 371, King Gogukwon of Goguryeo was killed in battle. At the height of its power, Baekje's influence extended over the West Sea. It even established forces in the Liaoxi region.

Goguryeo assumed leadership among the Three Kingdoms in the late 4th century. King Gwanggaeto (392~413) controlled Manchuria and began to pressure Baekje. King Jangsu (413~491) of Goguryeo relocated the capital to Pyeongyang (427) and occupied Hanseong and killed King Gaero in battle (475). Baekje moved its capital to Ungjin

[Photo] Discovery of the Tomb of King Munyeong

In 1971, the tombs of King Munyeong and his queen were discovered among ancient tombs in Gongju Songsan-ri. Inside the tomb, a number of burial accessories, including gold crowns, stone sculptures of animals, steles, and coins, were excavated.

〈Source: Korea Tourism Organization〉

[사진] 무령왕의 발견

1971년 공주송산리 고분에서 무녕왕과 왕비의 능이 발견되었다. 그 속에서 금관식과 돌짐승, 자석(誌石:무덤속에 넣은 비석), 동전 등 많은 부장품이 발견 되었다.

〈사진제공:한국관광공사〉

력을 통합하고 북으로 고구려를 공격하여 371년에 고국원왕을 패사시켰다. 이러한 국력을 바탕으로 백제는 서해를 건너 요서지역에 백제세력권을 형성하여 백제의 전성기를 맞았다.

그러나 4세기말 이후 삼국의 판도는 고구려가 주도하였다. 광개토왕(392~413)은 만주를 지배하는 한편 백제를 압박하기 시작하였고 장수왕(413~491)은 서울을 평양으로 옮긴 후 (427) 한성을 점령하여 개로왕을 패사시켰다(475). 이에 백제는 서울을 웅진(현재 공주)으로 옮긴 후 무녕왕(501~523)은 고구려를 공격하면서 외교를 통해 중흥을 꾀하였다. 이어 성왕이(523~554)은 다시 서울을 사비(泗沘:현재 부여)로 옮기며 국가를 재건시켰으나 신라에게 패사함으로서(554) 백제 부흥의 꿈은 사라져 갔다.

[6] 백제의 해외 진출

백제는 일찍부터 서해를 통한 해외진출을 꾀하였다. 근초고왕 때에는 중국의 진(晉)의 세력이 약화된 틈을 타서 요서 지방에 진출하여 백제군을 설치하였다. 백제는 또한 우세한

(currently Gongju), and King Munyeong (501~523) attacked Goguryeo and attempted to restore prosperity through diplomacy. King Seong (523~554) then relocated the capital again to Sabi (currently Buyeo) and rebuilt the state, but he was defeated and killed in battle (554) by Silla. Baekje's aspirations for prosperity were shattered.

[6] Baekje's Advances Overseas

From early on, Baekje was interested in moving into foreign lands over the West Sea. During the reign of King Geunchogo, Baekje took advantage of the weakness of the Chin Dynasty to advance into the Liaoxi region. Its strong navy enabled Baekje to also make inroads into Japan's Kyushu region. The Baekje were excellent navigators, and they established the maritime trade routes connecting China's Liaoxi and Shandong regions to Korea and Japan's Kyushu region. Baekje had such a great maritime presence that Baekje villages remain in China (Guangxi Zhuang Autonomous Region) and Japan (Miyazaki prefecture, Kyushu) to this day.

[7] Rise of Silla

Silla was the least developed of the Three Kingdoms because of its geographical isolation. In the 4th century, in the reign of King Naemul (356~402), Silla became a full-

해양 군사력을 바탕으로 일본의 큐슈지방에도 진출하였다. 백제인들은 발전된 항해술을 이용하여 요서·산동 지방과 한반도 및 일본 큐슈 지역을 연결하는 해상무역권을 형성하고 있었던 것이다. 백제인의 활발한 해상 활동으로 현재 중국(광서 장족자치구의 옹녕시 남부)과 일본(큐슈·미야자키현)에 백제 촌락이 남아있게 되었다.

[7] 신라의 발전

삼국 중에서 지리적 고립으로 후진성을 면치못했던 신라는 4세기경 내물왕(356~402)때에 국가 체제를 갖춘 후, 고구려의 간섭을 벗어나 6세기 법흥왕(514~540)대에는 불교를 받아들이고 정치 제도를 개혁하는 등 국가적 성장에 바탕을 마련하였다.

이어 진흥왕(540~576)대에는 한강 하류지역을 확보하고, 낙동강 유역에서 세력을 펴고 있던 가야(伽倻)를 정복하였으며, 북쪽으로는 함경도 지역까지 진출하여 그 기념으로 4곳에 순수비를 세워 삼국 통일의 기반을 마련하였다. 이러한 신라의 성장에는 국가와 민족에 충성

fledged state. In the 6th century, during the reign of King Beopheung (514~540), Silla became free from interventions by Goguryeo and laid a foundation for national growth by embracing Buddhism and initiating political reforms.

King Jinheung (540~576) secured the south of the Han River and conquered Gaya, which had influence over the area around the Nakdong River. To the north, Silla extended as far as Hamgyeong Province and set up statues at four sites, preparing the way for unification of the Three Kingdoms. The rise of Silla was partly driven by the spirit of the Hwarang warriors, who were dedicated to and sacrificed themselves for the country and its people. Renowned Hwarang warriors, including Sadaham, Gwanchang, and Kim Yu-shin, played a crucial role in Silla's unification of the Three Kingdoms.

Awareness of the Silla People
The awareness of the Silla people, epitomized in *Hwarangdo*, stressed patriotic loyalty to the country and filial duty to parents. Sacrificing one's life for the country was considered an act of both loyalty and filial duty.

하고 희생하는 화랑도 정신이 큰 힘이 되었다. 사다함 · 관창 · 김유신 등 대표적인 화랑은 신라가 삼국을 통일하는 대에 중추적인 역할을 하였다.

신라인의 국가의식
화랑도로 대표되는 신라인의 국가의식은 신하가 되려면 나라에 충성을 다하는 것이고 자식이 되려면 부모에게 효도를 다하는 것으로 생각하였다. 나라를 위해 목숨을 바치면 충 · 효를 함께하는 것으로 믿었다.

3. Silla's Unification of the Three Kingdoms and the South-North State Period

[1] Silla's Conquest of Baekje and Goguryeo

By the 7th century, Baekje and Goguryeo had fallen into turmoil due to insurgencies by noblemen and decline in royal authority. Silla took advantage of the situation to build up its power. Battles between Baekje and Silla served to intensify hostility between the two kingdoms, and Goguryeo became exhausted in its wars against Sui and Tang. Silla gained power under the leadership of Kim Chun-chu (who later became King Muyeol) and Kim Yu-sin. By allying with the Tang Dynasty, Silla conquered Baekje in 660 and Goguryeo in 668.

Loyal elements of Baekje and Goguryeo, nevertheless, continued to resist and tried to revive the two kingdoms. The restoration of Baekje with Japanese assistance failed due to internal conflicts and a defeat at the Battle of Baekchon River (663). Goguryeo's attempt at restoration turned into resistance against Tang as a result of Silla's pacification policy. Silla eventually put down the resistance from Goguryeo and Baekje and drew the people of the two kingdoms into resistance against Tang, finally achieving national unification for the first time in Korea's history.

3. 신라의 삼국통일과 남북국시대의 전개

[1] 신라의 백제 · 고구려 정벌

7세기에 들어와 백제와 고구려는 귀족의 반란과 정치적 혼란(왕의 실정)으로 국가적 혼란에 쌓였으며, 이 틈을 타 신라는 국력을 강화시켰다. 백제는 신라와의 전쟁으로 양국 간의 갈등이 심해졌고, 고구려는 수 · 당과의 전쟁으로 국력이 탕진되었다. 이에 신라는 김춘추(金春秋, 뒤에 太宗武烈王) · 김유신을 중심으로 국력을 집중시킨 후 당의 군사력을 이용함으로써 660년에 백제를, 668년에 고구려를 정복하였다.

그러나 두 나라에서는 부흥 운동이 일어났다. 일본의 지원을 받은 백제부흥운동은 내분과 백촌강 전투(663)에서 패함으로 실패하였다. 고구려부흥운동은 신라의 회유정책으로 대당항쟁에 합류하게 되었다. 그 후 신라는 백제 · 고구려 부흥 운동을 수습하고 제 · 려유민을 대당항쟁에 끌어들여 최초의 민족 통일을 완성하였다.

Showdown between Kim Yu-sin and Sojeongbang

In 660, Silla and Tang joined hands and agreed to conquer Baekje together. However, Silla was not able to accomplish its objectives by the promised date due to intense resistance from General Gyebaek of Baekje. Tang's commander in chief, Sojeongbang, pointed out that Silla had failed to keep its promise and tried to execute Silla's liaison officer. Kim Yu-sin stepped in and firmly declared that if the officer were punished for Silla's failure to keep the promised date, he would first wage war against Tang before conquering Baekje. Sojeongbang relented and took part in the joint operation. (*Samguk Sagi* Volume 5)

[2] Success of Ancient National Unification

Silla foiled the military ambitions of Tang, drove its forces off of the Korean Peninsula, and finally succeeded in unifying the entire peninsula in 676. Although unification was incomplete in that not all of the population and territory had yet been brought under control, a unified government was established for the first time and a single culture was created.

The Unified Silla embraced the people of Baekje and Goguryeo and appointed them to positions in government. Silla also drove out the Tang forces and established national independence and sovereignty. In particular, Silla assigned people of Baekje and Goguryeo to Silla's main central army (9th division) to realize national solidarity. The national territory was divided into nine *ju* (provinces) and five *sogyeong*

김유신과 소정방의 대결

660년 신라와 당은 백제정벌에 합동작전을 수행하였다.
그러나 신라는 계백(백제 장군)의 결사적인 저항으로 약속기일을 어길 수밖에 없었다. 이때 소정방(당군 총사령관)은 약속기일의 이행을 못했다고 신라의 연락관을 처형하려 하였다. 이때 김유신은 약속기일을 문책한다면 먼저 당나라군과 결전을 한 후에 백제정벌을 하겠다고 강경하게 나서자 소정방은 기가 꺾여 합동작전을 수행하였다. (「삼국사기」권5)

[2] 전근대 민족 통일의 실현

신라는 당나라의 군사적 야욕을 물리치고 당군을 한반도에서 축출하여 676년에 전근대 민족의 통일을 실현하였다. 비록 인구와 영토가 축소된 불완전한 통일이었으나, 비로소 처음 으로 통일 정부를 수립하고 하나의 민족 문화를 이룩한 것이다.

(secondary capital). The territories of each of the former three kingdoms had three *ju* and two *sogyeong* for balanced development.

[3] Prosperity of Unified Silla

King Munmu (661~681), who accomplished the unification, firmly established royal authority. His successor, King Sinmun (681~692), improved the bureaucratic system and established the first authoritarian monarchy. Then, King Seongdeok (702~737) demonstrated Silla's power overseas by forging close ties with Tang. Benefiting from this political stability, King Gyeongdeok (742~765) ensured that Unified Silla flourished through its unique bureaucratic system. Bulguksa Temple and Seokguram Grotto epitomize the glory and prosperity of Unified Silla.

Unified Silla not only accepted the cultures of Baekje and Goguryeo as well as Tang but also western culture and further developed the culture of the Korean people. Students and monks were sent to Tang to broaden the scope of Silla culture. Under a stable monarchy, Silla projected its independence and identity to the outside world and maintained societal stability for a long period of time.

통일신라는 백제 · 고구려 유민을 받아들여 신라의 관리로 등용하고 당군을 축출하여 민족의 자주성과 정통성을 확립하였다. 특히 신라는 백제 · 고구려 백성들을 신라의 중앙 군대 (9서당)에 편입시켜 민족 융합을 위해 노력하였으며, 전국을 9주 5소경으로 나누어 삼국의 옛 땅에 똑같이 각각 3주와 2소경을 두어 국가의 균형발전을 꾀하였다.

[3] 통일신라의 융성

신라의 통일을 완수한 문무왕(661~681)은 강력한 왕권을 확립하였고, 그 뒤를 이은 신문왕(681~692)은 새로운 관료 제도를 완비하여 최초로 전제 왕권을 이룩하였다. 이어 성덕왕 (702~737)은 당나라와 긴밀한 외교정책으로 국력을 대외적으로 과시하였다. 이러한 정치적 안정을 이어받은 경덕왕(742~765)은 신라의 독자적인 관료제를 통해 통일신라의 융성을 가져왔다. 이 시기에 나타난 불국사와 석굴암은 바로 통일신라의 번영을 뒷받침하는 것이었다. 통일신라는 제 · 려문화와 당나라의 문화 뿐 아니라 서역문화까지 수용하여 민족 문화를

[Photo] Bulguksa Temple

Bulguksa was built in a wish for a utopian nation of Buddhism. Daewoongjeon (he Land of Seokgamoni Buddha) and Geungnakjeon (the Land of Amitabha) are located at the east and west of the main courtyard. Birojeon and Gwaneumjeon stand to the north. To the south of Daewungjeon are two stone pagodas, Dabotap and Seokgatap.

⟨Source: Korea Tourism Organization⟩

[사진] 불국사

불국사는 불교의 이상 국가를 지향하는 뜻으로 건축되었는데 오른쪽에 대웅전(석가모니), 왼쪽에 극락전(아미타불), 북쪽에 비로전과 관음전이 있고, 대웅전 남쪽에는 다보탑과 석가탑이 있다.

⟨사진제공:한국관광공사⟩

발전시켰으며, 당나라에 유학생·구법승 등을 파견하여 신라 문화의 폭을 넓혔다. 특히 신라는 안정된 왕건을 바탕으로 대외적으로 자주성과 주체성을 나타내었으며 장기간의 평화를 구가하면서 안정된 사회를 유지하였다.

[4] Completion of Bureaucratic System

Unified Silla established a unique centralized bureaucratic system to support the monarchy. In the central government, 14 ministries directly reported to the king, and high-ranking officials enjoyed exclusive privileges while holding more than one position. There were administrations for nine provinces (*ju*) and five secondary capitals (*sogyeong*). The military was organized into nine central units (*seodang*) and 10 local units (*jeong*). Officials received stipends. These systems served as the prototype for traditional Korean society throughout the Goryeo and Joseon dynasties.

[5] Overseas Trade

Active diplomatic relations between Unified Silla and Tang led to frequent exchanges of diplomatic envoys, students, monks, and merchants, which further increased cultural and commercial exchanges. Silla imported silk, clothes, books, and stationeries from Tang and exported silk, hair, ginseng, statues of Buddha, and gold and silver products. This also encouraged increased smuggling. A Silla settlement called Sillabang was created in Shandong peninsula, the eastern region of Tang.

Towards the end of the Unified Silla period, both Silla and Tang experienced political turmoil, which led to the growth of the slave trade by appearing pirates. In 828

[4] 관료 제도의 완비

통일신라는 전제왕권을 뒷받침하기 위해 독자적인 중앙집권적 관료제를 마련하였다. 중앙 정부는 14관부가 왕에게 직속되었고, 고관들은 겸직제를 통해 귀족의 배타적 특권을 보장받았다. 지방 제도는 9주 5소경, 군사제도는 9서당(중앙군)과 10정(지방군)을 근간으로 하였으며, 관리들에게는 녹봉이 지급되었으며, 이 제도는 고려를 거쳐 조선에 이르기까지 계속되어 우리나라 전통 사회의 원형으로서 그 기반을 마련을 하였다.

[5] 해외 무역의 발달

통일신라와 당의 외교 관계가 활발해지자 외교 사절 · 유학생 · 구법승 뿐 아니라 상인들도 왕래가 빈번해져 문물의 교류가 잇따랐다. 당으로부터는 비단 · 의복 · 서적 · 문방구 등

(3rd year of King Heungdeok), Jang Bo-go established the Cheonghae Garrison on Wando Island to put an end to piracy and set up Beobhwawon, a temple in Chihshan Village, Shandong Province to protect the Silla people engaged in trade and maintain full control of trade between Japan and Tang. In fact, he made Silla the greatest maritime kingdom in the East. It is around this time when Sillabang was established on the Shandong Peninsula. Sillaso (autonomous agencies), Sillawon (Silla temples), and Sillagwan (Silla motels) were also built to support the active maritime and trade activities of the Silla people.

[Photo] Beophwawon

In 825, Jang Bo-go built Beophwawon in Chih-shan in order to provide maritime safety for the Silla people and control their trade. The temple can house about 500 people and had enough land to harvest about 500 sacks of grain each year.

[사진] 법화원

825경에 장보고가 신라인의 해상안전과 해상무역을 통제하려는 목적으로 적산에 세운 법화원에는 500여명이 거주할 수 있었으며 매년 500섬의 곡식을 수확하는 토지(장전)가 있었다.

이 수입되었고, 신라에서는 비단·두발·인삼·불상·금은 제품들을 수출하였다. 그에 따라 밀무역도 성해서 당나라 동쪽 산둥도에는 신라인들이 집단으로 거주하는 신라방이 설치되었다.

통일신라 말기, 신라와 당의 정치가 혼란해짐에 따라 해적이 등장하여 노예무역이 번창하게 되자 장보고는 828년(흥덕왕 3년) 완도에 청해진을 두고 해적을 소탕하고, 나아가서 그는 산동성 적산촌에 법화원(法花院)을 세워 신라인의 해상 안전과 일본과 당과의 무역을 독점하여 동양 최대의 해상 왕국을 건설하였다. 그러므로 산둥반도의 회하 일대에 신라방(신라인들의 집단 거주지)이 나타났으며, 신라소(자치 기관)·신라원(신라 사찰)·신라관(신라 숙박소)이 설치되어 신라인의 활발한 해상 및 해외 활동을 뒷받침하였다.

[6] 통일신라와 당

통일신라는 백제·고구려 정벌 이후 한때 당나라와 전면 전쟁을 하였으나, 그후 상호간

[6] Unified Silla and Tang

After conquering Baekje and Goguryeo, Unified Silla later engaged in an all-out war against Tang, but the two declared a truce due to political situations. The two countries established amicable ties and frequently exchanged envoys, students, monks, and merchants. As a result, Silla embraced Tang and western cultures and sent students to Tang to study and further promote cultural exchanges.

Silla's King Seongdeok (702~737) and Tang's Hsuan Tsung (712~755) maintained friendly relations and engaged in active bilateral cultural exchanges. Silla broadened the scope of its culture by accepting western culture as well. Silla envoys introduced Tang culture not only to Silla but also to Japan and served as a bridge in shaping East Asian culture. Most significantly, Seol Jung-eop (a grandson of Wonhyo) went to Japan and spread Buddhism by Wonhyo and Confucianism by Seol Chong (the father of Seol Jung-eop).

[7] Founding of Balhae and the South-North State Period

After the downfall of Goguryeo, refugees from Goguryeo strived to restore their nation in Manchuria. In 698, Dae Jo-yeong, a former general of Goguryeo, led a group of followers and founded a kingdom in Tungmoushan, Jilin Province. The kingdom

정치적 입장으로 휴전을 하였다. 양국은 친선관계를 맺고 사신·유학생·승려·상인들이 빈번하게 왕래하였다. 이로써 당과 서역 문화가 수용되었으며, 숙위학생(宿衛學生)이라는 유학생이 당에서 공부하며 문화적으로 많은 교류가 있었다.

특히 성덕왕(702~737)은 당의 현종(712~755)과 친선관계가 이룩되어 양국간에는 많은 문화교류가 있었으며, 서역의 문화까지 받아들여 신라문화의 폭을 넓혔다. 신라 외교사절은 당나라 문화를 신라 뿐 아니라 일본에까지 전달하여 동아시아 문화 형성에 다리 노릇을 하게 되었다. 무엇보다도 설중업(원효의 손자)은 일본에 건너가 원효의 불교와 설총(설중업의 아버지)의 유학을 보급시켰다.

[7] 발해(渤海)의 건국과 남북국시대

고구려가 멸망한 후에도 만주 지역에서는 고구려 유민들의 부흥 운동이 끈질기게 계속되었다. 고구려의 장군이었던 대조영(大祚榮)은 고구려 유민들의 부흥 운동을 선도하여 길

was named Balhae.

Balhae which was formed by the governing class of Goguryeo refuses was able to keep Tang in control and unify the Malgal people. At one point, it grew into a huge empire extending into what is today the Russian Maritime Territory to the east and bordering with Silla to the south. It recovered most of the former territories of Goguryeo and was dubbed as "The Prosperous State of East." In Northeast Asia, Silla and Balhae flourished in the south and north and continued the so-called South-North State Period for the next two hundred years.

[8] Domains of Balhae

Balhae inherited the legacy of Goguryeo and ruled Manchuria. Its vast territory extended to the Liao River to the west and the Songhua River to the north. It went beyond the Ussuri River, south of present day Khabarovsk, and occupied the Russian Maritime Territory. To the south, Balhae and Unified Silla were separated by a border connecting Pyeongyang and Wonsan Bay. Solbin-bu was to the south of Khanka Lake (Xingkai Lake) in the Far East, while Anbyeon-bu and Hiwon-bu were to the east and north of the lake. This is proven by sites and remains of Balhae discovered in these regions.

Balhae first made Tungmoushan its capital but soon moved the capital to Guguk (Dunhua city Youngseung remains), castle city since Tunmoushan was strategically

림성(지린성) 동모산에서 698년에 나라를 세웠으니, 이것이 바로 발해다.

고구려 유민이 지배층을 이루고 있었던 발해는 당을 견제하고 말갈족을 통합함으로써 동쪽으로는 연해주에 이르고 남쪽으로는 신라에 접하는 대제국을 건설하여, 이른바 해동성국으로서 고구려의 옛 영토를 대부분 수복하였다. 이로써 이후 200여 년 동안 동북아시아 지역에서는 신라와 발해가 남과 북에서 경쟁적으로 발전해가는 이른바 남북국시대의 형세를 이루게 되었다.

[8] 발해의 영역

발해는 고구려를 계승한 만주의 지배자였다. 그 영토는 서쪽으로는 요하에 이르렀고 북으로는 송화강에 이르러, 현재 하바로브스크 남쪽으로 우수리강을 건너 연해주 지방을 차지하였다. 남쪽으로는 통일신라와 평양~원산만을 경계로 하였다. 현재 극동의 한카호(싱카이호) 남쪽에는 솔빈부가, 그 동쪽에는 안변부가, 그리고 북쪽에는 회원부(懷遠府)가 있었다.

favorable for military defense but not suitable as a capital. Later, the capital was moved again to Junggyeong (Helong), which was located on the plain by the Haeran River. It benefitted from a milder climate and was a center of transportation.

After political stabilization, King Mun (737~793) relocated the capital northward to Sanggyeong (Ningan, Heilongjiang Province) in order to control the northern Malgal

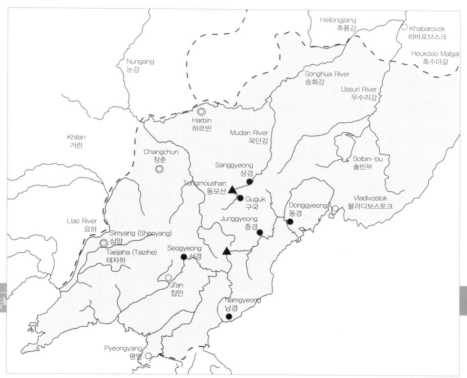

[Map] Domains of Balhae
[지도] 발해의 영역

현재 이 지방에서 발굴되는 발해의 유적과 유물이 이를 증명한다.

발해는 처음 동모산에 도읍을 정하였으나, 곧 구국(돈화시 영승유적)을 서울로 삼았다. 동모산은 방어에는 유리하였으나 서울로는 부적합하였으므로 그곳에서 가까운 평지성인 구국으로 옮긴 것이다. 이후 다시 해란강 유역의 평야 지대로서 기후가 온난하고 교통의 중심지인 중경(화룡현 서고성)으로 도읍을 옮겼다.

어느 정도 정치적 안정을 꾀한 문왕(737~793)은 북방의 흑수말갈을 통제하기 위래 서울을 다시 상경(흑룡강성 영안현)으로 옮겨 대제국의 수도로서 면모를 갖추었다. 상경은 목단강과 흘한해(경박호)의 풍부한 해산물과 목단강 유역의 넓은 평야에서 생산되는 농산물을

tribes, and Sanggyeong assumed the aspects of the capital of a great empire. It has easy access to abundant catches of fish from the Mudan River and Huhanhai Lake (Jingpo Lake) and also to agricultural products produced on the vast plains around the Mudan River, making it the center of prosperity for Balhae. Later, the capital was moved to Donggyeong (Hunchun) but returned to Sanggyeong, which remained the center of Balhae until its collapse.

[9] Balhae's Political Systems

In order to control its vast landmass, Balhae had three chancelleries (*seong*) and six ministries (*bu*) in the central government and set up five secondary capitals (*gyeong*), 15 major towns (*bu*), and 62 provinces (*ju*) for local administration. This system was completely unlike that of Tang. In particular, Jeongdang-seong, which is equivalent to Sangseo-seong of Tang, was divided into the Left and Right *sajeong*, which resulted in six *bu* and two sectors, for checks and balances.

Since the Balhae people had a firm belief in continuing the tradition of Goguryeo, they were confrontational towards Tang and Silla, but they proactively accepted Tang culture. Balhae was able to create a unique culture that was elegant, sophisticated, magnificent, and sound by accepting Tang culture on the foundation of Goguryeo culture. Although Balhae moved its capital several times for defensive purposes, Sanggyeong was the center of Balhae, the ruler of Manchuria.

바탕으로 발해 융성의 기틀이 되었다. 그 후 서울을 동경(훈춘시 팔련성)으로 옮겼다가, 상경으로 되돌아가서 멸망할 때까지 그곳이 발해의 중심지가 되었다.

[9] 발해의 정치제도

발해는 광대한 영토를 다스리기 위하여 중앙에 3성6부를 두고, 지방에는 5경 15부 62주를 설치하였다. 그러나 이러한 제도는 당나라의 그것과는 전혀 달랐다. 특히 당의 상서성에 해당하는 정당성 밑에 좌ㆍ우 사정을 두어 6부를 2부분으로 나누어 권한을 상호 견제시켰다.

발해는 고구려를 계승한다는 의식이 뚜렷하였으므로 당이나 신라와는 대립적인 자세를 취하였다. 그러나 당의 문화를 받아들이는 데에는 항상 적극적이어서, 발해는 고구려 문화의 바탕 위에 당 문화를 받아들여 부드럽고 세련되며 웅장하고 건실한 독자적인 민족문화를 건설하였다. 특히 수도를 여러 번 옮기면서 나라를 지켰으나 만주의 지배자인 발해의 중심 서울은 상경이었다.

[10] Features of Balhae History

As the successor to Goguryeo, the people of Balhae believed they were descendents of the heavenly god. Balhae was also a powerful state feared by neighboring countries, which is evidenced by an attack on Tang (Tengchou) in 732.

Today, however, China argues that Balhae was a Chinese government, while the Russians believe it was a Malgal state and Japan claims that Balhae was its vassal state. There can be no denying that Balhae had been founded by Goguryeo people and that "The Prosperous State of the East" had a distinctly Korean culture. In all letters Balhae sent to Japan, kings of Balhae were referred to as kings of Goguryeo.

Balhae was the last independent country of Koreans to rule Manchuria. It was not simply the successor to Goguryeo but, as a major state in Manchuria, a strong power that confronted Tang's hegemony and preserved *ondol* (underfloor heating) and *meju* (fermented soybeans). This fact is supported by a recording in the New History of Tang, which states "Balhae occupied a vast landmass and was feared by many states in Northeast Asia." Balhae kings had independent reign titles. When the Khitan brought down Balhae, they completely destroyed Sanggyeong.

[10] 발해사의 성격

발해는 고구려의 계승자로서 천손 의식을 갖고 있었고, 주변 나라가 두려워한 존재였으니, 732년 당나라(등주)를 공격한 데에서도 이 사실이 나타나 있다.

그러나 현재 중국은 발해를 자기들의 지방정권이라 부르고, 러시아에서는 말갈족의 나라로 생각하며, 일본은 자신의 부용국이라고 주장하지만 발해는 어디까지나 고구려인이 세운 나라였고, 우리 민족문화를 간직한 '해동성국(海東盛國)'이었다. 발해는 언제나 일본에 보낸 문서에서 발해왕을 고구려국왕이라 하였다.

발해는 우리 역사상 마지막으로 만주를 지배했던 나라였다. 동시에 단순히 고구려의 계승국이 아니라, 만주의 주인공으로서 당의 천하질서에 맞서며 온돌과 메주를 끝까지 지킨 강국이었다. 「신당서」의 "큰 영토를 개척했으며, 동북 여러 나라들이 두려워 신하를 칭하였다."는 기록이 이를 뒷받침한다. 따라서 역대의 발해왕은 독자적인 연호를 사용하였으며, 거란이 발해를 멸망시킨 후 상경성을 철저히 파괴시킨 사실에서도 그것을 엿볼 수 있다.

[11] Decline of Unified Silla

Since the late 8th century, power struggles for the throne continued in Unified Silla, and the bone-rank (*golpum*) system collapsed while the order of central government was broken down. In the 9th century, chaos in the central political systems led to the emergence of regional powers (*hojok*). These *hojok* owned vast farmlands and commanded private armies. Peasant uprisings continued to erupt all over the kingdom. In the end, the social turmoil led to the establishment of Later Baekje and Later Goguryeo in the "Later Three Kingdoms Period." Unified Silla was thus divided and thrown into turmoil. With the collapse of the bone-rank system, many at the head-rank six level left for China to study and embrace Chinese culture. Some monks chose to join the new Buddhist sect of Zen (*seon*) Buddhism in a move to break away from the establishments of Silla's society. Ultimately, a few elite members including Choi Chi-won joined local forces (*hojok*) and promoted new ideology combining Buddhism, Confucianism, and *fengshui* principles, clearing the way for the rise of the Goryeo Dynasty. The founding of the Goryeo Dynasty was, thus, a reuniting of the Korean people and marked the establishment of a medieval society.

[11] 통일신라의 쇠퇴

통일신라는 8세기 말 이후 왕위 쟁탈전이 계속되고 골품제가 붕괴되면서 중앙 질서가 무너졌다. 9세기에 이르러 중앙 정치의 혼란에 따라 지방세력(호족)이 등장하여 각기 광대한 농장과 많은 사병(私兵)을 거느리면서 할거하였다. 각처에서 농민 반란이 일어나고 결국 후백제 · 후고구려가 성립됨으로써 후삼국 시대가 나타났다. 따라서 통일 국가는 다시 분열되어 혼란을 맞게 되었다. 골품 제도의 붕괴에 따라 6두품에 속한 세력들은 중국 유학을 통해 중국 문화를 받아들였으며, 일부 스님은 새로운 불교인 선종에 귀의하여 신라사회로부터 스스로 벗어나려는 운동에 앞장섰다. 최치원(崔致遠)을 비롯한 소수의 지식인 집단은 결국 지방 세력(호족)과 결탁하는 한편, 불교 · 유교 · 풍수 사상의 결합을 통한 사상의 흐름을 주도하여 고려 왕조의 방향을 제시하였다. 따라서 고려왕조의 성립은 민족분열을 재통일한 역사적 사건이며, 한국사에 있어서 중세사회의 시작이 된다.

4. Ancient Korean Society and Culture

[1] Ancient Korean Society

The Three Kingdoms Period represents ancient Korean society. The social systems at the time were very rigid. At the very top of the ruling class were the kings and their queens. Immediately below them were the aristocrats, who were at the center of politics, the economy, and culture. Most of the common people were peasants, and they bore heavy duties to the state in the form of high taxes, military service, and corvee labor. The lowest social class was the slaves. They were forced to live in certain quarters (*hyang, so, bugok*) and were not treated with human dignity.

Royal authority was absolute, and the monarchy was firmly backed by the bureaucratic system and law. It was also backed by Buddhism, which united the people into one. Along with Chinese culture and western culture, Buddhism contributed greatly to the development of Korean culture.

The people of Goguryeo were courageous and high-spirited. A typical house had quarters reserved for sons-in-law (*seook*) and storage space (*bugyeong*), and people enjoyed singing and dancing. The people of Baekje also enjoyed writing, made inroads into China and Japan and developed a variety of foods. Silla made decisions on major state affairs, such as the election of kings or engaging in wars at *hwabaek*, a council of nobles. These decisions required unanimous votes.

4. 한국의 고대사회와 문화

[1] 한국고대사회의 성격

한국 고대사회를 대표하는 삼국시대는 엄격한 신분사회였다. 지배계급의 최상층에는 왕족과 왕비족이 있었고 다음에는 귀족층이 정치 · 경제 · 문화를 독점하였다. 평민층은 대부분 농민이었고 이들은 과중한 의무(세금 · 병역 · 부역)를 지고 있었고, 맨 아래층의 노예는 특정지역(향 · 소 · 부곡)에 거주하면서 인간적인 대우를 받지 못하였다.

고대사회는 왕권이 절대적이었으며 관료제도와 율령이 이를 뒷받침 하였다. 이러한 절대왕권을 뒷받침한 것이 불교였으며 국민을 하나로 뭉쳐주었다. 특히 불교는 중국문화와 서역문화와 함께 민족문화 발전에 기여하였다.

용감하고 활달한 기상을 가진 고구려인들은 집 안에 사위집(서옥 · 壻屋)과 창고(부경 · 桴京)를 두었으며, 노래와 춤을 좋아하였다. 백제인들은 글 읽기를 좋아하였고, 해외진출을

[2] Golpum System

Silla had a unique social class system called *golpum* (bone-rank), which was similar to the caste system of India. The *golpum* system originally had the levels of seonggol

[Photo] Relief Image of Buddha in Seosan

[사진] 서산마애석불

통해 중국과 일본에 진출하였으며 다양한 음식문화를 발달시켰다. 신라는 특히 왕의 선출이나 전쟁 등 국가 중대사를 화백이라는 귀족대표회의에서 만장일치로 결정하는 전통을 갖고 있었다.

[2] 골품제

신라 사회는 인도의 카스트제도와 같은 골품이라 불리는 특이한 신분 제도를 가지고 있었다. 골품제는 원래 왕족인 성골(聖骨)과 진골(眞骨), 그 밑의 6·5·4두품(頭品)으로 구성되어 있었다. 그러나 진덕여왕 이후 성골이 소멸되고 진골이 왕이 되었으며, 그 아래 6두품이 하층귀족층으로 사회·문화 활동을 주도하였으나 폐쇄적인 신분 제도의 한계 때문에 중국에 유학을 하거나 승려의 길을 택하였다.

골품제는 신라가 초기 국가에서 중앙집권적인 고대 왕국으로 발전해 가는 과정에서 부족장들을 중앙의 통제 하에 예속시키기 위해 세력에 따라 차별을 두고 일정한 신분을 부여하

(hallowed bone) and *jingol* (true bone), which were both for members of the royal family, and lower *dupum* (head ranks) six, five, and four. However, in the reign of Queen Jinseok, the *seonggol* level was discontinued and the *jingol* lineage led to the throne. The lower *dupum* six, the noble lineage, was at the center of social and cultural activities, but members of these levels often chose to go to China to study or become monks to avoid the limitations imposed by the restrictive class system.

The *golpum* system was established as Silla became a full-fledged kingdom with centralized power. In the process of its development, Silla had to assign people to certain classes and grant limited power accordingly in order to bring the tribal heads under control. Once the *golpum* system was in place, official positions and social activities were determined according to one's social class. In Silla society, *golpum* functioned as a strict class system determining one's role in society. This rigid *golpum* system hindered the further development of Silla society, and *dupum* six started to oppose the *golpum* system.

[3] Development of Buddhism

In ancient countries, Buddhism was embraced and encouraged by kings as a social ideology. Buddhism was first adopted in Korea in 372 during the reign of King Sosurim of Goguryeo. It was originally a religion for the aristocracy but gradually spread to the common people. Since then, the governments built temples and celebrated various

는 과정에서 성립되었다. 골품제가 확립됨에 따라 신분에 의해 관직과 사회생활에 차등이 있게 되었다. 신라 사회는 골품이 사람의 사회적 역할을 결정짓는 엄격한 신분 제도로 운영되었다. 이러한 골품제는 신라 사회를 발전시키는데 제한적 요소가 되었음으로 골품제에 대한 반발은 6두품으로부터 시작되었다

[3] 불교의 발달

불교는 고대 국가의 사상적 이념으로 왕의 장려로 수용되었다. 우리나라에 불교가 처음 들어온 것은 고구려 소수림왕때인 372년으로 초기에는 귀족 종교였으나 점차 백성들에게도 전파되어 국민의 의식을 높여 주었다. 이후 국가에서 사찰을 만들어 여러 가지 불교 행사를 거행하면서 국민의 단합과 문화발전의 바탕이 되어 불교가 국교로 자리잡게 되었다.

불교는 국민정신을 통일하여 호국사상을 고양시켰을 뿐만 아니라 탑파와 불상과 같은 불교 예술을 발달시켰다. 특히 부처의 사리를 봉안하는 일종의 무덤을 뜻하는 탑은 백제와

Buddhist events to bolster national unity and further cultural development. Accordingly Buddhism became the national religion.

In addition to promoting spiritual unity for national defense, Buddhism also advanced Buddhist art, including pagodas and Buddhist statues. Pagodas were used to enshrine relics (sari) and were especially well developed in Baekje and Silla.

In Baekje, the wooden pagoda at the site of Mireuksa Temple and the five-story stone pagoda at the site of Jeonglimsa Temple still stands. Silla left behind the brick pagoda of Bunhwangsa Temple and many stone pagodas. The stone pagodas of the Three Kingdoms are symbolic remains of stone artistry, and they are extremely well preserved.

The Three Kingdoms worshiped Buddhist statues. A refined and elegant relief carving of Buddha from Baekje survives. Above all The form of statues of half-seated Maitreya in meditation was transmitted to Japan, spreading the outstanding artistry of the Three Kingdoms.

[4] Wonhyo and Uisang

Buddhism continued to flourish in Unified Silla. The most renowned and accomplished monks who had the greatest influence in Silla were Wonhyo and Uisang. Wonhyo took the lead in spreading Buddhism and disseminated the teachings of Buddhism to the noble class as well as to the common people. Wonhyo suggested a

신라에서 크게 발달하였다.

백제의 탑은 목탑 형식을 취한 미륵사지탑과 정림사지 5층 석탑이 남아있으며, 신라는 벽돌 탑의 모습을 취한 분황사지탑과 많은 석탑을 남기고 있다. 삼국의 석탑은 지금까지도 옛 모습을 그대로 간직한 석조예술의 상징적 유적이다.

삼국은 불상을 조각하여 숭배하였으며, 특히 백제는 세련되고 우아한 서산마애석불을 남기고 있다. 특히 삼국시대의 미륵반가사유상은 일본에 전래되어 삼국인의 뛰어난 예술 감각을 전파시켰다.

[4] 원효와 의상

신라의 불교는 통일신라에 이르러 더욱 번창하였다. 이때에 가장 큰 업적과 영향을 남긴 고승은 원효와 의상이었다. 원효(元曉)는 불교의 대중화에 앞장서서 귀족으로부터 평민에 이르기 까지 불교 교리를 전파하였으며 전쟁과 갈등을 극복하고 평화와 화해의 정신을 제시

spirit of peace and reconciliation while overcoming wars and conflicts. As a free-spirited man of action, he effectively promoted Buddhism.

Uisang stressed training of the inner mind through strict discipline and rigorous asceticism. He envisioned interactions of the one and the whole. He practiced and supported absolute royal authority and placed the people within a single boundary. Both Wonhyo and Uisang displayed the spirit of mutual harmony and elevated Silla Buddhism a step further.

A Poem by Wonhyo

When patching up a garment, a small needle is enough.
No need for a long sword.
When it rains, a small umbrella is enough.
No need to cover the entire sky.
Little things should not be considered trivial.
Depending on their nature, all things - both big and small - are valuable.

하면서 일체의 구속을 거부한 행동의 실천자로서 불교의 대중화에 기여하였다.

의상(義湘)은 엄격한 수행과 철저한 수도자의 정신을 통해 인간의 내면을 강조하였다.

그는 하나와 전체를 상호 의존케 함으로써 전제 왕권과 백성을 하나의 테두리 속에 묶어 전제 왕권을 뒷받침하였다. 이와 같이 원효와 의상은 신라 불교를 한 차원 높게 발전시켜 융합과 조화의 정신을 보여주었다.

원효의 시

옷을 기울 때는 작은 바늘이 필요하지
긴 칼이 있어도 소용이 없다.
비를 피할 때는 작은 우산으로 족하며
온 하늘을 덮는다 해도 소용이 없다.
그러므로 작다고 가벼이 볼 것이 아니라
그 근성을 따라서는 큰 것이나 작은 것이 다 보배이다.

[5] Development of Buddhist Arts

The flourishing of Buddhism resulted in great development of Buddhist art and architecture. The people of Silla demonstrated exquisite skill in crafting stone pagodas, Buddhist statues, and temple bells. The utmost of Buddhist art is represented by Bulguksa Temple and Soekguram Grotto. Bulguksa Temple symbolizes the Buddhist utopia of Silla people and represents the past, present, and future world within a single space. The harmony of Seokgatap Pagoda and Dabotap Pagoda indicates the coexistence of royal authority and Buddhism. In 1966, during maintenance work on Seokgatap Pagoda, the oldest extant document printed with woodblock type, the *Mugujeonggwangdaranigyeong* Sutra, was discovered inside the pagoda.

Seokguram Grotto represents Silla's Buddhist temples. It is a man-made stone grotto, and various Buddhist figures are carved into the inner walls. At the center sits a statue of Buddha, which is a symbol of Buddhist art. It has a generous-looking and graceful face and an aura of religious mysticism. Seokguram Grotto is inscribed on the UNESCO World Heritage List.

Another type of artwork that represents Buddhist art is the temple bell. *Seongdeokdaewangsinjong* (Emille Bell), which is currently exhibited at the Gyeongju National Museum, is Korea's largest temple bell. Its surface is decorated with beautiful patterns, and dragon patterns adorn the sound pipe on the top of the bell. A big depression on the bottom of the bell was made for clear, graceful resonance.

[5] 불교 예술의 발달

불교의 번창으로 많은 예술이 발달하였다. 특히 탑파 · 불상 · 범종의 제작 등에서 신라인의 솜씨는 뛰어났다. 불교 예술의 극치는 불국사와 석굴암이다. 불국사는 신라인의 불교적 이상을 나타낸 사찰로서 과거 · 현세 · 내세의 세계를 한 울타리 안에 표현한 것이며, 석가탑과 다보탑의 조화 속에 왕권과 불교가 공존하려는 뜻을 나타내고 있다. 1966년에는 석가탑 보수 공사 중 석탑 안에서 세계 최고(最高)의 목판 인쇄물인 무구정광대다라니경이 발견되었다.

신라 불상을 대표하는 것은 석굴암이다. 석굴암은 인공굴을 파고 그 벽면에 각종 불상을 조각하였고 중앙에 여래상을 안치시키고 있다. 이 부처는 자애롭고 아름다운 얼굴과 종교적인 신비감에다 자연의 미까지 결합된 불교 예술의 상징으로 세계의 문화유산으로 보호받고 있다.

이러한 불교 예술을 대표하는 또 하나의 작품으로 범종이 있다. 현재 경주박물관에 보존되어 있는 성덕대왕신종(에밀레종)은 우리나라 최대의 범종으로 표면의 아름다운 무늬와 윗

[Photo] Seokguram Grotto
〈Source: Korea Tourism Organization〉

[사진] 석굴암
〈사진제공·한국관광공사〉

[6] Sculpture of the Three Kingdoms

During the Three Kingdom Period, not only the Buddhist arts but also sculpture was also well developed. A gold and bronze Baekje incense burner was discovered in an ancient tomb in Neungsan-ri, Buyeo in 1993. The burner is supported by a prop adorned with dragon carvings. The lid is decorated with mountains and on top stands of a precious bead a phoenix with its wings fully stretched out. This piece is considered to be the quintessence of Baekje art.

A gold crown worn by Silla kings consists of a top part adorned with various decorations and a head band with long chains. This not only demonstrates the exquisiteness of Silla art, but also displays the extravagance of the nobility of ancient society. The beauty of sari (remains of monks after cremation) cases placed in stone pagodas also shows the refined style and skill of the Silla people.

[7] Murals of the Old Tombs of Goguryeo

In Goguryeo tombs, burial chambers were built with stone and covered with soil. The four walls of a burial chamber were decorated with murals depicting scenes from the life of the deceased such as deceased hunting, wrestling, fighting in battle, and entertaining guests. The ceiling was used to express life after death, and an image of

부분에 용 무늬의 음통이 있고, 종 아래에는 큰 홈을 파서 종소리가 울려서 은은하고 청아하게 퍼지게 하였다.

[6] 삼국의 조각예술

삼국시대에는 불교예술 뿐 아니라 다양한 조각예술이 발달하였다. 백제의 금강대향로는 1993년에 부여군 능산리 고분에서 발견되었는데 용을 조각한 받침 위에 중복된 산봉우리의 뚜껑과 날개를 편 봉황이 구슬을 딛고 서있어 백제예술을 대표한다.

한편 신라왕이 쓰던 금관은 다양한 장식을 갖고 있는 윗부분과 긴 드리게를 달고있는 관테가 있어 신라예술의 솜씨를 나타내고 있어 고대사회 귀족들의 사치스런 모습을 보여준다. 그 외 탑 속에 넣은 사리(스님의 화장 뒤에 남은 유골)함은 그 아름다움 역시 신라인의 멋과 기교를 엿보게 한다.

[Photo] Mural of a Procession on the Eastern Wall of Goguryeo Anak Tomb No. 3

The deceased (presumed to be King Gogukwon) is riding a horse-drawn cart accompanied by a procession of warriors, honor guards, wrestlers, and music bands

[사진] 고구려 안악 3호분 '전실동벽' 의 행렬도 : 벽화

주인공(고국원왕설)이 마차를 타고 가고 무사 · 의장대 · 수박(手搏:傳統武藝) · 악대 등이 하나의 행렬을 이루고 있다.

[7] 고구려의 고분 벽화

고구려에는 돌로 현실을 받들고 흙을 위에 덮는 흙무덤이 발달하여 현실의 사방 벽에 벽화를 그렸다. 벽화에는 사냥 · 씨름 · 전쟁 · 접객 등의 주인공의 현실 생활을 그대로 나타냈으며, 천장에는 사후의 삶을 표현하여 학 · 용을 타고 승천하는 모습을 그렸다. 특히 고구려 벽화에는 4신도(청룡 · 백호 · 주작 · 현무)와 날개달린 물고기, 사람 얼굴을 한 새와 소 등을 그려 중국 문화와는 다른 특성을 보여준다. 더구나 해와 달 그림에는 까마귀와 두꺼비가 함께 등장하고 있어 고구려만의 독자적인 문화를 나타내고 있다. 현대 세계문화유산으로 보호되고 있다.

the deceased ascending to heaven on a crane or a dragon was drawn. Murals of Goguryeo also depicted four spirits (blue dragon, white tiger, red phoenix, and black turtle), winged fish, birds, and cows with human faces. These murals are very different from Chinese murals. Moreover, the sun and the moon were accompanied by three-legged crows and toads, displaying the uniqueness of Goguryeo culture.

The royal tombs of Goguryeo are inscribed on the UNESCO World Heritage List.

[8] Culture of Baekje

Blessed with mild climate and beautiful landscape, Baekje left behind a refined culture. The tombs of King Muryeong (501~523) and his queen were discovered in 1971. Gold crowns and stone sculptures of animals were excavated, confirming the development of splendid Baekje art. The Triad Buddha in Seosan is a relief carving of three Buddhist figures in rock. The smiling bodhisattva statue at the center has symbolic significance in Baekje Buddhist art.

[9] Transmission of the Three Kingdoms' Culture to Japan

The culture of the Three Kingdoms was transmitted to Japan and laid a foundation for the creation and development of ancient Asuka culture. Of the Three Kingdoms,

[8] 백제의 문화

백제는 온화한 기후와 아름다운 산천으로 세련된 문화를 남기고 있다. 특히 1971년에 무령왕(501~523)의 릉이 발견되어 왕과 왕비의 금관식·돌짐승 등이 출토되어 화려한 예술발달을 확인할 수 있었다. 그리고 백제의 「서산마애석불」은 바위에 새긴 3부처상으로 특히 미소짓는 중앙의 본존여래상은 백제 불교예술의 상징적 존재이다.

[9] 삼국 문화의 일본 전파

삼국 문화는 일본에 건너가서 고대 일본 아스카 문화의 형성과 발전의 기초가 되었다. 그중에서도 가장 두드러진 활약을 보인 사람들은 백제인이였다. 이러한 사실은 일본 국보 1호인 고류지[광륭사(廣隆寺)]의 목조미륵반가사유상과 우리나라의 금동미륵보살반가사유상의

[Photo] Gilt-Bronze Half-seated Maitreya
in Meditation in Meditation
Baekje, late 6C~early 7C (National Museum of
Korea)

[사진] 금동미륵보살반가사유상
백제,6세기 후반~7세기 전반 (국립중앙박물관)

[Photo] Wooden Half-seated Maitreya
Japan (Koryuji)

[사진] 목조미륵반가사유상
일본 (고류지)

Baekje had the greatest influence. This is verified by a fact that the Wooden half- seated Maitreya in Meditation at Koryuji Temple of Kyogo (Japan National Treasure No.1) is similar to the Gilt-Bronze Half-seated Maitreya in Meditation in Korea. The only difference between the two is material: the Baekje work is gilt-bronze; the Japanese counterpart is made of wood. Otherwise, their shapes and features are identical.

Ajikgi and Wangin of Baekje taught the Japanese people the Chinese characters and the Confucian concepts of loyalty and filial duty. They played an instrumental role in establishing the ancient state system of Japan by educating the Japanese on academic studies and technology. Many other monks also went to Japan and propagated Buddhism.

Goguryeo also had a great influence on Japan. Heja, a Buddhist monk of Goguryeo, tutored a Japanese crown prince. Damjing, a famous painter, conveyed not only paintings but also knowledge of how to make paper and ink sticks. He also drew a famous mural in the Golden Hall at Horyuji Temple, which Japanese people are proud of.

Silla culture was transmitted to Japan as well. At that time, Japan sent a number of envoys, scholars, and monks to Silla to learn about its advanced culture. During Unified Silla, Seol Jung-eop, a son of Seol Chong, introduced both Buddhism and Confucianism to Japan and spawned the creation of Hakuho culture. Well-made Silla ships enabled Japanese envoys and monks to travel to and from China. Jang Bo-go also helped Japan accept Chinese culture.

모습에서 엿볼 수 있다. 양자는 재료(백제는 청동, 일본은 나무)만 다를 뿐 외형과 특징이 똑같다.

백제의 아직기(阿直岐)와 왕인(王仁)은 일본인들에게 한문과 유교의 충효 사상을 가르쳐 주었다. 그리고 학문과 기술로써 일본인들을 교화하여 고대 국가의 체제를 확립하는데 결정적인 역할을 하였다. 그 외 많은 스님들도 일본에 건너가 그곳에 불교를 전파시켰다.

고구려도 일본 문화에 많은 영향을 끼쳤다. 고구려의 승려 혜자(惠慈)는 일본의 성덕태자(聖德太子)에게 학문을 가르쳤고, 담징(曇徵)은 그림은 물론 종이와 먹의 제조 방법까지 전해주었다. 일본인들이 자랑하는 호류지[법륭사(法隆寺)]의 금당 벽화도 담징이 그린 것이다.

신라의 문화도 일본에 전해졌다. 당시 일본은 많은 사신·학자·승려 등을 신라에 보내 선진 문화를 배워 갔다. 특히 통일 신라 때 설총의 아들인 설중업(薛仲業)은 불교 뿐 아니라 유학을 전해주었으며 하쿠호 문화를 일으켰다. 무엇보다도 일본인들은 신라인이 만든 우수한 신라선(新羅船)으로 견당사와 구법승(求法僧)들이 중국을 왕래하였으며, 장보고(張保皐)의 도움으로 중국 문물을 받아들일 수 있었다.

[10] Culture of Balhae

Balhae developed a unique culture by absorbing Tang culture on a basis of Goguryeo culture. Buddha statues, stone lanterns, and buildings were made of basalt, a volcanic stone, and such stone lanterns remain in Sanggyeongseong. Balhae culture can be studied through relics excavated in the Russian Maritime Territory (especially Ussuriysk). The Balhae people preserved their national tradition by developing *ondol* (under-floor heating system) and *meju* (fermented soybeans).

[10] 발해의 문화

발해는 고구려 문화를 바탕으로 하고 당의 문화를 결합시켜 독특한 문화를 개발하였다. 특히 화산 폭발로 나타난 현무암으로 불상·석등·건물을 조성하였으니 현재 상경성에 남아있는 석등에서 엿볼 수 있다. 발해문화는 현재 연해주 일대(특히 우수리스트)에서 발굴되는 유물에서 그 모습을 알 수 있으며, 특히 온돌을 개발하고 콩을 길러 메주(발효식품)를 개발하여 민족의 전통을 유지하였다.

[Photo] Hunmin Jeongeum
[사진] 훈민정음 〈사진제공·한국관광공사〉

Korean Medieval Society and Pre-Modern Society

한국중세사회의 발전과 근세사회의 전개

1. Reunification and Aristocratic Culture of Goryeo

[1] The Later Three Kingdoms

Unified Silla reached its peak in the 8th century and began to decline in the 9th century. The ruling class fell into political strife, and regional powers (*hojok*) gradually wrested power from the central government. The most serious cause of Silla's decline was power struggles for the throne among aristocrats of the *jingol* (true bone) lineage. In provincial areas, *hojok* exercised increasing autonomy, and peasant uprisings continued. In the process, royal authority was greatly weakened, and society fell into turmoil.

A few leaders united the rebels, declared themselves kings, and established new states. Prime examples are Gyeon Hwon and Gung Ye. Gyeon Hwon founded Later Baekje (892~936) on the former territory of Baekje, and Gung Ye set up Taebong (Later Goguryeo: 901~918). This marked the end of about 220 years of Unified Silla and the beginning of a new period of chaos: the so-called Later Three Kingdoms period.

1. 민족의 재통일과 고려의 중세귀족문화

[1] 후삼국의 분열

8세기에 전성기였던 통일신라는 9세기 이후 점차 지배층이 분열하고, 지방에서 중앙정부에 저항하는 호족세력이 성장함에 따라 점차 쇠퇴의 길을 걷게 되었다. 무엇보다도 진골 귀족 사이에 왕위 쟁탈전이 벌어지고, 지방에서는 호족세력의 독립과 농민 반란이 빈발하였다. 이러한 과정에서 왕권이 약화되고 사회는 혼란에 빠지게 되었다.

이러한 반란 세력을 규합하여 왕을 호칭하면서 나라를 세우는 세력들이 나타났는데, 그 대표적인 인물이 견훤(甄萱)과 궁예(弓裔)였다. 견훤은 백제의 옛 땅에서 후백제(892~936)를, 궁예는 태봉(후고구려, 901~918)을 세웠다. 그리하여 한반도는 신라의 통일 후 220여년 만에 다시 삼국이 정립하는 혼란기(후삼국시대)로 접어들게 된다.

[2] Reunification of the Korean People

It was Wang Geon who put an end to the chaos of the Later Three Kingdoms and founded a unified state. He was originally a follower of Gung Ye, but with the backing of *hojok* and new elites who studied in China, he managed to uphold tradition and culture and founded Goryeo in 918.

Goryeo secured authority as a legitimate state when Silla surrendered in 935 and absorbed the refugees of Balhae, which had been overthrown by the Khitans, broadening the path for national unity. Goryeo also sought to regain the former territories of Goguryeo. In 936, Goryeo conquered Later Baekje and achieved the great work of reuniting the Korean people.

[3] Development of the Goryeo Dynasty

Wang Geon (918~943) was able to secure authority as a legitimate successor when King Gyeongsun surrendered. He set up a western capital (Pyeongyang) in an attempt to restore the former territories of Goguryeo and pressed ahead with the effort to reclaim them. He stabilized society by firmly establishing it on Buddhism and *Feng shui* principles.

King Gwangjong (949~975), the successor of Wang Geon, laid a foundation for a

[2] 민족의 재통일

후삼국의 혼란을 수습하고 통일 국가를 세운 이는 왕건(王建)이다. 왕건은 처음에는 궁예의 부하였지만, 호족의 세력을 바탕으로 기존의 전통과 문화를 이어받아 중국에서 공부한 신 지식층의 지지를 받아 918년에 고려를 건국하였다.

고려는 935년에 신라의 투항으로 정통국가로서의 권위를 확보한 후 때마침 거란에 의해 멸망하였던 발해의 유민들을 받아들여 민족융합의 길을 넓혔다. 또 고구려 옛 땅을 회복하려는 북진 정책을 폈고, 후백제를 936년에 정벌하여 민족 재통일의 대업을 이룩하게 되었다.

[3] 고려 왕조의 발전

왕건(918~943)은 경순왕의 항복으로 정통 국가로서의 권위를 갖게 되었고, 고구려의 옛

new dynasty by liberating those who had been enslaved illegally and introducing the first civil service examination system in 958. With the help of Choi Seung-no, King Seongjong (981~997) institutionalized the educational and political systems through Confucian policy and overhauled the bureaucratic systems to build the framework for a medieval state.

[4] Completion of Governance System

Goryeo completed the framework of a medieval society by establishing a governance system that was different from Silla (ancient society). Its central administrative organization had three *seong* and six *bu*. As special agencies, Goryeo had Jungchuwon (political and military administration), Dobyeongmasa (the highest council), and Eosadae (an audit agency).

Central Government Organization of Goryeo

The highest administrative organizations of Goryeo were three *seong*, and the prime minister was called Munhasijung. Six *bu*, which collectively were equivalent to the cabinet, consisted of *yi-bu* (home affairs), *byeong-bu* (national defense), *ho-bu* (finance), *ye-bu* (education and diplomacy), *hyeong-bu* (justice), and *gong-bu* (construction).

땅을 회복하기 위해 서경(평양)을 설치하고 북진 정책을 실시하였으며, 불교·풍수 사상으로 사회를 안정시켰다.

왕건을 이은 광종(949~975)은 불법적으로 노비가 된 사람을 해방시키고 958년에 과거 제도를 처음으로 실시하여 새 왕조의 기틀을 마련하였다. 성종(981~997)은 최승로의 도움으로 유교 정치를 통해 교육·정치 제도를 파견하였고 관료 제도를 정비하여 중세 국가로서의 기틀을 마련하였다.

[4] 통치 체제의 완비

고려는 신라(고대)와는 다른 통치체제를 통해 중세사회의 기틀을 완비하였다. 중앙에는 3성6부를 두어 중앙행정부를 구성하고 그 외 특수기관으로 중추원(정치·군사행정)과 최고 회의 기관으로 도병마사를 두었으며 비행을 감독하는 어사대를 두었다.

고려는 국호에 나타나 있는 바와 같이 고구려를 계승한다는 의식이 강하였으므로, 고구

As evidenced in its name, Goryeo strongly believed in upholding the legacy of Goguryeo. Thus, it restored the former domains of Goguryeo and accepted refugees from Balhae. As a stronghold for expanding to the north, Goryeo set up Seogyeong (western capital) in Pyeongyang and ruled over the country. In addition, it designated military administrative zones named "*gye*" in the northern border region and the northeast coastal region. The southern regions were divided into five *do* (province).

[5] Flourishing of Aristocratic Culture

Goryeo promoted Buddhism as the state religion. It built guardian temples and held various Buddhist festivals. The educational and civil examination systems were developed according to the principles of Confucianism. Principles of *Feng shui* - a belief that topography is a strong determinant of one's destiny - had influence in broadening the aristocratic culture.

The people of Goryeo applied their substantial artistic talent and creativity to produce beautiful ceramics, most notably *sanggam cheongja* (inlaid celadon). The *cheongja* of Goryeo projected the elegance of the Goryeo aristocracy through beautiful shades of color and a variety of patterns (animals, plants, and clouds). In 1234, Goryeo invented the world's first printing movable metal type. Goryeo also created the Tripitaka Koreana, which is inscribed on the UNESCO World Heritage List. It is the world's greatest Buddhist cultural asset on which sutras (Buddha's teachings), the

> ### 고려의 중앙조직
>
> 고려의 최고행정기구는 3성(실제는 2성)이고 수상은 문화시중이다. 내각에 해당하는 6부는 이부(내무) · 병부(국방) · 호부(재정) · 예부(교육 · 외교) · 형부(법무) · 공부(건설)등이다.

려의 옛 영토를 수복하고 발해유민을 받아들였다. 고려는 북방 진출의 거점으로 평양에 서경 (西京)을 설치하였을 뿐만 아니라, 북방 국경 지대와 동북 해안 방면에는 계(界)라는 군사적 행정구역을 두고 그 이남 지방에는 5도라는 일반 행정구역으로 통치하였다.

[5] 귀족 문화의 융성

고려는 불교를 국가지도 이념의 기초로 삼아 호국사찰을 짓고 각종 불교 행사를 거행하였다. 그리고 유교를 정치 이념으로 하여 교육 · 과거 제도를 발전시켰다. 또한 산세와 지형

[Photo] Octagonal Nine-story Pagoda at Woljeongsa Temple
⟨Source: Korea Tourism Organization⟩

[사진] 월정사 8각 9층탑
⟨사진제공:한국관광공사⟩

이 인간의 길흉과 관계가 깊다는 풍수지리설을 결합시켜 귀족 문화의 폭을 넓혔다.

고려인들의 예술적 재능과 창의력은 상감청자라는 아름다운 도자기 문화를 이룩하였다. 고려청자는 아름다운 색과 다양한 무늬(동물 · 식물 · 구름)를 통해 고려귀족 사회의 멋을 남기고 있다. 그리고 1234년에는 세계 최초로 금속 활자를 발명하였다. 또한 불경을 집대성하여 팔만대장경이라는 세계 문화재를 남겼다. 이것은 부처님의 말씀(경)을 비롯하여 불교의 교리(율)나 그 해설(론)을 나무판에 새긴 세계 최대의 불교 문화재로서 현재 해인사에 남아 있다. 그 외 탑을 만들어 다양한 불교 예술을 남겼으니, 월정사 8각9층탑이나 경천사지탑 등이 대표적이다.

[6] 역사의 편찬

역대 왕들은 자신의 업적을 기념하기 위하여 역사를 편찬하였다. 삼국 시대에도 있었고 고려 초에도 실록(왕의 역사 기록)을 남겼으나, 거란의 침입으로 타버렸다. 1145년에는 김부

Vinaya (Buddhist precepts), and Abhidharma (commentaries on the sutras and Vinaya) are engraved on woodblocks, and it is currently preserved at Haeinsa Temple. Other Buddhist art forms remaining today are pagodas, including the octagonal nine-story pagoda at Woljeongsa Temple and a pagoda at the site of Gyeongcheonsa Temple.

[6] Historiography

Throughout the ages, kings tended to document their greatest achievements, and such records were made in the Three Kingdoms Period. *Sillok* (official records on royal history) were documented in early Goryeo, but they were destroyed by fire during an invasion by the Khitans. In 1145, Kim Bu-shik wrote a history book titled *Samguk Sagi* (*History of the Three Kingdoms*). It reports major events of the Three Kingdoms; describes social and political systems, geography, customs, garments; and tells the biographies of about 70 leading figures such as Kim Yu-sin, Gwan Chang, Choi Chi-won, and Uljimundeok. This is the oldest history book on Korea extant today, and it had great influence on next generations. *Samguk Yusa* (*Memorabilia of the Three Kingdoms*), written by Ilyeon (monk) during the period of Mongolian occupation, includes the mythical story of Dangun.

식 등이 「삼국사기」라는 역사책을 편찬하였다. 여기에는 삼국의 주요 사건을 비롯하여 제도 · 지리 · 풍속 · 복식 등에 대한 설명과 김유신 · 관창 · 최치원 · 을지문덕등 70여 명의 인물전기가 기록되어 있다. 이 책은 현존하는 우리나라 최고의 역사책으로 후대에 큰 영향을 끼쳤다. 한편, 몽고 간섭기에 일연(승려)이 쓴 「삼국유사」에는 단군 신화가 기록되어 있다.

[7] 외교와 해외 무역의 발달

고려는 외국 문화의 수용과 무역 활동에 아주 적극적이었다. 송(北宋:960~1127)과의 관계는 여진에 대항한다는 뜻도 문화적 의미도 컸다. 송과는 바다를 통한 문화 교류나 무역에서 가장 가까운 관계를 유지하였다. 고려가 송에 수출하는 물품은 주로 금 · 은 · 구리 · 화문석 · 유기 · 종이 · 먹 · 인삼 등이었고, 송으로부터 수입하는 물품은 책 · 비단 · 약재 · 악기 · 향로 등이었다.

고려의 해외 무역은 송 뿐만 아니라 거란과 여진 외에 아라비아에까지 미쳤다. 특히, 아

[Photo] Goryeo Celadon

[사진] 고려청자

라비아와의 교역을 통해서는 수은·향로·약품 등을 구입하였다. 개성의 관문인 벽란도(예성강 입구)는 당시 아라비아 상인들까지 출입하는 국제무역항이었고, 고려(Corea)의 이름은 이들을 통하여 서양에까지 알려지게 되었다. 이로서 고려는 국제사회에 눈을 뜨게 되었다.

[8] 교육과 과거 제도

고려의 최고 학교는 국자감이란 4종류의 국립종합 대학이다. 992년에 설치한 이 대학에는 신분에 따라 입학이 자격이 달랐으며, 주로 유교 경전과 한문을 배웠다. 그리고 일반 평민은 기술 계통의 학문을 배웠고 지방에도 학교(향학)가 있었다. 그리고 사립학교로서 12공도라는 것이 있었다.

958년에 실시된 과거제도(인물 선발 제도)는 한문의 문장 시험(진사과)과 유교 경전(명경과)으로 대별되고, 기타 의학·지리·산수 등 기술 시험이 있었다. 이러한 과거 시험은 어디까지나 귀족들에게만 자격이 주어졌으며, 3차에 걸친 복잡한 절차에 의해 일반인들은 응

[7] Development of Diplomacy and Overseas Trade

Goryeo avidly embraced foreign culture and engaged in foreign trade. Its relations with the Song Dynasty (Northern Song: 960~1127) were significant for forging a military alliance against the Jurchens and for cultural exchange. Song was the geographically closest partner for cultural exchange or trade by sea. Goryeo mainly exported gold, silver, copper, seagrass mats, brassware, paper, ink, and ginseng to Song and imported books, silk, medicine, musical instruments, and incense burners.

Goryeo also traded with Khitan, Jurchen, and as far as Arabia. It imported mercury, incense burners, and medicine from Arabia. Byeongnando (the mouth of the Yeseong River), a gateway to Gaeseong, was an international trade port frequented by Arabian merchants. The name "Corea" became known to the Western world through these merchants and it was through this connection that Goryeo opened its eyes to the international community.

[8] Education and Civil Service Examinations

Goryeo's highest educational institutions were four types of national universities collectively called *Gukjagam*, established in 992. Eligibility for admission varied depending on social class. Students mostly studied the Confucian classics and Chinese

시할 수 없었다. 더구나 5품 이상의 귀족 자제는 시험을 보지 않고 바로 관직을 맡을 수 있었는데 이것을 음서(蔭敍)라 하였는데 이러한 음서제도는 귀족사회의 특징이었다. 그리고 장교시험인 무과(武科:무과)는 없었다.

[9] 귀족 사회의 발달

고려는 귀족사회이다. 왕족과 고위직을 독점한 귀족들은 관직·토지·지식을 독점한 특권계급으로 가문을 이루어 고려 왕조의 지배층을 형성하였다. 이들 귀족 가문은 자기들끼리 결혼을 함으로써 배타적인 통혼권(通婚圈)을 형성하여 특권을 유지하였다.

귀족 밑으로 기술직과 하급 관료층인 중류계급이 있고, 그 아래 평민(농업·상업·어업·공업)과 천민계급이 있었다. 천민에는 노예, 뱃사공, 광대, 화척(禾尺·조선시대의 백정) 등이 있으며, 이들은 천민부락(향, 소, 부곡)에 살았다.

characters. Common people studied technological disciplines. Local areas had public schools called *hyanggyo*, and there was a private school system of 12 academies called *gongdo*.

The civil service examination held in 958 had two main parts: jinsa-gwa (composition in Chinese characters) and *myeonggyeong-gwa* (Confucian classics). Exams on medicine, geography, and mathematics were also administered. Only aristocrats were eligible to take these exams; common people could not realistically take them due to the complicated procedures involving three rounds of tests. Moreover, a special privilege called "*eumseo*" was given to sons of aristocrats at the rank of 5 *pum* or higher. They were appointed as government officials without having to take civil service exams, and this *eumseo* system was an integral feature of the aristocrat society. There was no exam for selection of military officers.

[9] Development of Aristocratic Society

Goryeo was an aristocratic society. The royal and noble families who monopolized government positions, ownership of land, and knowledge formed clans with special privilege and ruling class of Goryeo Dynasty. The noble families inter-married to maintain their vested interests.

Below the aristocrats was the middle class composed of engineers and lower government officials; common people engaged in farming, commerce, fishing, and

2. 북방민족과의 항쟁과 중세사회의 변화

[1] 거란과 여진의 격퇴

고려가 성립될 때 중국에서는 거란족이 요(遼:946~1125)나라를 세우고 926년에 발해를 멸망시키면서 북방의 위협적인 존재가 되어 있었다. 고려는 이들을 오랑캐로 여겨 강경한 북

서희와 소손녕의 대결

993년에 거란(요)의 장군 소손녕이 '고려는 신라 땅에서 일어났으며 고구려 땅이니 우리 것이니 땅을 내놓으라' 고 주장하였다. 이때 서희 장군은 '우리나라는 고구려를 계승하였음으로 국호를 고려라 칭하였으니 당신의 나라 서울인 동경(지금의 요양)도 우리영토이다.' 라고 끝까지 맞섰다.

industry; and the lower class consisting of slaves, boatsmen, performers, and butchers. There were quarters where only lower class people lived called *hyang*, *so*, and *bugok*.

2. *Resistance to the Northern Tribes and Changes in Medieval Society*

[1] Repulsion of Khitan and Jurchen

When Goryeo was being founded, the Khitans established the Liao Dynasty (946~1125) in China and overthrew Balhae in 926. Liao emerged as a threat in the

---

Confrontation between Seo Hee and So Son-nyeong

In 993, Liao general So Son-nyeong proclaimed, "Since Goryeo was founded on the former land of Silla and the domains of Goguryeo belong to us, return the land to us." Then, Goryeo general Seo hee rebutted, "Goryeo is the successor of Goguryeo. Therefore, your capital Donggyeong (currently Liaoning) is also our territory."

방정책을 추진하였다. 이에 거란은 성종12년(993)에 대군을 끌고 침입하였으나 서희 장군은 담판으로 이를 물리쳤으며, 현종 9년(1018)에는 10만 거란군의 침입을 강감찬 장군이 전멸시켰다(귀주대첩). 이로써 고려 영토는 압록강 유역까지 확대되었다.

거란을 격퇴한 이후, 고려는 외족의 침입을 막기 위해 천리장성(압록강 입구~원산만)을 쌓았으며 수도 외각에 성곽(나성)을 축조하였다. 그 후 만주 일대의 여진족(금:1115~1234)이 다시 강성해졌으므로 윤관은 특수군대(별무반)를 조직한 후 여진을 정벌하여 그들을 두만강 밖으로 몰아내고 함경도 지역으로 진출하였다. 이때 윤관이 설치했던 9성 중에 공험진은 두만강 건너 연변지역이라는 주장이 재기되고 있다.

[2] 귀족 사회의 모순

고려 사회의 지배계급은 여러 세대에 걸쳐 가문(clan)을 이룩하여 고위관직을 독점함으로써 많은 특권을 행사하였다. 그들은 학문과 지식·토지·관직을 독점하였으며 음서와 공

north, and Goryeo regarded Liao as a country of barbarians and sought to expand northward. In response, the Khitans mobilized a huge army and invaded Goryeo in the 12th year of King Seongjong (993). Goryeo General Seo Hee managed to repulse the attack. In the 9th year of King Hyeonjong (1018), a 100,000-man Khitan army launched an attack, but General Kang Gam-chan utterly defeated it at the Battle of Guiju. This allowed Goryeo to expand its territory to the north as far as the Amnok River basin.

After repelling the Khitans, Goryeo constructed the Thousand Li Great Wall (Cheollijangseong) connecting the mouth of the Amnok River and Wonsan Bay for national defense. Fortresses were built around the capital. Later, the Jurchens (Jin: 1115~1234) in Manchuria became a threat, and Yun Gwan organized special troops to conquer Jurchen. He chased them north of the Duman River and secured a presence in Hamgyeong Province. Yun Gwan then built nine fortresses, and some believe that Gongheomjin Fortress was in Yanbian.

[2] Corruption of Aristocratic Society

The ruling class of Goryeo society enjoyed many special privileges by forming exclusive clans over several generations and monopolizing the highest government positions. They monopolized academic sector, educational opportunities, and land ownership, and were granted *eumseo* and *gongeumjeon* (special land offered to high-ranking officials). They were exempted from taxes and military duty. Despite such

음전(고위 관직에게 주는 특별 토지)을 받는 특권층이었다. 이들은 면세·면역권을 갖고 있었는데, 상호 대립과 충돌을 일삼다가 이자겸의 난(1126)과 묘청의 난(1135)을 거치면서 고려 귀족사회의 모순이 심화되었다.

[3] 귀족들의 반란

고려 사회는 12세기에 접어들면서 자체의 모순이 나타나 흔들리기 시작하였다. 특히 명문 가문을 중심으로 문벌을 형성하여 그들 사이에 정권 쟁탈전이 일어났으며, 이자겸의 난과 묘청의 난으로 그 모순이 노출되었다. 1170년에 일어난 무신 정변은 고려를 밑바닥부터 흔들어 놓은 역사적 사건이었다. 특히 무신들은 평소 문신에 비해 대접을 못 받고 있던 사실에 불만을 품고 있었다. 거란, 여진 등 계속된 외침의 시련 속에서 무신들의 지위는 향상되었지만 사회적 대우가 그에 미치지 못하자 불만이 커지게 되었다. 1170년에 상장군 정중부(鄭仲夫) 등은 정치가 문란해진 틈을 타서 쿠데타를 일으키고 정권을 장악하였다.

privileges, they often engaged in confrontations and conflicts with each other. Two incidents, the Treason of Yi Ja-gyeom (1126) and the Revolt of Myocheong (1135), served to exacerbate the corruption of the Goryeo aristocracy.

[3] Revolts of Aristocrats

At the onset of the 12th century, Goryeo society began to reveal its internal conflicts and fell into a state of disorder. Prominent families engaged in increasingly intense power struggles, and conflicts became evident through the Treason of Yi Ja-gyeom and the Revolt of Myocheong. Musinjeongbyeon (a revolt by military officials) in 1170 was a historical event that shook Goryeo to its very foundations. Military officers had long been mistreated and seen as of lower status than civil officials. They gained stature for having repelled several consecutive invasions by the Khitans and Jurchens, but were dissatisfied with their social treatment. In 1170, Commander Jeong Jung-bu took advantage of the strife to stage a coup d' e-tat and seize power.

[4] Military Rule and Slave Uprising

Jeong Jung-bu was succeeded by Yi Ui-bang, Yi Eui-min, and Gyeong Dae-seung. Their rule was followed by the dictatorship of Choi Chung-heon (1196~1258). They

[4] 무신의 집권과 노예의 반란

정중부 이후 이의방·이의민과 경대승을 거쳐 최충헌의 무단 독재(1196~1258)까지 100여 년간 무신정권이 수립되어 정치적 권한과 경제적 부를 독점하여, 문신중심의 귀족사회는 무너졌다.

무신 정변에 의해 문신 중심의 귀족 지배질서가 붕괴되자, 전국 각지에서는 농민과 천민들이 반란을 일으켰다. 농민들은 귀족들의 과도한 수탈에 저항하여 난을 일으켰고, 만적

> **만적의 난**
>
> 1198년에 최충헌의 노예였던 만적은 '무신란 이후 국가의 대신들은 전부 천민에서 나왔으니, 대신들이라고 처음부터 씨가 있는 것이 아니다. 우리는 각기 상전을 죽이고 노예문서를 불태워서 천민(노예)을 없게 하자'고 반란을 일으켰다.

exercised military rule and monopolized political authority and economic wealth for about 100 years. The influence of the aristocracy led by civil officials was at its lowest ebb.

When the rule of the aristocracy collapsed as the result of Musinjeongbyeon, the peasants and lower class rose in revolts all over the country. The peasants revolted against excessive exploitation by the aristocrats. Lower class people including Manjeok launched a movement for liberation from their social status. The largest slave uprising for freedom was the Revolt of Manjeok in Gaegyeong in 1198.

[5] Resistance Against the Mongols

The military regime had become entrenched by the early 13th century. At this time, the Mongols (1206~1388) conquered nearly all of known Asia and began to invade Goryeo in 1231. The Mongols staged no fewer than six invasions of Goryeo over several decades. In desperation, Goryeo moved its capital to Ganghwa Island and braced itself for

(萬積)을 비롯한 천민들은 혼란해진 사회 분위기를 이용하여 신분 해방을 위한 운동을 전개하였다. 특히 1198년에 개경에서 일어난 만적의 난은 신분 해방을 외친 대표적인 노예 반란이었다.

[5] 대몽 항쟁

무신 정권이 안정되어 갈 무렵인 13세기 초반에 아시아 대륙을 모두 차지한 몽고(1206~1388)는 1231년에 고려를 침략하기 시작하여 전후 6차에 걸쳐 고려를 유린하였다. 고려는 육전에 강한 몽고군을 피해 서울을 강화도로 옮기는 등 장기적인 전쟁태세를 갖추었다. 특히 몽고군은 우리나라의 문화재를 약탈·분탕시켜 대장경이나 황룡사 9층 목탑 등이 소실되었다.

그중에서도 몽고군에 대항하여 끈질기게 조국 수호 전쟁을 전개했던 계층은 정부군이 아니라 농민과 천민 등 일반 민중들이었다. 이러한 감투 정신은 지배층이 몽고에 굴복한 이

a protracted war. In the course of many battles, the Mongols exploited and destroyed numerous cultural assets of Goryeo, including the Tripitaka Koreana and the Nine-story Wooden Pagoda at Hwangryongsa Temple.

It was not the government army but the common people including peasants and lower class people who put up the greatest resistance to the Mongols. Their spirit was readily apparent in their organization of special troops called *sambyeolcho*, even after the ruling class had surrendered to the Mongols. They moved their base of operations to Jindo Island and then to Jeju Island and continued the fight against the Mongols to the last.

[6] Goryeo Under Mongol Control

Goryeo continued its struggle against the Mongols from Ganghwa Island but finally surrendered in 1270. The capital was then moved to Gaegyeong, and Goryeo was subjected to Mongol political control for about 70 years. The kings had to marry Mongolian princesses, and Mongol political systems were established. In fact, the highest administrative organizations, three '*seong*', were replaced with one '*bu*', while the six '*bu*' was changed into four '*sa*'. Wordings used at the royal court were modified.

The Mongols also tried to conquer Japan twice, but both attempts failed, only making Goryeo suffer even more. Goryeo ultimately lost the land north of Cheollyeong and Jabiryeong as well as Jeju Island. During this period, Western (Arabian) culture was introduced, broadening the perspectives of the Goryeo people.

후에도 삼별초(三別抄)라는 특수 군대를 조직하여 몽고에 대항하였다. 그들은 중심지를 진도 · 제주도로 옮기면서 최후의 한 사람이 남아 있을 때까지 몽고와의 항쟁을 계속하였다.

[6] 몽고 간섭하의 고려

고려는 강화도에서 몽고와의 투쟁을 계속하였으나, 1270년에 몽고의 힘에 굴복하였다. 따라서 강화도에서 서울을 개경으로 옮기고 70여 년간 몽고의 정치적 간섭을 받게 된다. 왕은 몽고인 부인을 얻었고, 정치 제도를 몽고식으로 바꾸고 특히 최고 관부인 3성을 1부로, 행정 6부를 4사로 고쳤으며 궁중에서 쓰는 용어를 바꾸기까지 하였다.

또한 2차에 걸쳐 일본을 정벌하려 했으나 고려에 피해만 주고 실패하였으며, 철령과 자비령 이북의 땅과 제주도를 빼앗기는 수모를 당하였다. 그러나 이 시기에 서역(아라비아)의 문화가 전래되어 고려인의 세계관이 확대되었다.

[7] Reformed Policies by King Gongmin

King Gongmin (1351~1374) was initially under the control of Mongolia. He was encouraged by the people's spirit of resistance, and in the late 14th century when Yuan (China under the Mongols) was declining, he launched an anti-Yuan independence movement in full scale. He was succeeded in regaining the lands that had been taken away by the Mongols and purged pro-Yuan figures.

The objectives of King Gongmin's anti-Yuan and independence movement were to purge the pro-Yuan faction and eliminate the Mongolian government system (restore the three *seong* and six *bu*), restore the northern territories, and pursue reforms. However, his reformed policies faced strong opposition and ended in failure, and the country was plunged into a crisis once again as a result of foreign invasions and raids by Honggeon tribes and Japanese *waegu* (pirates).

[8] Social Changes in Late Goryeo (Medieval Age)

King Gongmin succeeded in freeing Goryeo from Mongol rule, but the country was beset by invasions by Honggeon tribes from the north and raids by Japanese waegu from the south. Exacerbating the situation, the aristocratic families, the incumbent ruling class, owned vast farms and exercised power as a pro-Yuan faction. New

[7] 공민왕의 개혁 정치

몽고의 간섭을 받았던 공민왕(1351~1374)은 국민들의 항몽 정신에 힘입어 14세기 후반에 원(元)이 쇠약해진 틈을 타서 빼앗긴 영토를 되찾고, 친원파를 숙청하는 등 반원자주정책을 대대적으로 추진하였다.

공민왕의 반원·독립개혁운동은 우선 친원파를 숙청하고 몽고식 관제를 폐지(3성 6부로의 환원)하는 동시에 몽고가 지배하던 북방 영토를 회복하였다. 그러나 그의 개혁정치는 반대 세력에 부딪혀 실패하였으며, 계속된 이민족(왜구·홍건적)의 침입으로 고려 왕조는 또다시 커다란 위기에 봉착하게 되었다.

[8] 고려 말(중세사회)의 사회 변동

공민왕은 몽고의 지배를 벗어나 민족의 독립을 되찾았으나 북방의 홍건적, 남방의 왜구

progressive bureaucrats that emerged from local areas were anti-Yuan, and confrontations between the two groups intensified.

In midst of such conflicts, Yi Seong-gye, a successful military leader, partnered with the newly emerging class to initiate land reform. On the occasion of the Wihwa Island incident (1388), Yi seized power and founded the Joseon Dynasty. This marked the end of medieval society and the beginning of modern society on the Korean Peninsula.

3. Founding of the Joseon Dynasty and the Development of a Pre-Modern State

[1] Social Changes in late Goryeo

For the late Goryeo period was a time of conflicts in transition to pre-modern society, many political influences, who wished to restore order, emerged. One of them was newly emerging group of progressives who studied neo-Confucianism and had extensive experience in government administration.

Another group that emerged in late Goryeo period was the militarists who have gained power through effectively controlling the external aggressions from China and Japan. The militarist group, led by Yi Seong-gye, suppressed incumbent aristocrats by

들이 계속 침입하여 국가적 위기는 계속되었다. 더구나 기존 집권 세력인 권문세족은 넓은 농장을 소유하고 친원파로 군림하였다. 지방 출신으로 진보적인 신진 관료층은 신흥사대부 계층으로 반원세력으로 양파의 갈등이 심해졌다.

이러한 갈등 속에서 군사적으로 성공한 이성계는 신흥 세력과 연합하여 토지 제도를 개혁하고, 위화도 회군(1388)으로 고려 왕조의 실권을 장악한 뒤 마침내 새로이 조선 왕조를 건설하게 된다. 이로서 우리사회는 중세사회에서 근세사회로 발전되어갔다.

3. 조선왕조의 성립과 근세국가의 발전

[1] 고려 말의 사회 변화

고려 말기는 새로운 시대(근세사회)를 향한 갈등기였으므로, 이러한 혼란과 어려움을 극

forming coalitions with the other newly emerging group and, later, founded Joseon Dynasty as a key political player of the late group period. The corrupt land ownership system and frequent invasions from Japan and China contributed to the fall of the Goryeo.

[2] Significance of the Founding of Joseon

The Joseon was founded through an alliance between the militarists and new literati. Under the reign of King Wu of late Goryeo, Yi Seong-gye, the leader of the militarists, led the troops to invade Ming Chins and reached as far as the Amnok River. He withdrew the troops (Wihwado Turnaround Incident, 1388) and, with the support of new literati such as Jeong Do-jeon, founded Joseon Dynasty (1392).

Contrary to Goryeo, the social position of the common people was much elevated. And a new society has formed by taking Confucianism as governing philosophy instead of Buddhism. The founding of Joseon was not simply a beginning of a new dynasty. But it signified the transition of hereditary aristocratic society to bipartisan bureaucratic society. And it also was the beginning of a pre-modern society. The national territory was expanded, people's national pride strengthened, the national wealth and military power grew, and the social status of peasants improved, confirming the legitimacy and of the Korean people of Joseon.

복하고자 하는 새로운 세력들이 등장하였다. 이들이 바로 신진사대부(新進士大夫)들이었다. 이들은 성리학을 공부한 학자이면서 행정 실무에도 밝은 진취적인 사람들이었다.

한편, 고려 말에는 홍건적과 왜구의 침입을 격퇴함으로써 실력을 쌓아 가는 새로운 무장 세력(武裝勢力)들도 등장하였다. 이들 이성계로 대표되는 무장세력은 기존의 권문세족을 압도하여 신흥세력과 손잡고 고려 말의 주인공으로 조선을 건국하였다. 특히 토지제도가 문란해졌으며, 왜구·홍건적의 침입으로 국가위기가 닥쳐왔다.

[2] 조선건국의 의의

조선은 이러한 무장 세력과 신진사대부 세력이 힘을 합쳐서 건국되었다. 무장 세력을 주도한 이성계는 고려 우왕 때 명나라를 공격하기 위하여 압록강까지 진군하였다가 되돌아와 (위화도 회군, 1388) 고려의 정권을 장악하고, 새로운 토지 제도(과전법)를 공포한 후 정도전 (鄭道傳) 등의 신진 사대부의 도움을 받아 조선을 건국하였다.(1392)

[3] Development of Joseon

King Taejo (Yi Seong-gye) moved the capital to Hanyang (today's Seoul) to bolster the legitimacy of the new dynasty. He also constructed Sungnyemun (Namdaemun). After overcoming the Revolt of Princes in early days, King Taejong (1400~1418) laid out a framework of a state by implementing laws such as Prohibition of private armies, Introduction of *Sinmungo* (a drum to beat for grievances and injustices) and *Hopae* Vae (identification card law).

King Sejong (1418~1450) later established Jiphyeonjeon (Hall of Worthies) to promote academic study and created Korea's unique alphabet system, Hunmin Jeongeum. He also invented a water clock and sundial and advanced the sciences. Korea's border expanded as far as the Amnok River and the Duman River, and movable type printing press was improved for mass publication. During the reign of King Sejong, traditional Korean music was to the brilliant achievement compiled into *Aak*.

The Joseon Dynasty reached its prime during the reign of King Seongjong (1469~1494) when *Gyeongguk Daejeon* (*National Code*) was fully completed. Composed of six statutes on government personnel, finance, protocols, military affairs, legal affairs, and civil engineering, *Gyeongguk Daejeon* described the political and social systems of the Joseon Dynasty and provided the traditional Korean society with a framework of a pre-modern society.

조선왕조는 고려 왕조와는 달리 백성의 지위가 크게 향상되었으며, 불교 대신 유교사상을 신봉하여 새로운 사회를 이룩하였다. 조선 건국은 단순한 역성혁명(易姓革命)이 아니라, 문벌 귀족 사회에서 양반 관료 사회로의 이행을 의미하는 동시에 근세사회로의 변화가 이룩되었다. 특히 국토가 확장되고 국민의식이 향상되었으며, 부국강병과 농민층의 지위 향상을 가져와 민족의 정통성과 영속성을 확인하였다.

[3] 조선의 발전

태조(이성계)는 새로운 민족 국가의 정통성을 강조하기 위해 수도를 한양(오늘의 서울)으로 옮겼으며 숭례문(남대문)을 건설하였다. 국초의 왕자의 난과 같은 시련을 극복한 태종(太宗, 1400~1418)은 사병(私兵)의 폐지, 신문고(申聞鼓, 억울한 사정을 호소하기 위해 치는 북)의 설치와 호패법(戶牌法, 주민등록증) 실시 등으로 국가의 기틀을 마련하였다.

이어 세종(世宗, 1418~1450)은 집현전을 두어 학문을 연구하게 하였으며, 우리민족의 독창

[Photo] Sungnyemun

Located in Seoul and widely known as Namdaemun, Sungnyemun was completed in 1398 and renovated in 1447 (29th year of King Sejong). It was destroyed by arson on February 10, 2008 and is currently under reconstruction.

⟨Source: Korea Tourism Organization⟩

[사진] 숭례문

숭례문은 서울의 남대문으로 1398년에 완성된 후 1447년(세종 29)에 개축하였다. 2008년2월 10일에 불타버려 현재 복원중이다.

⟨사진제공:한국관광공사⟩

[4] Creation of Hunmin Jeongeum

After completing the nation's infrastructure, King Seojong founded an academic research facility called Jiphyeonjeon (Assembly Hall of Virtue) and directed scholars, such as Sin Suk-ju and Seong Sam-mun, et al., to invent Humin Jeongeum (*hanguel*),

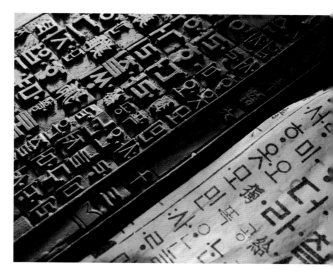

[Photo] Hunmin Jeongeum Korea Aphabet
〈Source: Korea Tourism Organization〉

[사진] 훈민정음
〈사진제공:한국관광공사〉

적인 문자인 훈민정음(訓民正音)을 창제하였다. 왕은 물시계·해시계 등을 발명하여 과학을 발전시키고 압록강과 두만강까지 국경을 확장시킨 후, 금속활자를 개량하여 많은 책을 간행하였다. 또한 우리나라의 전통음악을 정리하여 아악을 완성하여 조선의 황금기를 이룩하였다.

이어 성종(成宗, 1469~1494)대에 이르러 「경국대전(經國大典)」을 완비하여 조선 왕조의 황금기를 이룩하였다. 「경국대전」은 6개의 법전으로서 인사·재정·예의·군사·법률·토목 등 조선 왕조의 정치·사회 제도를 정리하여 근세사회로서 한국 전통사회의 기틀을 마련하였다.

[4] 훈민정음의 창제

세종은 나라의 기틀을 완성한 후 민족적 긍지와 자부심을 나타내기 위해 집현전이라는 학문연구소를 두고 신숙주·성삼문 등 학자들을 시켜 우리 고유문자인 훈민정음(한글)을 제작·반포하게 하였다. 이로써 우리 민족은 중국의 한자 대신 자국의 글자를 지닌 문화민족으

Korea's own lettering system, and to publish it in order to demonstrate national pride and excellence. Thus, Korean people took pride in owning their own writing system in lieu of borrowed Chinese writing system. For the distribution and the promotion of broad acceptance of newly created Hunmin Jeongeum, King Sejong wrote *Yongbioecheonga* (*Songs of Flying Dragons*: a eulogy cherishing the virtues of ancestors and praising the foundation of the Joseon Dynasty) and *Seokbosangjeol* (*Biography of Buddha*) using *hangeul* in 1477.

[5] Establishing the National Boundaries

Goguryeo (37 B.C.~668) and later Balhae (698~926) controlled a vast area that stretched into Manchuria and the Russian Maritime Territory, but the landmass of Korea had been reduced to the Korean Peninsula by the Unified Silla period. The northern border of Unified Silla connected Pyeongyang and Wonsan, and that of Goryeo ran along the Amnok River and through the Hamheung area.

King Sejong placed four outposts in Amnok river area and six camps in the Duman river area to push the Jurchens out to the north of the rivers and expanded national territory. By the late 15th century, King Sejong completely incorporated Amnok river area and Duman river area into Joseon's domain and, by relocating population to the region, contrived to achieve the balanced national development.

로서의 긍지를 갖게 되었다. 세종은 훈민정음을 보급 · 시행하기 위해 1477년에는 「용비어천가」(태종대까지의 조상의 덕을 기리고 조선 왕조 건국을 찬양한 노래)와「석보상절」(석가의 일대기)을 한글로 편찬하였다.

[5] 국토의 완성

고구려(기원전 37~668)나 발해(698~926) 시기에 우리나라는 만주와 연해주까지 지배하였지만 통일신라 이후 그 영토가 한반도로 축소되었다. 통일신라 때 평양~원산까지 진출하였고, 고려 시대에 와서 압록강~함흥 일대로 확장되었다.

세종은 압록강 유력에 4군을, 두만강 유역에 6진을 설치하여 여진족을 강북으로 쫓아내고 영토를 크게 넓혔다. 그 후 성종 때인 15세기 말에 압록강과 두만강 유역을 완전히 우리 영토로 편입시키고 남쪽의 주민을 북방으로 이주시켜 국토의 균형발전을 꾀하였다. 이로서 우리나라의 국토가 완성되었다.

[Map] Expansion of national territory

[지도] 우리나라의 영토확장 과정

[6] 정치 제도

　　조선은 유교적인 민본 정치를 바탕으로 평민의 지위가 향상된 근세사회이다. 조선의 정치 제도는 「경국대전」을 근거로 하여 유교적인 정치 이념을 구현할 수 있도록 짜여 있었다. 중앙에는 오늘의 내각에 해당하는 의정부(議政府)와 6조가 있어서 모든 정치를 관장하였고, 정책 결정과 행정의 잘못을 비판하는 사헌부(司憲府)와 왕을 비판하는 사간원(司諫院)이 별도로 설치되었다. 그 외 양반의 범죄를 다스리는 의금부와 평민의 죄를 관장하는 포도청, 그리고 오늘의 서울특별시에 해당하는 한성부가 있었다.

　　지방에는 관찰사를 책임자로 하는 8도를 두었으며, 군(郡) 아래 가장 말단 기구인 현에까지 수령이 파견되어 중앙집권정치를 실시하였다. 특히 이 시기는 백성들의 주장과 건의를 받아들이는 민본정치(民本政治)를 시행하였다.

[6] Political System

Joseon was a pre-modern society where the commoner's social status was much elevated due to Confucius democratic political philosophy. Its political systems were structured to execute Confucian political ideology based on *Gyeonggukdaejeon* (*National Code*). Uijeongbu, equivalent to today's cabinet, and Yukjo, meaning six ministries, overviewed the overall political affairs. Apart from that, Saheonbu that checked government's administrative policies and decision-making and Saganwon that criticized King's political behavior were independently operated. In addition, there were Euigeumbu, which dealt with criminal affairs of *Yangban* (noble class), Podocheong, which managed commoner's criminal and Hanseong-bu that was equivalent to today's capital city government.

The local area was divided into eight *do* (province), each of which was headed by a governor. The centralized administration was in place, and even chief magistrates for *hyeon*, the smallest administrative unit below *gun* (county), were appointed centrally. Especially during this period, the political process focused heavily on the citizenry: suggestions and arguments by the people were duly heard and acted upon by the government.

[7] 사회구조

조선사회의 신분은 초기에는 양인(良人)과 천인(賤人)으로 구별되었지만, 시대가 지남에 따라 '분화가 이루어져 양반 · 중인 · 상민 · 천민의 4등급으로 나뉘어졌다. 양반은 과거를 통해 관직에 나갈 수 있는 계층으로, 학문과 지식을 독점할 수 있는 계급이었다. 그 외 막대한 부(토지)를 독점한 유산 계급이었고, 면세 · 면역을 갖고 있는 특권 계급이었다.

지배 계급 아래에는 중인이 있었는데, 이들은 통역 · 의술 · 천문 · 예술 등 기술관이나 말단 관직에 취임하는 사람들이었다. 양인은 농민 · 상인 · 수공업자 등으로서 조세의 납부와 군역의 의무를 졌다. 천민 중에서 특히 노비는 고려시대와 마찬가지로 매매 · 상속 · 양도될 수 있는 하층민이었다.

[7] Social Structure

In the early years of the Joseon Dynasty, society was largely divided into two social classes: *yangin* (freeborn) and *cheonin* (lowborn). Over time, however, it was subdivided into four classes: *yangban*, *jungin*, *sangmin*, and *cheonmin*. The *yangban* were the nobles, who were eligible to take civil service exams and be appointed as government officials. They monopolized academic and educational sector. In addition, they were bourgeois class that accumulated massive wealth through inheritance and were privileged class that were exempted from tax and duties.

Below the ruling class was the *jungin* (middle class), which mostly consisted of technical specialists such as interpreters, medical personnel, astrologists, fine artists, and low-ranking government officials. The *yangin*, commoners, consisted of farmers, merchants, and craftmen whp were subject to tax dues and military service duties. Among the *cheonmin* class, slaves especially were low class subjects who were often traded, inherited as property and sold just as in Goryeo Period.

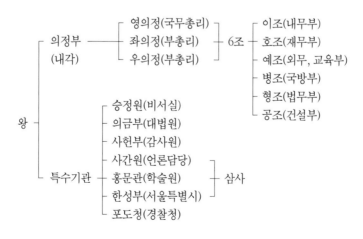

[표 2] 조선의 중앙관제(괄호 안은 현재관직)

왕
- 의정부 (내각)
  - 영의정(국무총리)
  - 좌의정(부총리)
  - 우의정(부총리)
  - 6조
    - 이조(내무부)
    - 호조(재무부)
    - 예조(외무, 교육부)
    - 병조(국방부)
    - 형조(법무부)
    - 공조(건설부)
- 특수기관
  - 승정원(비서실)
  - 의금부(대법원)
  - 사헌부(감사원)
  - 사간원(언론담당)
  - 홍문관(학술원)
  - 한성부(서울특별시)
  - 포도청(경찰청)
  - 삼사 (사헌부, 사간원, 홍문관)

[Table 2] The Central Government of Joseon (position today)

```
                    ┌ Yeong-uijeong (Prime Minister)              ┌ Ijo (Ministry of Internal Affairs)
          Uijeongbu ┤ Jwa-uijeong (Deputy Prime Minister) ┬ 6 jo ┤ Hojo (Ministry of Finance)
          (Cabinet) └ Wu-uijeong (Deputy Prime Minister)          ├ Yejo (Ministry of Foreign Affairs,
                                                                   │       Ministry of Education)
                                                                   ├ Byeongjo (Ministry of Defense)
                                                                   ├ Hyeongjo (Ministry of Justice)
                      ┌ Seungjeongwon (Office of the President)    └ Gongjo (Ministry of Construction)
                      ├ Uigeumbu (Supreme Court)
   King ─┤            ├ Saheonbu (Board of Audit and Inspection)
                      ├ Saganwon (PR office)
          Special    ├ Hongmungwan (National Academy of Sciences) ┬ 3 sa
          Institutions├ Hanseongbu (Seoul City Government)
                      └ Podocheong (National Police Agency)
```

[8] 군사 제도

조선 시대에는 농병 일치제(부병제)인 일종의 국민개병제로서 16~60세까지 평민 남자에게 병역의 의무가 있었다. 군역에 나가지 않는 남자[봉족(奉足)]는 군역자의 경비를 담당하였다. 모든 군대는 중앙군(5위)과 지방군(육군과 해군)으로 나뉘었고, 지방군의 책임자는 그 지방 수령이 겸직하였다.

그 후 세조 때는 군사적 요충을 중심으로 군사 제도를 개혁하여 자체 방위 제도로 전환하였으며, 연락망은 봉수제와 역마제가 있었다. 16세기 이후에는 국민개병인 군사제도가 무너져서 임진왜란 이후에는 모병제가 실시되었다.

[9] 서울의 모습

조선 왕조의 서울인 한양은 북쪽으로는 북악산, 남쪽으로는 남산, 동쪽으로는 낙산, 그리

[8] Military System

During the Joseon Dynasty, peasants were required to serve in the army. Every male commoner aged between 16~60 was drafted for military service. Those who did not serve in the military (*bongjok*) were in charge of providing financial support for the drafted soldiers. The army was divided into the central army (five *wee*) and local army (army and naval forces). The local army was headed by the magistrates of each region.

Later, King Sejo initiated a military reform that primarily converted points of strategic importance to self-sustaining localized defence system and employed *Bonsuje* (fire/smoke beacons) and *Yeokmaje* (horseback messenger system) as communication network. After the 16th century, the draft-based military system fell apart and was replaced by a draft system.

[9] Profile of Seoul

Hanyang (Seoul), the capital of Joseon, was a geopolitically strategic location as it was flanked by Mt. Bugak to the north, Mt. Nam to the south, Mt. Nak to the east, and Mt. Inwang to the west. To the south of Seoul, the Han River flows from east to west. The outer boundary of Seoul is surrounded by Mt. Acha (east), Mt. Deokyang (west), Mt. Gwanak (south), and Mt. Bukhan (north) like a folding screen.

고 서쪽으로는 인왕산이 있으며 남쪽으로는 한강이 흘러 지정학적으로 요지이다. 이러한 서울의 외곽에는 아차산(동)·덕양산(서)·관악산(남)·북한산(북)이 병풍처럼 둘러싸고 있다.

조선왕조는 서울 주위를 성곽으로 싸고 4대문과 4소문을 두었으며, 경복궁·창덕궁·덕수궁 등의 궁궐을 세웠다. 궁궐의 동쪽에는 종묘(왕의 조상 제사)를 두었고, 서쪽에는 사직단, 서·곡식의 신)을 두었으며 중앙의 종로 사거리에는 종루를 세워 밤10시부터 새벽4시까지 통행을 금지하였다. 당시 서울의 인구는 약10만 명이었다.

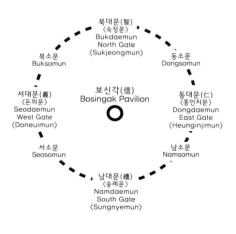

[Map] Seoul in Joseon
[지도] 조선시대의 서울

The Joseon Dynasty built walls around the capital placing four main gates and four auxiliary gates, and constructed royal palaces such as Gyeongbokgung, Changdeokgung and Deoksugung. To the east royal palaces, there was Sajikdan (an altar to worship the gods og land and grain). At the intersection of the main streets, Jongo intersection, a belfry was built to enforce curfew between 10 am and 4 am. The population of Hanyang at the time was estimated about 100,000.

[Map] Seoul in Joseon
[지도] 조선시대의 서울

[10] Education and Civil Servant Recruitment System of Joseon

Each kingdom in Korea had its own educational institutions. Goguryeo had Taehak, Unified Silla had Gukhak, and Goryeo had Gukjagam, a university. For the first time in Korean history, Joseon differentiated the levels of education: *seodang*

[10] 조선의 교육 · 과거 제도

우리나라의 교육제도는 고구려의 태학, 통일신라의 국학이 있었고 고려시대에는 국자감이라는 종합 대학이 있었다. 조선시대에는 처음으로 각급 학교가 분리되어 서당(초등학교)과 4학 · 향교(중학교), 그리고 성균관(대학 과정)이 구분되었으며 주로 한자교육이 중심이었다.

대학은 과거 1차 시험 합격자(생진과)가 입학하여 한문(유교 경전)을 배웠으며, 기타 전문 교육 기관으로 전의감(의대) · 사역원(외국어대) · 관상감(천문학) · 형조 부설(법대) · 호조 부설(상대)) 등이 있었다.

과거 제도는 문관 시험과 무관 시험, 그리고 중인 계층이 응시하는 기술관 시험으로 나누어 실시하였으며 복잡한 절차(3단계)로 시행되었다. 문관 시험(문과)은 양반 자제가 주로 응시하였고, 무관 시험(무과)에는 평민이나 지방 세력가의 자제가 응시할 수 있었으므로 문관 시험(문과)이 중시되었다. 기술관 시험(잡과)은 주로 양반의 서자나 중인층이 응시하였는데 2차까지만 있었다. 조선시대의 관리는 원천적으로 과거에 합격한 자들이 임명되었으나, 2품

(elementary school), *Sahak* and *hyanggyo* (middle school), and Seonggungwan (university). These institutions mainly taught Chinese characters and literature.

University education was provided to those who have passed the first round of civil service examinations, *saengjin-gwa*, for Chinese literature (Confucian scriptures) education. And there were other high education institutions of specialized disciplines such as Jeoneuigam (medicine), Sayeogwon (foreign languages), Gwansanggam (astronomy), Hyungjobuseol (law) and Hojobuseol (commerce).

There were separate civil service examinations for officials, military officials, and technical specialists. The last one was for the *jungin* class. Sitting for an exam was a complex affair, and there were three rounds of exams. Civil official exams (*mungwa*) were mostly taken by the sons of *yangban*, while the military official exams (*mugwa*) were open also to the sons of common people or local influentials. Therefore, the civil official exams were considered more prestigious. Most of those who sat for the technical exams (*jabgwa*) were sons of mistresses of *yangban* or. There were only two rounds of these exams. In principle, only those who passed the civil service examinations were appointed as government officials, but the sons of senior officials ranked 2 *pum* or higher were given privileges called *muneum*.

이상의 고위관리 자제는 문음이라는 특전이 있었다.

[11] 토지와 조세 제도

조선 시대에는 전 시대와 마찬가지로 토지의 소유권을 국가가 가지고 있었고 개인에게는 징세권·경작권만 있었다. 따라서 모든 토지는 공전(公田)과 사전(私田)으로 나뉘었다. 전자는 국가에 소속된 토지이며, 후자는 개인에게 소속된 토지로 관리에게 지급된 땅(과전)이나 공신에게 준 땅(공신전) 등이 있다. 그 후 세조 12년(1466)에는 현직자에게만 토지를 주게 되었다. 그러나 그 후 토지 제도는 점차 모순을 낳게 된다.

조선 시대의 조세 제도는 우선 토지 경작자가 납부하는 조세(소작료)를 비롯하여하여 지방 특산물인 공물, 그리고 남자(16~60세)들의 병역과 부역(노동)이 있다. 그러나 이러한 국가에 대한 의무는 양인(평민)들만이 지고 있었다.

[11] Land and Tax System

Just as in other earlier dynasties, all land was owned by the state. Individuals only had rights to collect fees or to cultivate the land. Thus, all land was categorized as either *gongjeon* or *sajeon*. The former was allocated for government's official use and the latter was assigned to individuals for personal use. *Sajeon* consisted of *Gwajeon*, given to government officials, and Gongsinjeon, given to meritorious individuals. Later, since the 12th year of King Sejo (1466), the land was given strictly to incumbent government officials only. After the change, however, the land system brought about ever-growing contradictions.

Taxation and duty to the Joseon state included land taxes (rent), which were paid by cultivators; *gongmul*, tribute of local specialties; and military service, and corvee labor, which applied to males aged between 16 and 60. These taxes and duties were borne only by the *yangin* (commoners).

[12] Commercial Activities in the early Joseon Period

In *yangban*-led Joseon society, merchants or handicraftsmen were disregarded, and most people were mostly self-sufficient. For these reasons, commerce was underdeveloped. Moreover, commercial activities were restricted due to limitations in

[12] 조선 초의 상업 활동

양반 사회인 조선에서는 상인(merchants)이나 수공업자(handicraftsman)는 천시되었고, 국민들이 주로 자급자족 생활을 하였으므로 상업은 위축되었다. 더구나 화폐 유통의 불가능, 교통수단의 미비로 상업 활동이 제한되었다. 서울 한복판에는 육의전(六矣廛)이라는 공공 시장(비단 · 종이 · 어물 등)이 있었으나 주로 양반층이 이용하였다.

도시와 지방에서는 5일에 한 번씩 장(Fair)이 열려 물품이 유통되었는데 이를 담당한 상인을 보부상(褓負商)이라 불렀다. 주로 일용 잡화를 판매하는 이들은 전국적인 조직망을 가지고 활동하였다.

[13] 양반사회의 모순

조선의 양반 사회가 기반을 마련하면서 양반 귀족들은 정치적 · 학문적 · 경제적 특권을

circulation of currency and the lack of transportation means. At the heart of Seoul was a public market called *yukeuijeon*. It was frequented mainly by *yangban*, and silk, paper, and fishery products were traded.

In cities and rural areas, local markets opened every five days for trade their goods. The merchants who participated in such markets were called bobusang. The bobusang, distributors of general merchandise, operated with national networks.

[13] Breakups in *Yangban* Society

As the *yangban*-led society became established in Joseon, the *yangban* enjoyed more political, academic, and economic privileges. The number of *yangban* increased due to the inheritance of government positions, an increase in the number of meritorious subjects, and the exclusive right to take the civil service exams. However, national government revenue began to decline because the *yangban* were exempted from taxes and military service. The *yangban* eventually began to have conflicts and confrontations among themselves to protect their vested interests.

Politically, the *yangban* occupied all high government positions. Economically, they owned vast lands and farms. Socially, they established exclusive clans and confronted each other. Extreme parochialism among schools, clans, and regions led to purges and factional strife. The *yangban* tried to protect their interests and rights through *hyangyak* (village rules) and *seowon* (private academies).

누렸다. 특히 관직의 세습, 공신의 증가, 과거의 독점 등으로 양반층은 수적으로 증가하였으나, 그들의 면세·면역으로 국가 수입은 감소하였다. 따라서 양반층은 자신의 권익을 보호하기 위해 대립·갈등을 일으켰다.

양반들은 정치적 특권으로 고관을 독점하였고 경제적으로는 많은 토지와 농장을 가졌으며, 사회적으로는 파벌 위주로 배타적인 가문을 이루어 대립·항쟁을 일삼았다. 따라서 학파·가문·지역 간의 분열이 나타나 사화·당쟁으로 이어졌고 양반들은 향약·서원 등을 통해 자신들의 권익을 옹호하였다.

[14] 사화와 붕당정치의 전개

조선을 개국하는데 도움을 준 유학자들은 점차 구세력이 되어 주요 관직을 독점하였고, 새로 등장한 신진 계열은 기존의 권력을 타파해야 살아갈 수 있었다. 여기에 학자·관료간의 대립으로 4대 사화(士禍)가 계속되었다. 연산군(1494~1506)은 2차에 걸친 살육을 감행하였고, 이

[14] *Sahwa* and Factional Politics

Confucian scholars who contributed to the founding of Joseon continued to occupy all key government positions, and newly emerging forces had to overthrow the incumbent leaders in order to survive. Scholars and government officials were also confrontational with each other. This led to four major literati purges (*sahwa*). King Yeonsangun (1494~1506) executed two rounds of bloody purges, and more scholars and government officials were executed in following purges. The 16th century was a dark age in the political arena.

Conflicts over key positions in the central government ultimately provoked factional strife (factional politics). The factional strife originated from the structural contradictions of *yangban* society, and it intensified despite mediation by Yi yi (Yulgok: 1536~1584). The 17th century is marked as a period of factional politics.

In the 18th century, King Yeongjo (1724~1776) and King Jeongjo (1776~1800) adopted policies designed to prevent factional strife (Tangpyeongchaek), but confrontations and hostility among bureaucrats continued. This situation was a result of the structural problems of Joseon Dynasty, and the factional strife gradually escalated into more complicated rivalries involving power struggles, the designation of the crown prince, and the practice of ancestor worship.

어 계속된 숙청으로 많은 학자 · 관료들이 피살되어 16세기는 정치의 암흑기가 전개되었다.

그 후 중앙의 주요 관직을 둘러싼 갈등은 당쟁(정치적 대립: 붕당정치)으로 이어졌다. 양반 사회의 구조적 모순에서 생겨난 조선 시대의 당쟁은 이이(율곡, 1536~1584)등의 조정에도 불구하고 치열해져 17세기에는 붕당정치의 시대가 되었다.

따라서 18세기의 영조(1724~1776) · 정조(1776~1800)의 당쟁 방지 노력[탕평책(蕩平策)]도 소용없이 관료층 간의 대립과 불화는 끊이지 않았다. 이것은 조선 왕조의 구조적 모순에서 일어난 정쟁(政爭)이었다. 그러나 점차 당쟁은 권력 투쟁이나 왕세자 책봉, 그리고 전례문제(제사) 등과 어우러져 복잡한 파쟁을 야기하게 되었다.

[15] 유교의 발달

고려 말에 들어 온 유교(주자학)는 조선사회의 사상적 바탕이 되었으며, 점차 도덕적 원리와 명분을 강조하게 되면서 조선사회의 윤리와 도덕에 기준이 되었다. 이러한 유교의 번창

[15] Development of Confucianism

Confucianism (Chu Hsi School) was introduced in the late Goryeo period and served as the philosophical foundation of Joseon society. As gradually emphasizing strong moral principles and justice, it bacame ethical and moral standards of Joseon. Although Confucianism thrived the development of human ethics and academic studies. It also fueled confrontation and factionalism among schools and triggered purges, factional strife, and social problems.

Due to the development of Confucianism, moral discipline of individuals was emphasized to the utmost, and the norms on the essence of the universe and human beings were practiced and respected. However, differences in practices and theories led to the establishment of different schools, which confronted each other and caused social problems.

[16] *Hyangyak* and *Seowon*

One of virtues stressed in Confucianism is collaboration and friendship among neighbors. Confucian scholars enacted *hyangyak*, a set of rules to educate the peasants in their hometowns and promote their mutual assistance. This began with the good intention of fostering cooperation among neighbors, but eventually devolved into a

으로 인간의 도리와 학문의 발전을 가져왔으나, 학파의 대립 · 파벌을 조성하여 사화 · 당쟁 · 사회적 문제도 일으켰다.

이러한 유교의 발달로 개인의 도덕수양이 강조되고 우주와 인간의 실체에 대한 규범과 그에 따른 수행과 성찰이 중시되었다. 그러나 그 방법과 이론의 차이에 따라 학파가 생기고 대립이 나타나 사회적으로 문제도 발생하였다.

[16] 향약과 서원

유교의 덕목에는 이웃 간의 협조와 친선을 강조하는 풍속이 있었다. 유학자들은 자기 고향에서 농민을 교화하고 상호 부조하는 규약인 향약(鄕約)을 만들어 실시하였다. 그러나 이것은 이웃 간의 협조라는 좋은 결과는 있었지만 결국 자기 세력을 기르고 농민을 통제하는 수단이 되었다.

한편, 학자들은 지방에서 덕망 깊은 인물을 제사하고 청소년을 교육시키기 위해 서원(書

means of building power and controlling the peasantry.

Scholars set up *seowon* (private academies) to worship virtuous figures and educate youth. *Seowon* helped to enlighten the peasants and improve their knowledge. However, it is also true that they fueled factional strife.

[17] Yi Hwang and Yi Yi

Ever since Confucianism (Neo-Confucianism) was introduced from China in the late Goryeo Period, it continued to evolve and reached its peak in the 16th century. Two leading Confucian scholars were Yi Hwang (1501~1570) and Yi Yi (1536~1584).

Yi Hwang emphasized that the foundation of the universe lies in the inner moral fiber and beliefs of human beings, while, Yi Yi claimed that the foundation of the universe was more materialistic and emphasized participation in everyday politics. Yi Hwang led the Yeongnam School and provided a base for the formation of Chu Hsi scholarship in Japan, serving as a standard for Japanese Confucianism. As a leader of the Giho School, Yi Yi mediated factional strife and warned of the danger of invasion by Japan. Yi Hwang is memorialized by Dosan Seowon in Andong; Yi Yi is memorialized by Munhoe Seowon in Baecheon.

院)을 세웠다. 그러나 이 서원은 농민을 개화시켜 농촌의 지식수준을 높여 주었으나, 당쟁의 근원지가 되었음은 부인할 수 없다.

[17] 이황과 이이

고려 말 중국으로부터 유교(성리학)가 전래된 후 점차 발전되어 16세기에 이르러 절정을 이루었는데, 이를 대표하는 학자가 이황(李滉, 1501~1570)과 이이(李珥, 1536~1584)였다.

이황은 우주의 근원을 인간의 내면적 도덕과 신념에 두어 이를 강조하였으며, 이이는 우주의 근원을 문질적인 면에 두어 현실정치 참여를 강조하였다. 전자는 영남학파를 형성한 후 일본 주자학에 기반을 제공하였으며 일본 유학의 기준이 되었으며, 후자는 기호학파의 영수로서 당쟁을 조정하고 왜군 침략의 위험성을 경고한 바 있다. 이황을 제사하는 서원은 도산서원(안동)이며, 이이를 제사하는 서원은 문회서원(배천)이다.

4. *Japanese Invasion and Changes in Late Joseon Society*

[1] Overcoming the Japanese Invasion

In the 16th century, Joseon fell into political turmoil brought on by purges and factional strife and neglected national defense. Seizing the opportunity, Toyotomi Hideyoshi, who unified Japan, invaded Joseon in 1592 on the pretext of conquering Ming. The invasion devastated Korea, and numerous valuable cultural assets were taken

4. 외족침입의 극복과 조선후기사회의 변화

[1] 왜란(倭亂)의 극복

16세기에 이르러 조선은 사화 · 당쟁에 휘말려 정치적 분열로 국방을 게을리하였다. 여기에 일본을 통일한 도요토미 히데요시(豊信秀吉)는 명나라 정벌의 구실로 1592년 조선을 침략(임진왜란)하였다. 이에 국토는 황폐화되고 귀중한 문화재는 빼앗기거나 불탔다. 부산

away or destroyed by fire. The Japanese army captured Seoul only 18 days after landing in Busan. They continued to move northward along two routes and occupied Pyeongyang as well as Hamgyeong-do. Ming mediated and a truce was reached, and the Japanese army withdrew. However, Japan soon launched another invasion against Joseon. With the support of Ming, Joseon was eventually able to repel the Japanese.

Noteworthy about the war effort was the formation of volunteer units. Volunteer soldiers took up arms under retired government officials, Confucian scholars, and monks, but the main force of the corps was peasants. Hyujeong and Yujeong, renowned Buddhist monk-generals, fought off Japanese troops all over the Korean Peninsula. Along

[Photo] Turtle Ship
Featuring a dragon's head and an ironclad body, this was the greatest armored ship of the time and crucial in defeating the Japanese navy. Admiral Yi upgraded the early version of turtle ship from early Joseon, as shown here.
〈Source: Korea Tourism Organization〉

[사진]거북선
머리는 용의 모습을 하고 배를 철갑으로 덮은 거북선은 당시 최대의 무장 선박이었다. 이 배는 조선 초의 거북선을 이순신이 개조 한 것으로 일본군을 물리치는 데 큰 힘을 발휘하였다.
〈사진제공:한국관광공사〉

이순신

임진왜란 때 해군을 이끈 이순신(1545~1598)은 왜군의 수군을 전멸시킨 불후의 명장이다. 그는 거북선을 개조하여 실전에 응용하여 한산도 · 노량 해전 등 남해안 일대에서 왜군을 전멸시켰다. 특히 남해안의 지형과 조류를 이용한 교묘한 작전과 훌륭한 전술로 왜병의 북상을 저지하였으나 노량 해전에서 전사하였다. 그는 전쟁의 와중에서도 「난중일기(亂中日記)」를 썼고 다음과 같은 시를 남겼다.

　　　고요한 바다에 가을빛 저무는데
　　　찬바람이 놀란 기러기 진영 높이 나르는구나
　　　근심 속에 잠 못 이루는 밤
　　　새벽달이 칼끝을 비치네

에 상륙한 왜군은 18일만에 서울을 함락시키고 두 방향으로 북진하여 평양과 함경도까지 약탈하였다. 이어 명나라의 조정으로 휴전이 성립되어 왜군이 퇴각하였으나 일본군은 재차 침입하였고, 명나라의 지원과 조선군의 반격으로 이들을 물리쳤다.

Yi Sun Sin

Admiral Yi (1545~1598) is a legendary commander who led the Korean navy during the Japanese invasion of 1592. He utterly defeated the Japanese navy in the South Sea with his upgraded version of turtle ships. By applying clever strategies and outstanding tactics that took advantage of the topography and tides of the South Sea, he stymied the northward advance of the Japanese. Yi was later killed during the Battle of Noryang. During the war, Yi kept a journal, War Diary, in which he wrote the following poem.

> The Sun falls onto the vast sea in autumn,
> A flock of wild geese, startled by coldness, flies high up into the sky,
> During a restless night in agony,
> The dawn moon sheds light on swords.

with the victory by the naval forces led by Admiral Yi Sun-sin, resistance by these volunteer corps was decisively instrumental in throwing back the Japanese.

The Japanese plundered countless cultural treasures, and ceramic artists were abducted to Japan to advance Japanese ceramic skills. In 1607, diplomatic ties between Joseon and Japan were re-established at the request of Japan.

[2] Dispatch of Delegations

The Japanese invasion severed the diplomatic ties between Joseon and Japan. At

이 전쟁을 극복하는 과정에서 특히 주목할 만한 사실은 향토방위를 위해 전국 각지에서 의병이 스스로 봉기하였다는 점이다. 의병은 전직 관리나 유학자 · 승려 등이 주도하였지만 자발적으로 일어난 농민들이 주축을 이루었다. 특히 휴정과 유정(惟政)은 승장(僧將)으로서 각처에서 왜병을 물리쳤다. 왜란 때에 이들 의병의 항쟁은 이순신(李舜臣) 장군이 이끄는 수군의 승리와 맥을 같이하여 왜군을 격퇴하는데 결정적인 공헌을 하였다.

일본은 이 와중에서 우리의 문화재를 약탈해 갔으며, 특히 도공들을 납치하여 일본 도자기 기술을 발전시키는 계기를 만들었다. 그러나 1607년 일본의 요청으로 국교가 재개되었다.

[2] 조선통신사의 파견

임진왜란 이후 조선과 일본은 국교가 단절되었다. 그러나 도쿠가와 막부가 세워져 일본의 요구로 1607년(선조40)에 국교가 재개되었으며 1609년에 기유조약이 체결되어 부산포가 개항되었다. 조선정부는 일본의 요구로 1607년부터 1811년(순조11)까지 12차의 통신사를 파

the request of Japan, bilateral relations were resumed in 1607 (40th year of King Seonjo), by that time the Tokugawa shogunate had been established. In 1609, the Giyu Treaty was signed, and Busan port was opened. At the request of Japan, the Joseon government dispatched royal delegations (*tongsinsa*) 12 times from 1607 through 1811 (11th year of King Sunjo). The missions were huge groups of about 500 delegates, which included writers, painters, and calligraphers. They would made up compositions and calligraphies during their stay in Japan. They were welcomed by the Japanese and they helped greatly to advance Japanese culture.

[Photo] Joseon delegations to Japan

[사진] 조선통신사

견하였다. 이때의 일행은 약500명 규모로 문인 · 화가 · 서예가가 포함되어 가는 곳마다 글과 글씨를 써주었고 일본에서는 이들을 거국적으로 환영하여 일본문화를 크게 계승시켰다.

[3] 호란과 북벌계획

1616년에 중국에서는 명이 망하고 청나라가 들어섰다. 이때 조선 정부(광해군)의 자주 · 독립 외교에 불만을 품은 후금(후에 청)은 1627년에 조선을 침략하였는데, 이를 정묘호란(丁卯胡亂)이라 부른다.

1636년에는 청 태종(누르하치)이 10만 대군을 이끌고 침입하였고 (병자호란), 조선은 끝까지 저항하였으나 결국 항복하게 된다. 이때부터 청은 조선 정부에 여러 가지 부당한 요구를 하였다. 청나라에 볼모로 잡혀 갔던 효종(1649~1659)은 군사를 훈련하고 신식무기를 제작하여 청을 징벌하려는 계획을 세웠으나, 재위 10년만에 세상을 떠남으로써 무위로 끝나고 말았다.

[3] Qing Invasion and Northern Expansion Plan

In 1616, the Ming Dynasty collapsed and the Qing Dynasty took over China. By the time, Later Chin (renamed Qing later on), discontent with Joseon government's (King Gwanghaegun) independent diplomatic policy, invaded Joseon in 1627. This invasion is known as Jeongmyo Horan.

In 1636, Emperor Taizu (Nurhaci) of Qing invaded Joseon again (Byeongja Horan) with an army of 100,000 troops. Joseon resisted but was eventually compelled to surrender. Qing then made many unjust and absurd requests to Joseon. King Hyojong (1649~1659), who had been held hostage in Qing, drafted a plan for training the army and upgrading weaponry to conquer Qing. The plan was never put into action because he passed away in the 10th year of his reign.

[4] Joseon's Conquest of Southeast Russia

In the 17th century, the Russian Romanov Dynasty aggressively encroached southward on Qing and occupied lands as far down as the Heilong River basin. At the request of Qing, in 1654, Joseon sent General Byeon Geup and a force of about 150 shooters to ally with Qing forces. This combined force repelled the Russian army in Hutung (present-day Yilan near the Heilong River). Then, in 1658, together with the Qing

[4] 조선의 러시아 남동 지역 정벌

17세기 러시아 로마노프 왕조는 적극적인 남하정책으로 청나라 영토인 흑룡강 일대까지 침범하기 시작했다. 조선은 청의 요청으로 1654년에 변급(邊岌)장군이 조총군 150여 명을 이끌고 청군과 함께 후퉁(好通 · 지금의 흑룡강성 의란)에서 러시아군을 격퇴하였다. 이어 1658년에도 신유장군은 청군과 함께 흑룡강 유역(동강시)까지 진출하여 러시아군을 물리쳤다. 이를 나선정벌(羅禪征伐)이라 부른다. 이러한 승리는 조선이 병자호란 이후 북벌을 철저하게 준비해 온 결과였다.

[5] 정치 · 군사 제도의 개혁

임진 · 병자란 이후 조선 정부는 피폐해진 국가를 재건하기 위해 많은 개혁을 시도하였

army, General Sin Yu advanced northward near the Heilong River and drove away the Russian forces. This incident is called Naseon Jeongbeol. These victories were attributable to rigorous preparation by Joseon for northern expansion after Byeongja Horan.

[5] Political and Military Reforms

After going through invasions by Japan and Qing, the Joseon government launched a series of reforms to rebuild the devastated country. Politically, the Uijeongbu was replaced by the Bibyeonsa, which functioned as the highest institution for administrative and military affairs until 1865.

In the military, the conventional ineffective 5 *wi* (command) system was eliminated, and the 5 *gunyeong* (army garrison) system was established. The key feature of the military reform was replacement of recruitment with universal conscription that applied even to *yangban* and slaves as well as to commoners. The newly established 5 *gunyeong* system included Hulnyeon Dogam (military training command), Geumwiyeong (royal court guards), and Eoyeongcheong (capital guards).

[6] Economic Reforms

The state's financial condition was very poor after the two invasions by Japan and

다. 우선 정치 제도는 종래 의정부 제도를 개혁하여 비변사라는 행정·군사 최고 기관을 두었으며, 1865년까지 존속하였다.

이어 군사제도는 종래의 유명무실한 5위 제도를 폐지하고 5군영 제도를 두어 모병제에 입각한 군사 제도를 개혁하고, 양반·평민·노예까지 포함한 전국민 개병제(皆兵制)를 실시하였다. 이때 신설한 5군영 제도에는 신병 훈련을 위한 훈련도감, 궁중을 지키는 금위영, 서울을 지키는 어영청 등이 있었다.

[6] 경제 제도의 개혁

두 번의 전쟁(일본·청의 침입)으로 국가 재정이 피폐해졌으므로 우선 세제를 개혁한 후, 모든 세금을 쌀로 통일하여 바치는 대동법(1608~1708)을 실시하였다. 전국적 실시가 100년이나 걸렸으나, 그 결과 국가 수입은 늘었지마는 농민 부담은 오히려 그 대신 가중되고 공물 청부업자(공인)가 등장하였다. 동시에 군역의 복무 대신에 베를 납부케 하는 균역법

Qing. The government initiated tax reforms and then introduced the Daedongbeop (Land Tax Act: 1608~1708), which stipulated payment of all taxes in rice. It took over 100 years to roll out the new plan to the entire nation, and even though the national revenue increased, the burden on the peasants became heavier. Tax collectors (*gongin*) emerged. The Gyunyeokbeop (1750) system, which allowed people to pay taxes in cloth in lieu of rendering military service, was also announced. However, these reforms spawned corruption and various side-effects, which increased the burden on the peasants even more, ultimately leading to peasant uprisings.

[7] Development of Agriculture and Commerce

The government launched a number of agricultural and commercial reforms in an effort to secure financial resources. Expansion of irrigation systems (reservoirs) and improved farming techniques such as double-cropping and rice transplanting resulted in higher productivity. Some farmers became wealthy enough to hire farmhands. Commercial crops including ginseng, tobacco, chili, and cotton were cultivated. Potatoes and yams were raised in preparation for poor harvest years.

As a result of active application of new farming techniques, some *yangban* and commoners with large lands emerged as wealthy farmers. Many other farmers lost their lands and ended up as tenant farmers or laborers. In the process, population migration, rising disparity in wealth distribution, and increasing awareness of farmers prompted

(1750)을 실시하였다. 그러나 그에 대한 갖가지 부정과 폐단은 농민의 부담만 가중시켰고 결국 농민 반란이 일어나는 원인이 되었다.

[7] 농업과 상업의 발전

정부는 국가의 재원 확보를 위래 농업과 상업의 개혁에 힘쓰게 되었다. 우선 농업의 발달은 수리시설(저수지)의 확충과 이모작이나 모내기 및 농업방법의 개선으로 생산량이 확대되어 머슴을 고용하는 부농까지 생기게 되었다. 특히 인삼·담배·고추·목화 등 상업 작물이 재배되었고, 흉년을 대비하기 위해 감자·고구마가 보급 되었다.

새로운 농사 기술을 적극적으로 수용한 결과 양반과 평민 중에서 토지를 많이 소유하여 지주(부농)로 성장하는 사람들이 생겨나는 반면에, 많은 농민들은 땅을 잃고 소작인이 되거나 노동자로 전락하였다. 이러한 과정에서 인구 이동, 빈부 차이, 농민 의식의 성장은 사회 전반에 걸친 변화를 초래하였다.

significant changes in society overall.

Some 1,000 markets were opened in the capital city and local areas, which led to the emergence of free merchants who accumulated capital. Economic changes such as the creation of a free market, the rising class of free merchants, growth in trade, and development of handcrafts and mining were all indicators that the Joseon society was modernizing.

[8] Development of Silhak

In the late Joseon period, the political and economic changes resulted in significant changes in scholarship, which is called *silhak*. A number of problems of the time were identified, and solution for reformation were suggested. An especially great challenge was reforming agriculture and commerce. The importance of Korean history was also strongly emphasized.

The agro-economic policy was led by Yu Hyeong-won (1622~1673). He argued for eliminating the civil service exams and for reform of the land and tax systems. He also suggested the establishment of an ideal state through the equal distribution of land. His suggestions were refined by Jeong Yak-yong (1762~1836), who urged building collective farms.

Mercantilism was advocated by the Northern school, whose members had been to Qing. In his travel journal, *Yeolha Ilgi*, Park Ji-won (1737~1805) stressed social reform

서울과 지방의 각지에는 1,000여 개의 장시(場市)가 열리게 되고, 이를 배경으로 하여 자본을 축적하는 자유 상인들이 생겨나게 되었다. 특히 자유 시장의 발전, 자유 상인의 대두, 무역의 발달, 그리고 수공업과 광업의 발달 등으로 나타나는 경제적 변화는 한국 사회가 스스로 근대화하려는 발전적인 모습이라고 할 수 있다.

[8] 실학의 발달

조선후기에 이르러 정치·경제의 변화에 따라 학문상에도 큰 변화가 나타났으니 이것을 실학이라 부른다. 현실사회의 여러 문제점을 지적하고 그 개혁방안이 제시되었는데 특히 농업과 상업에 대한 개혁이 큰 과제였으며 우리나라의 역사에 대한 중요성이 강조되었다.

우선 중농주의적인 견해는 유형원(1622~1673)으로 대표되는데 토지·세제 뿐 아니라 과거제도폐지를 주장하고 토지의 균분제를 통해 이상국가 건설을 제시하였다.

이러한 견해는 정약용(1762~1836)에 의해서 완성되었는데 그는 집단농장제를 주장

by enriching the nation and stabilizing the livelihood of the people through the
introduction of new technology and the promotion of commerce and industry.

[9] Significance of *Silhak*

Silhak departed from the earlier unrealistic and impractical theories and focused on
practical and useful thought. Its significance lies in that it was scholarship for enriching
the nation and improving the livelihood of the people through a scientific and critical
approach. Therefore, *silhak* not only embraced agro-economic policies and
mercantilism, but also took a nationalistic approach toward Korea's history and
language.

하였다.
    이에 대해 중상주의적 견해는 청나라를 다녀온 북학파의 주장으로서 박지원(:朴趾
源,1737~1805)은 자신의 여행기(열하일기)속에서 기술도입과 상공업의 장려로 부국강병 ·
민생안정을 통한 사회 개혁을 강조하였다.

[9] 실학의 의미

    실학은 현실과 유리된 공리공담에서 벗어나 실질적이고 유용한 것을 추구하였다. 따라
서 부국강병, 민생안정을 위한 학문으로서 과학적이며 비판적이라는데 의미가 있다. 그러므
로 중농주의와 중상주의 입장뿐 아니라 국어, 국사 뿐 아니라 우리나라 지리를 강조함으로써

Although *silhak* had limitations of neo-Confucianism, its proactive reformative orientation led to enlightenment thought and provided momentum for modernization. In particular, *silhak* not only stressed the importance of institutional reforms but also Korean history and geography. Kim Jeong-ho completed Korea's first modern map.

[10] New Trends in the Arts

Since *Silhak* also influenced painting, there was a movement to shift from the conventional Chinese-style paintings such as landscape paintings and portraits to the unique style of paintings portraying the everyday lives of the common people and Korea's scenic beauty. Genre paintings such as *Seodangdo* (*School*) and *Ssireumdo* (*Wrestling*) by Kim Hong-do, genre paintings featuring common people by Sin Yun-bok, and *Inwangjaesaekdo* (*After Rain at Mount Inwang*) by Jeong Seon are especially renowned. Kim Jeong-hee contributed to the development of calligraphy through his unique Chusache style.

민족의식과 국사의 중요성을 인식하여 민족사학의 발달에 기여하였다.

특히 실학이 성리학의 한계를 지니고 있지만 적극적인 현실개혁 사상은 그대로 개화사상으로 연결되어 근대 사회로의 계기를 마련하는데 바탕이 되었다. 특히 실학은 이러한 현실 개혁뿐 아니라 우리나라의 역사 · 지리를 강조하여 한국사의 정통성을 내세워 김정호는 최초의 근대적 우리나라 지도를 완성하였다.

[10] 예술의 새 경향

실학은 회화에도 영향을 주어 종래의 산수화, 인물화 등 중국화풍의 모방에서 벗어나려는 움직임이 일어났다. 일상생활, 서민의 애환과 우리나라의 독창적인 산수화를 개척하였다. 특히 김홍도의 풍속화(서당도 · 씨름도), 신윤복의 인물 풍속도, 정선의 인왕제색도가 유명하다. 그리고 김정희는 독창적인 추사체로 서예의 발전을 가져왔다.

[Photo] Kim Hong-do's painting
〈Source: Korea Tourism Organization〉

[그림] 김홍도
〈사진제공:한국관광공사〉

[11] Cultural Renaissance by King Yeongjo and King Jeongjo

In the 18th century, supported by *silhak*, King Yeongjo (1724~1776) and King Jeongjo (1776~1800) strove to protect and revive culture. In an attempt to put an end to factional strife, King Yeongjo appointed government officials from various factions equally and published many books. King Jeongjo established Gyujanggak (palace library) to encourage academic research and discussion. He upgraded the movable type to increase the volume of publications and protected scholars and gave them especially good treatment. King Jeongjo also constructed Hwaseong Fortress in Suwon in memory of his father Sado Seja and built a magnificent pre-modern city. This period was an age of enlightenment for Korea and the second renaissance following the first one during the reign of King Sejong in the 15th century.

[12] Changes in the Class System

The social and economic changes in the late Joseon Dynasty triggered change in its social class system. The most noticeable changes were a sharp rise in the number of *yangban* households, a relative decline in the population of commoners, and a drastic reduction in the number of slaves or lowborns (virtual abolition of slavery). In addition to such upward social mobility, the *jungin* class also made appeals to allow them to

[11] 영조 · 정조의 문화 진흥

실학을 뒷받침한 18세기에는 영조(1724~1776)와 정조(1776~1800)의 문화 보호와 진흥책이 있었다. 영조는 당쟁을 없애기 위해 여러 당파를 고르게 등용하였고 많은 책을 간행하였다. 정조는 규장각(奎章閣)을 두고 학문을 연구 · 토론케 하였으며, 활자를 개량하여 많은 책을 출판하여 학자들을 보호 · 우대하였다. 특히 정조는 아버지(사도세자)를 위해 수원에 화성(華城)을 건설하여 화려한 근세도시를 만들었다. 이러한 영조 · 정조 시대는 우리나라의 계몽 시대에 해당하는 시기로 15세기의 세종대에 이은 제2의 문예 부흥기라고 할 수 있다.

[12] 신분제의 변동

조선 후기의 사회 · 경제적인 변화는 신분제의 변동을 가져왔다. 신분제의 변화 모습 중

hold high government positions.

Some commoners moved up in status and became *yangban* by buying their positions in the government. Slaves increasingly ran away. In the course of such social changes prompted by the collapse of the class system, the awareness of peasants had improved significantly.

[13] Introduction of Western Civilization

In the early 17th century, Joseon envoys traveled to and from Beijing. During these exchanges, they brought a number of Western products such as maps of Europe and clocks to Joseon, while they opened their eyes to western world. Catholicism came to Korea when Yi Su-gwang introduced Matteo Ricci's *True Principles of Catholicism*. At first, this new religion was adopted by the most politically disadvantaged people of Joseon, the *jungin*, but it gradually spread to the general population.

The government banned Catholicism for fear that its doctrine rejected Confucian ethics and promoted equality. The believers were persecuted brutally (one of four major persecutions). In the early 19th century, the government rounded up and executed Catholic leaders. In 1839, French Father Maubant, Father Chastan, and Bishop Imbert were also executed. However, the introduction of *seohak* (Western Learning) played a critical role in broadening the awareness and global view of the Joseon people.

에서 두드러진 현상은 양반 호수가 급증하고 평민 계층이 상대적으로 줄어들었으며, 천민 계층인 노비가 급격히 감소(노비제의 해체)했다는 사실이다. 이러한 신분의 상승 운동과 더불어 중인들은 자신들도 고위 관리가 될 수 있게 해달라고 통청운동(通淸運動)을 일으켰다.

농민층의 분해에 따른 상민층이 양반으로 상승하는 방법에는 돈을 주고 관직을 사거나 도망쳐서 천민의 굴레로부터 벗어나기도 하였다. 이러한 신분질서의 붕괴에 따른 사회 변화 과정에서 농민의식은 크게 향상 되었다.

[13] 서양 문물의 수용

17세기 초에 이르러 조선의 사신들이 베이징을 왕래하는 과정에서 유럽지도 · 시계 등 서양의 문물을 받아들이게 됨으로써 서양 세계에 눈을 뜨게 되었고, 이수광이 마테오리치의 천주실의를 소개하면서 천주교에 접하게 되었다. 처음에 이 종교는 정치적으로 불우한 계층이나 중인층에서부터 믿기 시작하다가 점차 백성들 사이에 퍼지게 되었다.

[Photo] Hwaseong Fortress
〈Source: Korea Tourism Organization〉

[사진] 화성
〈사진제공:한국관광공사〉

132

[14] Spread of *Donghak*

In the late 19th century, when the exploitation of the peasants became more severe, the rural economy collapsed and the peasants were agitated. Moreover, the government stepped up its oppression as the rapid spread of Catholicism weakened traditional values. This caused more and more peasants to turn to *Donghak*, which combined elements of traditional folk religions (shamanism and superstitions) with the chanting prayers for immortality.

Donghak was not simply an ideological belief system. It set forth anti-feudal (anti-class) and nationalistic (rejection of foreign forces) principles based on equality and humanism. The government executed its founder, but it was supported by the general population because it advocated the elimination of classes and the abolishment of slavery and the expulsion of the tyrannical *yangban*. The adherents of *Donghak* went underground to avoid government oppression and served as a nucleus of an anti-government movement, which led to the *Donghak* Revolution in 1894.

[15] Popular Uprisings

Although Joseon society was undergoing drastic change in both the cities and rural areas, government officials were still bent on exploitation and power struggles and did

정부는 유교 중심의 윤리관의 배격과 평등사상의 보급을 우려하여 천주교를 금지시켰으며, 가혹한 탄압을 자행하였다(4대 사옥). 19세기 초 정부는 천주교도를 체포하여 처형했는데 1839년에는 프랑스 신부인 Maubant, Chastan, Imbert 등도 희생되었다. 그러나 이러한 서학의 수용은 당시 백성들의 의식과 세계관을 확대하는데 큰 역할을 하였다.

[14] 동학의 유포

19세기 말 정부는 3정의 문란에 따른 착취가 심해지자 농촌은 파탄에 이르고 농민들은 동요하기 시작했다. 더구나 천주교의 급속한 확산으로 전통 사상이 혼미해지자 조정의 탄압은 강화되었다. 이에 농민층은 전통적인 재래 신앙(샤머니즘·미신)에 불로장생의 주술이 결합된 동학을 믿게 되었다.

이러한 동학은 단순한 사상 체계가 아니라, 사회평등과 인도주의에 입각한 반봉건(계급 타파)·민족주의적(외세 배격) 성격을 지녔으므로 정부는 그 창도자를 처형하였다.

not heed the social changes and hear the complaints of the peasants.

In the 19th century, after the years of King Yeongjo and King Jeongjo, under the "in-law governance" (*sedo* politics), the Three Administrations (land tax, military tax, and government loans), the backbone of government finance, fell into disorder and corruption among government officials became extensive. This exacerbated the hardships of the peasants and their discontent. Starting with the Revolt of Hong Gyeong-rae (1811), peasants staged a series of uprisings throughout the nation. In fact, after the Jinju Uprising (1862), peasants organized nationwide riots. Uprisings by peasants were significant as they indicated the growing power and awareness of the general populace.

[16] Dismantling of the Pre-modern Society

In the late 19th century, Joseon underwent a period of massive transformation. The traditional *yangban*-based political system was broken down by the in-law governance system. The collapse of the class system resulted in much greater awareness of the peasants. The disturbance to the class system had shaken the foundation of the Joseon Dynasty.

The *yangban* society of Joseon, which was based on the doctrines of Chu Hsi, was strictly a class society. But it was thrown into a crisis when it was challenged by Catholicism and *Donghak*, which both advocated equality and life after death.

그러나 동학은 계급타파 · 노비폐지 · 횡포한 양반배격 등을 바탕으로 백성들의 지지를 받으면서 정북의 탄압을 피해 지하로 숨어들어 점차 반정부 운동의 구심체가 되어 1894년 동학 혁명의 사상적 배경이 되었다.

[15] 민란의 발생

조선 사회가 도시와 농촌을 막론하고 크게 변모하고 있었음에도 불구하고, 조정의 관리들은 착취와 정권 다툼에만 열중하면서 변해가는 사회와 농민들의 불만을 받아들이려 하지 않았다.

특히, 영조와 정조 이후 19세기에 들어서서 세도 정치 아래에서는 국가 재정의 근본인 삼정(전정 · 군정 · 환곡)이 문란해지고 관리들의 부정부패가 극심하여 백성들의 고통과 불평불만이 높았다. 그리하여 전국 각지에서는 농민들이 중심이 되어 자신들의 처지를 개선하려는 홍경래의 난(1811) 이후 민란이 끊임없이 발생하였다. 더구나 진주민란(1862) 이후 농민

Consequently, the traditional Korean society was taken down and the pre-modern society collapsed from within. A new society was aborning, and the late 19th century is considered the incubation period of the modern age.

들은 전국적인 반란으로 확산되었다. 민란은 백성들의 힘과 의식이 그만큼 성장했다는 것을 의미하는 사건이었다.

[16] 근세 사회의 해체

19세기 말 조선 사회는 일대 변혁기에 들어섰다. 전통적인 양반 체제는 세도 정치에 의해 무너졌으며, 특히 신분상의 해체는 농민 의식의 성장을 가져왔다. 신분층의 동요는 조선 왕조의 기반을 흔들어 놓는 것이었다.

주자학을 바탕으로 한 조선양반사회는 엄격한 신분사회였으나, 평등과 내세관을 제시한 천주교와 동학이 도전함으로써 새로운 위기가 닥쳐왔다. 이에 한국 전통사회는 해체의 길을 걷게 되었고, 근세 사회는 안으로부터 무너지는 새로운 사회를 요구하는 시대정신을 맞게 되었다. 따라서 우리는 19세기 후반을 근대의 태동기라 부른다.

[Photo] Independence Gate ⟨Source: Korea Tourism Organization⟩
[사진] 독립문 ⟨사진제공 : 한국관광공사⟩

Challenges In Transition to Modern Society and Overview of Contemporary Society

근대사회로의 시련과 현대사회

1. Modernization and Subsequent Conflicts

[1] External incursion: Threat to Joseon

Joseon again fell into crisis in the mid-19th century. Internally, it experienced what became known as "in-law governance" and faced popular uprisings. Externally, foreign powers which are called, imperialism that is united with Capitalism and nationalism increasingly encroached on Joseon's sovereignty. These powers competitively made inroads into Asia in order to secure new markets and lay claim on sources of raw materials. They particularly sought to win railroad construction rights and mining rights. Under the pretext of protecting persecuted Catholic missionaries, the U.K., France, and the U.S. demanded that Joseon establish trade relations.

Western powers sent ships to the Korean coast and requested Joseon to open its ports, causing anxiety among the Koreans. In particular, an invasion by French warships (Byeong-in Yangyo), a sortie by American ships, and an attempted grave robbery by Ernest Oppert (a German) escalated feelings of xenophobia against the West. After people were enlightened by mission work of catholic priests and agitated their thought, this together with popular uprisings led society into serious chaos.

1. 근대사회의 추진과 갈등

[1] 열강의 침투와 조선의 위기

19세기 중반 이후 조선왕조는 안으로 세도정치와 민란이 이어지고 있었고 밖으로 자본주의와 민족주의가 결합된 제국주의 국가들이 다투어 침투하여 위기가 닥치고 있었다. 제국주의 열강들은 철도부설권·광산채굴권을 통해 상품시장과 원료공급지 확보를 위해 경쟁적으로 아시아에 들어닥쳤다. 특히 카톨릭 선교사들의 피살을 구실로 영국, 프랑스, 미국 등은 조선에 통상을 요구하였다.

특히 서양 열강들은 이양선(異樣船)을 앞세워 개국·통상을 요구하며 국민들을 불안하게 하였다. 특히 프랑스 함대의 침입(병인양요)과 미국 함대의 출현과 오페르트 도굴사건(독일) 등으로 서양인에 대한 배외열이 고조되었다. 특히 카톨릭 신부들의 선교활동 이후 사상의 동요가 나타나 계속된 민란과 함께 사회는 크게 혼란에 빠졌다.

[2] Closed-Door Policy of Regent Daewongun

In an effort to overcome these crises, Daewongun seized power on behalf of his young son, King Gojong (1864~1874). He then implemented reform measures like appointment of new officials, closure of private academies, imposition of taxes on the *yangban*, completing the legal code (Daejeong Hoetong), and the like. He also ordered for rebuilding Gyeongbok Palace to restore the dignity of the royal family.

On the grounds of preserving Confucian tradition, Regent Daewongun persecuted the Catholics. He repulsed the French fleet that had attacked in retaliation for the execution of French missionaries (Byeongin Yangyo) and an American fleet that had attacked to avenge the burning of an American merchant ship (Sinmi Yangyo).

In order to commemorate his closed-door policy, Regent Daewongun erected stone monuments all around the nation bearing a warning to the people about foreigners. The inscription on the monuments urged Koreans to fight back against Western barbarians. He autonomously tried to modernize the policy to maintain the worships and artillery and to strengthen national defense. However, his closed-door policy allowed easy and exclusive

Anti-Foreign Stone Monument

In 1871, to bolster his closed-door policy, Daewongun erected stone monuments in Seoul and throughout the country with a warning to the people about foreigners. The inscription on the monuments read "Western barbarians invaded our land, and we should fight back. Making peace with them is like selling out our country. Future generations should be protected against this danger."

[2] 대원군의 쇄국 정책

이러한 위기를 극복하기 위해 대원군은 나이 어린 고종을 대신하여 정권을 잡은 후 (1864~1874)에 인재 등용, 서원폐지, 세제 개혁(양반에게 징수)·법전 완비(대전회통) 등 개혁정치를 강행하고 경복궁을 재건하여 왕실의 위업을 회복시키고자 하였다.

또한 유교적 전통을 지킨다는 명분으로 천주교도를 살해하고 그 보복으로 침입한 프랑

척화비

대원군은 쇄국정치를 강화하기 위해 1871년에 서울과 전국요지에 서양인을 배척한다는 척화비를 세웠다. 그 내용은 '서양오랑캐가 침입하니 싸워야한다. 그들과 화해하는 것은 나라를 팔아먹는 것이니 이 사실을 후손에게 경고하는 바이다' 라고 되어있다.

[Photo] Anti-Foreign Stone Monument

[사진] 척화비

encroachment on Korea by Japan.

[3] Opening Doors and Ports

When Regent Daewongun was deposed in 1873, Queen Min assumed power and advocated the necessity of an open-door policy. The Unyo incident in 1875 led to Joseon's signing of the Ganghwado Treaty with Japan, and the two countries exchanged delegations.

스 함대를 패퇴시켰으며(병인양요), 미국의 상선 서면호를 소각시킨 사건으로 쳐들어온 미국 군함도 격퇴시켰다. (신미양요)

이러한 쇄국 정치를 기념하기 위해 대원군은 서양 오랑캐와 싸워야 한다는 척화비(斥和碑)를 각처에 세웠다. 대원군은 전함과 대포를 수리하고 국방을 강화하는 정책을 시도하는 자주적 근대화 노력은 있었으나, 외국과의 통상을 거부한 쇄국 정치는 결국 일본의 독점적 침투를 허용하는 계기가 되었다.

[3] 문호 개방과 개항

1873년 대원군이 정치에서 밀려나자 문호 개방의 필요성에 따라 정권을 잡은 민씨 정권은 개국정책을 내세웠다. 1875년의 운요오호 사건을 계기로 일본과 강화도 조약이 체결되어 양국간의 사절이 교환되었다.

이어 부산·인천·원산이 개항되었고, 미국(1882)·영국(1882)·러시아(1884) 등과 통

Following this Busan, Incheon, and Wonsan ports were opened. Joseon signed trade agreements with the U.S. (1882), the U.K. (1882), and Russia (1884) and opened its ports; Korea appear on the stage of the world. However, Joseon lacked knowledge of the outside world and was seriously challenged.

[4] Enlightenment Movement and Conflicts between Progressives and Conservatives

After opening its doors, the Joseon government sent envoys (1876) and a "gentlemen's sightseeing group" (Sinsa Yuramdan) (1881) to Japan and a delegation of students (Yeongseongsa) (1881) to Qing to actively embrace western civilization. Later, Joseon set up the Office for Extraordinary State Affairs (Tongrigiamumun), which resembles Qing's central government system. In the military, the Special Military Corp

운요오호(雲揚號)사건
일본은 조선정부가 통상을 거부하자 1875년에 운요오호를 조선에 보내 수로(水路)를 측정한 후 담수(淡水:맑은 물)공급을 위해 한강 하류를 거슬러 오면서 무력시위를 했다. 이에 강화도 포대가 발포하니 운요오호에서 포대를 파괴하고 민간인을 약탈하고 돌아간 후 사죄와 통상을 요구하였다.

상 조약을 맺어 문호를 개방함으로서 국제 무대에 한국이 등장하게 되었다. 그러나 국제사회에 대한 인식이 부족한 조선사회는 커다란 시련에 직면하게 되었다.

[4] 개화운동과 개화와 보수의 갈등

문호 개방 후 정부는 일본에 수신사(1876)와 신사유람단(1881)을, 청에 영선사(1881)를 각각 파견하여 선진 문물을 적극 수용하기 시작하였다. 이어 청나라의 중앙제도를 본 따 통리기무아문을 두었고 군사제도는 일본식의 신식 군대(별기군) 룰 조직하는 한편 서양 문물

(Byeolgigun) was organized according to the Japanese model.

In the meantime, conflicts between the conservatives, who wanted to preserve Confucian tradition, and the progressives, who wanted to initiate the open-door policy, intensified. Confrontation between Japan and Qing, each supporting one of these two camps, complicated the situation and led to the Military Mutiny of 1882 (Imo Gullan). The struggle between the conservatives and the progressives was further heightened by hostility toward Japan.

[5] Development of the "Defending Orthodoxy and Rejecting Heterodoxy" Movement

Since assuming power from Regent Daewongun, the Queen Min-led government

을 받아들여 개화 정책을 실시하였다.

이 과정에서 유교 전통을 고수하자는 보수 세력과 개화 정책을 추진하려는 개화 세력간의 갈등이 격화되었고, 여기에 이 두 세력을 뒷받침하는 일·청간의 대립으로 임오군란(1882)이 일어나게 되었다. 이러한 보수·개화의 갈등은 일본에 대한 불만으로 더욱 고조되었다.

[5] 척사 위정 운동의 전개

opened Joseon's doors to the outside world and initiated modernization. Trade agreements were signed and western civilization was introduced. In response, the conservative *yangban* led by Choi Ik-hyeon, who upheld the ideology of neo-Confucianism, launched a movement dubbed "Defending Orthodoxy and Rejecting Heterodoxy" (Wijeong Cheoksa). In their view, heterodoxy meant the open-door policy, while orthodoxy meant traditional Confucian principles. It was an ideological movement that opposed foreign forces and the open-door policy while preserving tradition.

The Confucian literati who led this movement criticized the government's open-

[Photo] Korea's First Delegation to Europe and the U.S.

[사진] 최초의 구미사절단

대원군 이후 집권한 민씨 정부는 외국과 문호를 개방한 후 통상 조약을 체결하고 서양 문물을 받아들여 근대화 정책을 추진해 나갔다. 이에 성리학의 이념을 강조하는 최익현 등 보수적인 양반 세력들은 척사위정운동(斥邪衛正運動)을 전개하였다. 척사위정운동은 나쁜 것(개화정책)을 물리치고 올바른 것을 지킨다(전통적인 유교적 질서)는 운동으로서 외세 배척과 개화정책을 반대하는 전통 유지의 사상운동이었다.

척사운동을 주도하는 유생들은 정부의 개화 정책을 비판하고, 일본을 비롯한 외국의 침략 세력을 규탄하는 상소를 잇달아 발표하여 여론을 주도하였다. 이러한 운동은 때마침 외국 세력 특히 일본의 정치 · 경제적 침탈에 고통을 당하고 있던 일반 백성들로부터 많은 호응을 받았다.

[6] 갑신정변

임오군란 이후 청의 간섭이 강화되자 우리나라에서 주도권을 잡으려는 청과 일본의 대립은 더욱 강화되었다. 이때 김옥균(1851-1893) · 박영효(1861-1939)등 개화파들은 일본세력

door policy. They appealed to public opinion by making a series of announcements that denounced foreign aggressors including Japan. The movement resonated strongly with the general public, which was suffering as a result of interference by the foreign powers, especially political and economic exploitation by Japan.

[6] Gapsin Jeongbyeon

Qing began to intervene more deeply in Joseon after the Military Mutiny of 1882, and confrontation between Qing and Japan for dominance over Joseon intensified. Backed by Japan, the progressives led by Kim Ok-gyun (1851-1893) and Park Yeong-hyo (1861-1939) attempted to eliminate the conservatives and initiate sweeping modernization, including the elimination of lineage and tax reforms. They attempted a coup d'etat in 1884 called Gapsin Jeongbyeon.

The coup was staged without public support or thorough preparation and ended in failure in just three days. Power reverted back to the conservatives, and the entire modernization effort became stymied as a result of the power struggle between Qing and Japan and the conflict of interests among Western powers, including Russia.

Qing gained the upper hand following Gapsin Jeongbyeon, but Japan regained influence through the Convention of Tianjin (1885) and by joining hands with Britain. Then, rivalries among the Western powers over Joseon continued to intensify as Russia emerged as a third power and Britain occupied Geomun-do Island in 1885.

에 의지하여 보수 세력을 제거하고 문벌폐지나 세제개혁 등 급진적인 근대화 운동을 추진하기 위하여 1884년에 쿠데타를 일으켰다. 이것이 바로 갑신정변(甲申政變)이다.

갑신정변은 국민적 지지 기반 없이 준비 없는 계획으로 일본과 청의 간섭만 불러들여 사흘 만에 실패로 끝났고, 정권은 다시 보수 세력에게 넘어갔다. 그 후 부터 청과 일본의 세력 갈등과 러시아를 비롯한 서구 열강의 이권 쟁탈로 인하여 근대화 운동은 효과를 거두지 못하였다.

갑신정변으로 청의 세력이 강화되자 일본은 텐진조약(天津條約 1885)으로 영국과 결탁하여 세력을 만회하였다. 이어 러시아가 제3세력으로 등장하였고 영국의 거문도사건(1885, Hamilton Accident)을 일으켜 우리나라를 둘러싼 열강의 각축이 치열하였다.

[7] 농촌의 파탄

개항 후의 조선의 농촌 사회는 일본의 경제적 침략으로 영국제 면제품과 일본제 공산품이 대량으로 유입되는 한편, 쌀과 콩이 일본으로 상당량 빠져나감으로써 농민들은 큰 고통을

[7] Breakdown of Rural Villages

After Joseon opened up to the world, peasants in rural villages suffered immensely. As a result of a Japanese economic invasion, British cotton products and Japanese manufactured goods flooded in, while a large volume of rice and beans flowed out to Japan. Naturally, the public seethed with anti-Japanese sentiment.

Rural villages were devastated by the economic duress, and the peasants' rage led to repulsion Western world and Japan. It was in this environment that the Donghak Movement, which promised equality and a future free from pain, readily gained support from the peasants. In particular, the public's discontent with Japanese exploitation of Korean agriculture led the Joseon government to announce a decree banning grain exports to Japan in 1889. This incident displayed the resentment of the peasants for having their grain taken away by Japan.

[8] Sino-Japanese War (1894-1895)

Through the Military Mutiny of 1882 and Gapsin Jeongbyeon in 1884, the rivalry between Qing and Japan for political and economic domination of Joseon led to the Sino-Japanese War. Japan defeated Qing, and as agreed in the Treaty of Shimonoseki (1895), Qing retreated from Joseon. Japan established its hegemony over Joseon and

당하게 되었다. 이에 따라 국민들의 반일감정은 더욱 고조되었다.

농촌사회의 파탄에 따른 농민들의 불만은 그런 상황을 가져온 서양과 일본의 저항으로 이어졌다. 이에 따라 평등과 고통 없는 미래를 기약하는 교리를 내걸고 농민을 상대로 포교 활동을 벌이던 동학이 갑자기 교세를 떨치게 되었다. 특히 일본의 경제침략에 대해 국민적 불만이 고조되어 방곡령사건(防穀令事件 1889)이 일어났다. 이 사건은 곡물이 일본으로 빼앗기고 있는 현실의 불만을 나타낸 것이다.

[8] 청일전쟁(1894-1895)

개항 이후 청·일 간에는 한국의 정치·경제를 지배하려는 야욕으로 임오군란(1882)·갑신정변(1884)을 거치면서 군사적 대립으로 이어졌다. 여기서 청·일 전쟁이 일어났으나 일본이 승리하여 시모노세키조약(1895)으로 청은 조선에서 물러났다. 이에 일본은 조선에서의 주도권을 확립하고 조선 지배의 기틀을 마련하였다. 그러나 다시 러시아의 도전을 받아 러·일전쟁(1904-1905)으로 이어졌다.

laid a foundation for its dominance. Later, however, Japan was challenged by Russia, eventually leading to the Russo-Japanese War (1904-1905).

[9] Donghak Movement

Peasant resistance against the political and economic exploitation of Japan exploded in the Donghak Movement in 1894. It first began as a religious movement to prove the innocence of its leader, Choi Je-wu, who was executed on false charges. However, it escalated into an uprising against the exploitive magistrate of Gobu County.

Led by Jeon Bong-jun, the peasants supporting *Donghak* demanded the punishment of corrupt government officials and protection of the nation against foreign

---

Political Reforms Proposed by *Donghak* Movement

Led by Jeon Bong-jun, *Donghak* Movement supporters occupied Jeonju and announced a 12-point political reform plan. Key demands were ① Punish corrupt governmenat officials and yangban ② Burn slave documents ③ Allow remarriage of widows ④ Abolish social classes, and ⑤ Distribute land equally.

[9] 동학혁명운동

일본의 정치·경제 침투에 대한 농민의 저항은 동학농민운동(1894)으로 폭발되었다. 이 운동은 억울하게 죽은 교조(최제우)의 누명을 벗기려는 종교운동에서 시작되었으나 지방수령의 착취에 봉기한 고부(전라도)민란으로 1894년에 폭발하였다.

전봉준(全琫準)을 중심으로 한 동학 농민군은 부정한 관리를 처벌하고 외국의 침략세력으로부터 나라를 지키겠다는 구호를 내걸고 봉기하여 전주를 점령하면서 마침내 전라남·북도를 모두 점령하고 지방혁명정부를 세웠다. 그러나 민중들의 대대적인 지지를 받았던 동

동학혁명의 정치 개혁안

정봉준의 동학혁명군은 전주를 점령하고 정치개혁안(12개조)을 발표하였다. 그 주요 내용은 ①탐관오리와 불량한 양반 처벌 ②노비문서 소각 ③과부의 재혼 허용 ④계급타파 ⑤토지균분 등이다.

invaders. They first occupied Jeonju but soon seized control of the entire south and north of Jeolla Province. They also established a revolutionary government. Although the movement was supported extensively by the public, the government partnered with the Japanese army and suppressed it. Nonetheless, the political reforms initiated by this movement, such as abolition of classes and distribution of land, were from the "bottom-up" results of any civil rebellion or anti-imperialist and nationalist movement.

[10] Reform of 1894, Gabo

Japan sent troops to Joseon under the pretext of suppressing the Donghak Revolution. Then, it demanded that Joseon reform the government. Accordingly, the Joseon government set up a special organization called Gunguk Gimucheo

Features of the Reform of 1894

① Socially, classes were abolished and abusive practices (early marriage and collective punishment of family members of criminals) were banned. ② Politically, civil service exams were banned, the central government system was revised (separation of Gungnaebu and Uijeongbu), and the judiciary became independent. ③ In the economy, taxes had to be paid in cash, and weights and measures were standardized.

학혁명운동은 일본군과 합세한 정부군의 탄압을 받아 결국 실패로 끝나고 말았다. 하지만 이들이 내세운 정치개혁안은 계급 타파, 토지의 분배 등 처음으로 시도된 '아래로부터의 시민 혁명'이었고 반제·민족운동이었다. 그러나 일본의 지원을 받은 정부군에 진압되었다.

[10] 갑오개혁

동학 혁명군 진압을 핑계로 군대를 파견한 일본은 조선 정부에 내정 개혁을 요구하였다.

갑오개혁의 내용

갑오개혁(또는 갑오경장)은 ①사회적으로는 계급타파, 악습(조혼, 연좌법)폐지 등을, ②정치적으로는 과거제도폐지, 중앙정치제도 개혁(궁내부와 의정부 구분), 사법권독립 등을, ③경제적으로는 조세를 현금으로 일원화(금납화)하였고 도량형을 통일하였다.

(Deliberative Council) and devised an overall reform plan which came to be known as the Reform of 1894, Gabo.

The reform brought changes to society, politics, and the economy. Socially, the class system was abolished and punishing the family members of criminals was prohibited. In the political realm, the central and local administration systems and judiciary were changed. In the economy, taxes had to be paid in cash, not in-kind. Such all-around reforms spurred the most rapid modernization in Korean history. However, the reforms were not carried out by the Koreans independently which allowed Japan to exert increasing influence.

[Photo] Jeon Bong-jun Under Arrest

[사진] 체포되어가는 전봉준

이에 정부는 군국기무처라는 특별 기구를 두고 전반적인 개혁안을 마련하였다. 이것을 갑오개혁(甲午改革, 1894)이라 부른다.

이 개혁은 사회적으로 신분제도와 연좌제의 철폐, 정치적으로는 중앙 · 지방 · 사법제도의 개편, 그리고 경제적으로는 금납화(세금을 화폐로 바침)등 한국사의 근대화 시발점이 되었다. 그러나 자주적인 개혁이 아니었고 결국은 일본 침투를 허용하게 되었다.

[11] 일 · 러의 각축과 을미사변

청일 전쟁의 승리(1895:시모노세키 조약)로 일본은 한국을 독점적으로 지배하게 되었다. 그러나 곧 이은 삼국의 간섭(러시아 · 프랑스 · 독일)으로 일본이 랴우둥반도(遼東半島)를 청에게 반환하자, 국내에는 일본세력의 약화라고 생각하여 다시 친러파가 대두하였다. 이에 일본은 을미사변(1895)으로 명성황후를 살해하고 친일 정부를 세워 새로운 개혁을 단행하였다(을미개혁).

[11] Rivalry Between Japan and Russia and the Incident of 1895

Japan's victory in the Sino-Japanese War (1895: Treaty of Shimonoseki) made Japan dominant over Joseon. However, when the Triple Intervention of Russia, France, and Germany forced Japan to return the Liaodong Peninsula to Qing, a pro-Russian faction perceived the situation as the weakening of Japan and emerged again in Korea. In response, Japan assassinated Queen Min in the Incident of 1895 (Ulmi Sabyeon) and established a pro-Japanese government to initiate new reforms (Reform of 1895).

The Reform of 1895 was a continuation of the Reform of 1894. It called for adoption of the solar calendar, change to the military system, and establishment of elementary schools. With this as a momentum, the assassination of Queen Min and an order for all Korean males to cut off their traditional topknots triggered a strong protests, which led to the emergence of armed volunteer resistance forces.

[12] Agwan Pacheon and Incursions by World Powers

Taking advantage of the Koreans' anti-Japanese sentiment after the Incident of 1895, Russia forcibly evacuated King Gojong to the Russian legation in 1896. Following this incident (Agwan Pacheon), the pro-Japanese faction was removed and a pro-Russian cabinet was set up. Then, the Russian special advisor to the Ministry of Finance,

갑오경장의 연장으로서 을미개혁은 양력을 사용하게 하고, 군사 제도를 고치고 소학교를 세우는 등 개혁을 시도하였다. 그러나 명성황후의 피살과 단발령의 실시로 한국민은 강력하게 반발하였다. 이를 계기로 한국민의 일본에 대한 저항은 무력에 의한 의병활동으로 전개되었다.

[12] 아관파천(俄館播遷)과 열강의 침탈

을미사변 이후 러시아는 한국민의 반일감정을 이용하여 1896년에 고종을 러시아 공사관으로 강제 피신시켰다. 이를 아관파천(俄館播遷, 1896)이라 부르는데, 여기서 친일파들을 제거하고 친러내각을 세운 후 알렉세프 재정고문이 한국의 정치와 재정권을 장악하게 되었다.

한 나라의 국왕을 외국 공사관으로 옮긴 것은 주권 국가의 체면을 손상케 한 것으로 독립협회를 비롯하여 국민들의 환궁 요구가 일어났다. 이에 따라 서구 열강은 기회 균등의 입장에서 다투어 경제적 침투를 하여 한국은 열강의 침탈 대상이 되었다. 일본 · 러시아 · 미국 · 영국 등은 철도 부설권과 광산 채굴권을 장악하여 한국 경제를 지배하기 위한 경쟁을 벌였다.

Alexeev, gained control of the political and financial affairs of Joseon.

Forcibly moving a king to a foreign legation was an act of humiliation to a sovereign state. The public, including the Independence Club, demanded the king's return to the royal palace. Western powers competed for economic concessions and demanded equal treatment, and Korea became a target for incursion by world powers. Japan, Russia, the U.S., and the U.K. won railroad construction rights and mining rights

[Table 3] Competition of World Powers Over Concessions

	Country	Description/Location	Year	Remarks
Railroad construction rights	U.S.	Seoul-Incheon Line	1896	Transferred to Japan
		Seoul streetcar system	1898	
	Japan	Seoul-Busan Line	1898	
		Seoul-Incheon Line	1899	
	France	Seoul-Uiju Line	1896	
Gold mining rights	U.S.	Unsan Gold-mine	1896	
	Russia	Gyeongwon Gyeongseong Mine	1896	
	Japan	Jiksan Gold Mine	1900	
	U.K.	Eunsan Gold Mine	1900	
	Germany	Danghyeon Gold Mine	1897	

[표 3] 열강의 이권 쟁탈

	나 라	내 용	연 도	비 고
철도 부설권	미국	경인선 부설권	1896	일본에 양도
		서울전차부설권	1898	
	일본	경부선 부설권	1898	
		경인선 부설권	1899	
	프랑스	경의선 부설권	1896	
금광 채굴권	미국	운산금광 채굴권	1896	
	러시아	경원,종성광산 채굴권	1896	
	일본	직산금광 채굴권	1900	
	영국	은산금광 채굴권	1900	
	독일	당현금광 채굴권	1897	

and raced against each other for dominance of the Korean economy.

[13] Activities by Independence Club

Fearing extinction, the exploitation by foreign power provoked the new intellectuals launched an independence and civil rights movement. The most active organization was the Independence Club led by Seo Jae-pil (1863-1951) and Lee Sang-jae (1850-1929). They promoted independence rights, civil rights and reform movements. The club tore down Yeongeun Gate symbolized toadyism, which had been used to welcome Chinese envoys, and erected the Independence Gate, which symbolized Korean sovereignty. It also published 'The Independent' as a medium for creating a wareness among the populace. In 1898, the club organized a mass rally

---

Independence Club's Resolution to the Government (Six Proposals)

① The government and people shall join hands to uphold royal authority and will not rely on foreigners. ② Agreements and treaties on concessions to foreign states shall be co-signed by ministers and the head of the Central Council. ③ State finances shall be managed by the Ministry of Finance, and budgeting and settlement of accounts shall be disclosed to the people. ④ Perpetrators of serious crimes should be brought to trial, but the human rights of the accused shall be protected. ⑤ The government shall require a majority of votes to approve appointment of a rank 1 or 2 official (chigimgwan). ⑥ The stipulated rules (14 Articles of the Guiding Principles for the Nation) shall be observed.

---

[13] 독립협회의 활동

제국주의 열강에 의한 이권 약탈로 국가의 존망에 위기를 느낀 지식인들은 자주·민권 운동을 전개하였다. 그 대표적인 단체가 서재필(1863-1951)·이상재(1850-1929)등이 주도한 독립협회(獨立協會)이다. 이 단체는 중국 사신을 맞이하는 사대주의의 상징인 영은문(迎恩

독립협회 대정부결의안(헌의6조)

① 외국인에게 의지하지 말고 관민이 합세하여 전제황권을 견고하게 할 것. ② 외국과의 이권에 관한 계약 과 조약은 각 대신과 중추원의장이 합동 날인하여 시행할 것 ③ 국가재정을 탁지부에서 전관하고, 예산과 결산을 국민에게 공표할 것 ④ 중대 범죄를 공판하되, 피고의 인권을 존중하여 자복한 뒤 시행할 것 ⑤ 칙 임관을 임명할 때에는 정부에 그 뜻을 물어서 중의(과반수)에 따를 것 ⑥ 정해진 규정(홍범14조)을 실천할 것(장정실천)

called Manmin Gongdonghoe to submit a resolution (Six Proposals) to the government and demanded independence and parliamentary democracy, but it was disbanded by the government.

Seeking independence (maintaining sovereignty, autonomous diplomacy), civil rights (voting rights), and reform (constitutional monarchy, new education, industrial modernization), the Independence Club called for parliamentary democracy. It was later disbanded by the government.

[Photo] Independence Gate

[사진] 독립문

門)을 헐고 그 자리에 독립국가를 상징하는 독립문을 세워 자주 독립, 민권 신장, 개화 혁신을 주장하였고, 「독립신문」을 발간하여 국민 계몽에 앞장섰다. 특히 1898년에 만민공동회라는 군중 대회를 개최하여 대정부 결의안(헌의6조)을 제출하고 민족 독립과 의회 민주주의를 주장하였으나 정부의 탄압으로 해산되었다.

독립협회의 사상은 자주독립의 추진(국가주권의 옹호, 자주중립외교), 자유민권의 실현(국민참정권), 자강개혁사상(입헌군주제·신교육·산업근대화)을 기반으로 하는 의회민주주의를 제창하였으나 정부의 탄압으로 해산되고 말았다.

[14] 대한제국의 성립

국왕이 러시아공사관에 있고 이권이 외국에 넘어가자 고종은 국민의 여망에 따라 러시아공사관에서 덕수궁으로 환궁하였다. 고종은 1897년에 독립국가로서 대한제국(大韓帝國:연호는 광무:1897~1910)을 내외에 선포하고 황제권 강화, 자주 외교, 교육 제도 개혁 등을 단행하였다.

[14] Founding of the Daehan Empire

Upon transferring the rights and interests to fpreign country, in response to the public's demand, King Gojong returned from the Russian legation to Deoksu Palace. In 1897, he announced the establishment of the Daehan Empire as an independent state and renamed the era of his reign as Gwangmu (1897~1910). He also took initiatives to strengthen imperial authority, handle diplomacy independently, and reform the educational system.

Emperor Gojong appointed a Northern Border Jiandao Controller to Jiandao (Manchuria) and a trade officer to Vladivostok and reformed the land system and family registration system. According to the New Education Decree, schools were opened and students were sent overseas to study. The Daehan Empire began to take shape as an independent state and pursued civil rights, but continued meddling by Japan and Russia made it very difficult to assert its sovereign rights.

[15] Russo-Japanese War (1904~1905) and Invasion by Japan

After the Triple Intervention (1895), Russo-Japanese confrontation intensified further as a result of King Gojong's flight to the Russian legation. Russia dominated Korean politics and increased its power by advancing southward. Feeling uneasy at the

특히 간도(만주)에 북변간도관리사와 블라디보스토크에 통상 사무관을 설치하고 토지 제도, 호적 제도 등을 개정하였다. 이어 신교육령에 따라 학교를 세우고 유학생을 파견하는 등 독립 국가의 면모를 갖추고 민권정치를 추구하였다. 그러나 당시 조선은 일본 · 러시아의 간섭으로 자주 국가로서의 주권을 지키기가 매우 어려운 상황이었다.

[15] 러 · 일 전쟁(1904~1905)과 일본의 침탈

삼국 간섭(1895) 이후 러 · 일 간의 갈등은 아관파천으로 더욱 첨예화되었다. 러시아는 한국에서 정치적 주도권을 잡고 남하 정책을 계속 추진하여 일본과 맞섰다. 이에 불안을 느낀 일본은 영 · 일 동맹(1902)으로 자신을 갖고 여순 공격으로 일 · 러 전쟁을 일으켰다.

전쟁에서 패하자 러시아는 미국 대통령 루즈벨트의 중재로 일본과 포츠머스 조약을 맺게 되었다. 이후 러시아는 한국에서 손을 떼고 영국 · 미국의 후원을 받은 일본의 독점적 지배가 시작되었다. 일 · 러 전쟁 직전인 1904년에 일본은 '한 · 일 의정서'를 강요하여 황무지 개간

situation, Japan established the Anglo-Japanese Alliance (1902). Eventually, the Russo-Japanese War broke out when Japan launched an attack on Port Arthur in Qing.

Japan handily defeated Russia during the war. With mediation by then U.S. President Theodore Roosevelt, Russia signed the Treaty of Portsmouth with Japan. Russia had to step back from Korea, and Japan, backed by the U.K. and the U.S., began to exert dominant influence over Korea. In 1904, shortly before the Russo-Japanese War, Japan forced Korea to sign the Korea-Japan Protocol, by which it took away Korean land on the pretext of reclaiming barren land. Following this, according to the First Korea-Japan Agreement signed in 1904, Japan began to exercise so-called "advisor governance."

Japan sent Megada as a financial advisor and Stevens as a diplomatic advisor to limit the authority of the Korean government and increase its dominance. Japan also changed the currency of Korea and introduced the Japanese currency.

[16] End of the Daehan Empire

With the signing of the Protectorate Treaty of 1905, Japan took away Korea's diplomatic rights and set up a Japanese Residency-General in Korea to handle domestic affairs. The public protested nationwide and the volunteer army engaged Japanese units in combat. In 1907, King Gojong sent delegates (Yi Jun, Yi Wi-jong, and Yi Sang-seol) to the Second Hague Peace Conference to protest the injustice of the Protectorate Treaty of 1905, but they were denied entry.

이라는 명목으로 국토를 약탈하였고 제1차 한일 협약(1904)으로 고문정치를 시작하였다.

일제는 제정고문에는 메가다를, 외교고문에는 Stevens를 파견하여 한국의 재정권과 외교권의 제한하고 그들의 지배권을 강화하였다. 이어 한국의 화폐제도를 정리하고 일본의 신화폐를 하용하게 하였다.

[16] 대한제국의 말로

일제는 을사조약(1905)으로 한국의 외교권을 박탈하고 통감부를 두어 한국의 내정간섭을 시작하였다. 이에 국민의 전국적인 저항과 의병항쟁이 나타났다. 고종은 1907년에 제2차 만국평화회의에 대표(이준 · 이위종 · 이상설)를 보내 을사조약의 부당성을 호소(헤이그밀사 사건)하려 했으나 회의 참석이 거절되었다.

이 사건으로 고종은 퇴위하고(1907) 순종이 즉위하였으나 곧 정미7조약(1907)으로 한국의 내정간섭(차관정치)이 시작되었다. 이어 1907년에 군대를 해산시키고 1910년에 한일합방

King Gojong was held accountable for this incident and abdicated the throne in 1907. He was succeeded by Sunjong. Soon, however, according to the Korea-Japanese Treaty of 1907, Japan began to interfere even more deeply in domestic affairs by appointing vice ministers. In 1907, Japan disbanded the Korean military, and in 1910, the Korea-Japan Annexation Treaty was signed, bringing the Daehan Empire to an end. This was the beginning of Japan's colonial rule of Korea (1910-1945).

[17] The Righteous Army's War

The Righteous Army (*uibyeong*) was a resistance movement of the Korean people against Japan's aggression. The spiritual foundation of this movement was the Confucian philosophy of rejecting heterodoxy. Many people readily gave up their lives in the fight against Japan.

으로 대한제국은 멸망하고 일본의 식민지시대(1910-1945)가 시작되었다.

[17] 의병전쟁의 전개

의병이란 일본의 침탈행위에 반대하여 일어선 한국민의 자주적인 저항운동이다. 이 운동의 정신적 바탕은 유교의 이단배척사상에 기초한 것으로 특히 일본을 죽음으로 반대한 민중운동이다.

의병의 1895년 일본이 명성황후를 시해하고 단발령(斷髮令)을 발표하자 끓어오르는 분

The movement was spawned by the assassination of Queen Min by the Japanese and the decree forcing men to cut their hair knots in 1895. Later, as Japan more aggressively seized sovereign rights by such means as the Protectorate Treaty of 1905, the Righteous Army, led by Choi Il-hyeon and Yu In-seok, rose up throughout the country and fought vehemently against the Japanese army.

When Japan disbanded the regular Korean army in 1907, the Righteous Army movement developed into armed resistance. A Righteous Army force of 10,000 fighters led by Yi In-yeong officially declared war on Japan and attempted to capture Seoul.

Japan suppressed the Righteous Army ruthlessly. The Japanese army was

[Photo] The Righteous Army
The anti-Japanese Righteous Army was led by Confucian scholars and mainly consisted of peasants. When the regular Korean army was disbanded in 1907, the Righteous Army began to wage armed resistance against Japan.

[사진] 의병군의 모습
항일의병은 유생을 지도자로 하여 농민층을 중심으로 구성되었으며, 1907년 군대 해산을 계기로 무력으로 항일 투쟁을 전개하였다.

노를 참지 못하고 일어났다. 그 후에 을사조약(1905)을 비롯하여 일본의 국권 침탈이 날로 악랄해지자, 최익현·유인석 등을 지도자로 하는 의병은 전국 각지에서 일어나 일본군을 상대로 치열한 전투를 전개하였다.

군대해산을 계기로 1907년에는 의병은 무장 항쟁으로 전개되어 이인영이 이끄는 1만여 명의 의병부대가 일본에 대해 정식으로 선전포고를 하고 서울진공작전을 벌이기도 하였다.

의병에 대한 일본군의 탄압은 무자비하였다. 일본군은 의병이 일어난 마을에 불을 지르고 양민을 학살하며 곡식을 빼앗는 만행을 서슴지 않았다. 일본군의 무자비한 탄압으로 국권을 회복하는 데는 실패했지만, 의병활동은 그 무대를 만주로 확장시키고 무장 독립 투쟁을 계속하였다.

[18] 국민들의 항일운동 전개

을사조약 이후 일본의 침약이 강화되자 국민들의 항일투쟁은 여러 방면에서 본격화되었

unreluctant to set fire to villages where the Righteous Army was organized, execute innocent civilians, and plunder their grain. Although the Righteous Army failed to restore Korea's sovereignty due to cruel suppression by Japan, it moved its base to Manchuria and continued their fight for independence.

[18] The People's Anti-Japan Movement

While Japan became more aggressive after the Protectorate Treaty of 1905, the Koreans continued with huge anti-Japanese protests in various forms. Jang Ji-yeon called the people to resist by writing an article titled "Today, We Lament" in the Hwangseong Newspaper. Min Yeong-hwan committed suicide leaving behind a writing titled "For 20 Million Koreans." Jo Byeong-se, Song Byeong-seon, and Hong Man-sik also took their lives as a sign of protest against injustice by Japan.

Jang In-hwan and Jeon Myeong-Un assassinated pro-Japanese Durham Stevens in San Francisco in 1908. An Jung-geun (1879-1910) assassinated Ito Hirobumi, the villain of the Japanese invasion, in Harbin in 1909. In the year 1907 in Daegu, a National Repayment Movement began to free the nation from the then-astronomical 13 million won debt owed to Japan. Citizens were urged to stop smoking and drinking and instead make donations.

다. 장지연은「황성신문」에서 `오늘은 통곡 한다'라는 글을 싣고 국민의 항쟁을 호소하였고, 민영환은 `이천만 동포에게 고함'이라는 글을 남기고 자살하였다. 그 외 조병세·송병선·홍만식 등도 일본의 부당성을 자살로서 나타내었다.

미국(Sanfrancisco)의 장인환·전명운은 친일파 Stevens를 살해하였고(1908), 안중근 (1879-1910)은 조선침략의 원흉인 이토 히로부미를 하얼빈에서 살해하기도 했다.(1909) 그리고 1907년 대구에서 국채보상운동으로 일본에 빌린 차관(1300만원)을 갚기 위해서 금주·금연운동을 일으키면서 의연금을 모집하였다.

[19] 애국 계몽 운동

의병 전쟁과 더불어 이 시기의 민족운동의 또 하나의 흐름은 애국 계몽운동이었다. 이 운동은 민족 산업을 일으켜 자립적인 경제 부강을 이룩하고, 교육과 언론·국학 운동(국사·국어)을 통하여 국민을 계몽하고 민족의식을 고취시켜 자주 독립을 쟁취하고자 한 운동이었다.

[19] Patriotic Enlightenment Movement

Apart from the Righteous Army, another major national movement during this period was the Patriotic Enlightenment Movement. It aimed to achieve independent nation by building economic strength through development of domestic industry and by creating mass awareness through education, the media, and Korean studies (history and language).

This movement was launched in a number of ways. Efforts were made to modernize education for the people, and over 5,000 educational institutions, including

Newly Opened Schools

In the early 20th century, the government introduced a new educational system. Hanseong Teachers' School (1908), Hanseong Middle School (1909), and Hanseong Foreign Language School were established. Missionaries had already established Baejae School (1885, Appenzeller), Ewha School (1886, Scranton), and Yeonhee College (1915, Underwood). Schools for girls such as Jeongsin (1895) and Baehwa (1898) were also founded. Then, other schools established were the Boseong and Yangjeong schools in 1905 and the Jinmyeong and Sookmyeong girls' schools in 1906. Daeseong School (An Chang-ho) and Osan School (Yi Seung-hun) were founded in rural areas. In Jiandao, Myeongdong School (Kim Yak-yeon) and Sinheung (Yi Si-yeong) were opened.

애국 계몽 운동은 여러 가지 방면에서 전개되었다. 특히 국민계몽을 위해 배재학당이나 이화학당 등 근대 교육을 발전시키려는 노력이 이어져 전국에 5,000여 개에 달하는 민족 교육 기관이 세워졌다.

이들 교육 기관에서는 민족의식을 고취하는 국사와 국어뿐만 아니라 근대적인 학문도 많이 가르쳐 국가 사회의 새로운 지도자를 양성해 냈다. 또한 애국 단체, 신문과 잡지 등을 통해 항일 운동을 고취하였다. 또한 천도교·대종교 등 민족종교가 나타났으며, 장로교·감

새로 생긴 학교들

20세기 초에 정부는 한성사범학교(1908),한성중학교(1909), 그리고 한성외국어학교를 세워 신교육을 실시하였다. 이미 선교사들이 배제학당(1885,Appenzeller), 이화학당(1886,Scranton), 연희전문(1915,Underwood) 등을 세웠고 정신(1895)·배화(1898)등 여학교가 세워졌다. 이때 한국인의 손으로 1905년에는 보성과 양정학교가, 1906년에는 진명과 숙명여학교가 세워졌다. 지방에는 대성학교(안창호)·오산학교(이승훈)가, 그리고 간도에는 명동학교(김약연)와 신흥학교(이시영)가 세워졌다.

Baejae School and Ewha School, were established all around Korea.

These institutions cultivated new leaders for the nation by teaching them not only Korean history and language to instill in them a strong sense of national consciousness, but also modern academic studies. Anti-Japanese protests were inspired by patriotic associations, newspapers, and magazines. In addition, nationalist religions such as Cheondogyo and Daejonggyo emerged. Christian churches, including the Presbyterian Church and the Methodist Church, built hospitals (Gwanghaewon by Allen) and schools.

[20] Dissemination of Nationalistic and Historic Outlook

The protest against the Japanese aroused patriotism and fostered a spirit of independence among the Koreans, because the Koreans have national superiority in

---

"Tragic History of Korea" by Park Eun-sik

Park Eun-sik once said, "A long time ago, someone said that nations always fall, but history lasts forever. That is, a country is the body (substance), and history is the mind (spirit). As long as the spirit lives, the body can sometimes be revived. Although the Jews are away from their homeland, they are never assimilated into foreign lands. But they have preserved their own history."

리교 등 기독교(신교)가 병원(광혜원;Allen) · 학교 등을 세워 전래되어 민족주의와 자유주의 사상을 길러주었다.

[20] 민족주의 역사관의 보급

일제의 침투에 대항하기 위해서 우리 민족의 우수성 · 주체성 · 독자성을 강조함으로써 민족의 독립과 얼(혼)을 되찾자는 민족의 역사관이 나타났다. 이러한 역사관은 민족주체성

박은식의「한국통사」

박은식은 " 옛사람이 말하되 나라는 반드시 멸망하나, 역사는 멸하지 않는 것이니라. 따라서 나라는 형(물질)이오 역사는 신(정신)이다. 신이 있어 멸망치 아니하면 형이 때때로 되살아날 수 있는 것이다. 유태인이 나라를 떠나있었지만 다른 나라에 동화되지 않은 것은 오직 그 유태교(역사)가 있었기 때문이다." 라고 하였다.

identity and independence. This further motivated the Koreans in their protest against the Japanese invasion.

Park Eun-sik (1859~1925) and Sin Chae-ho (1880~1936), the pioneers of nationalist history, highlighted the greatness of Korean history and called on the Korean people to understand how important and distinguished their history truly was. They also encouraged social reform and national independence. Although Park Eun-sik, Sin Chae-ho, and Jeong In-bo advocated different concepts, they all laid a spiritual foundation for the anti-Japanese independence movement. Such a nationalistic perspective on history was at the core of the anti-Japanese movement and this served to popularize the study of Korean history and lalso paved way for the development of modern study of history

Sin Chae-ho stressed the nationalist spirit through *hwarang* philosophy and valued the inter-relations of time, space, and people as three elements of history. Park Eun-sik claimed that since the soul of the people is immortal, we should search for it in history.

을 통해 민족의 각성과 항일운동의 바탕이 되었다.

민족사학의 선구자인 박은식(朴殷植, 1859~1925)과 신채호(申采浩, 1880~1936) 등은 우리 역사의 위대성을 강조하고 국사를 통해 국민의 자각과 사회 개혁 그리고 민족독립을 부르짖었다. 박은식은 혼, 신채호는 낭, 정인보는 얼을 찾아 항일·독립 운동의 정신적 바탕을 세웠다. 이러한 민족주의 사관은 국사를 대중화함으로서 항일운동과 국민 계몽에 앞장섰으며, 근대 역사학을 이끌었다.

신채호는 낭사상(화랑)을 통해 민족정신을 강조하였으며 역사의 3요인으로서 시간·공간·인간과의 관련을 중시하였다. 박은식은 민족의 혼은 영원히 죽지 않기 때문에, 그것을 역사에서 찾는다고 하였다.

2. Suffering of the Korean People and Independence Movement

[1] Japanese Military Rule

Upon seizing control of the Daehan Empire in 1910, Japan established the Government-General and took control of the political, military, and administrative affairs of Joseon. The Korean people were placed under Japanese colonial rule (1910-1945) and had to undergo a series of ordeals. The Government-General oppressed the independence movements of the Koreans through its military police and employed militarist politics in an attempt to root out the nationalist spirit. Japan banned the media and the right of assembly and indiscriminately arrested and imprisoned Koreans with intransigent attitude and opposing the Government-General. Patriotic activists fled to the U.S. (An Chang-ho, Rhee Syngman), Siberia (Russian Maritime Territory), and China (Manchuria: Yi Si-yeong and Yi Dong-nyeong). This marked the beginning of 36 years of suffering of the Korean people. Korean emigrants started new lives overseas and built bases for the independence movements.

2. 민족의 수난과 구국투쟁

[1] 일제의 무단 정치

1910년에 대한제국의 국권을 강탈한 일본은 조선총독부를 두어 조선의 정치 · 군사 행정을 장악하였다. 이로서 우리나라는 온갖 시련을 겪는 일제식민통치(1910-1945)를 받게 되었다. 조선총독부는 헌병경찰제를 통해 한국민의 독립 운동을 탄압하고 민족의식을 빼앗는 철저한 무단 정치를 강행하였다. 일제는 언론 · 집회를 금지하고 총독부에 반대 · 비협조하는 한국인을 무차별 체포 · 투옥하였으므로 뜻있는 애국지사들은 미국(안창호 · 이승만) · 시베리아(연해주) · 중국(만주:이시영 · 이동녕) 등지로 망명을 하였다. 여기서 36년간 민족의 시련이 시작되었고 고국을 떠난 해외 동포들은 그곳에서 새 삶을 개척하였고, 독립운동의 기지를 건설하였다.

[2] Land Survey Project (1910~1918)

Land in Korea had traditionally been owned by the state; private ownership of land had been unknown. Taking advantage of this, the Japanese announced a land registration system in 1910 and launched the Land Survey Project (1910~1918). All the unregistered or unclaimed land then became the property of Japan. In the end, 40% of all farmland in Korea was expropriated by Japan.

Numerous farmers lost nearly all of their land. The Oriental Development Corporation established by Japan monopolized commerce, mining, and banking and controlled the Korean economy. Land confiscated by the Government-General was now owned by Japan, and a part of this was distributed to Japanese migrants through the Oriental Development Corporation. Korean farmers who lost their land ended up living as slash-and-burn farmers or wanderers.

[3] Forfeit of Native Industry

In order to dominate the Korean economy, Japan set up the Oriental Development Corporation, which exploited farmers; monopolized forestry, mining, transportation, and cultivation of ginseng and tobacco; and controlled aviation, transportation, and communication facilities. Japan intended to prevent the rise of Korean capital. they also

[2] 토지조사사업(1910~1918)의 실시

한국에는 예부터 토지의 국유제(國有制)로 개인의 사유제가 없었다. 이를 이용하여 일제는 1910년에 토지 신고제를 통한 토지 조사 사업(1910~1918)을 실시하였다. 일제는 신고하지 않거나 못한 땅을 몰수하여 일본인의 소유로 만들어 한국의 전 경작지의 40%를 장악하였다.

이로서 농민들은 거의 토지를 상실하게 되었고, 일제가 만든 동양척식주식회사는 한국의 상업과 광산 · 은행을 독점하여 한국 경제를 지배하였다. 조선총독부에서 몰수한 토지는 국유지로 되어 그 일부를 동양척식주식회사에 일본 이주민에게 불하되었고 토지를 잃은 농민들은 거의가 화전민이나 유민으로 몰락하였다.

[3] 민족 산업의 박탈

일제는 한국경제를 지배하기 위해 동양척식주식회사를 세우고 농민을 착취하고 삼림 · 광

introduced a license system on the Company Law. This empowered Japan to dissolve native Korean companies. Japan also secured control over national finances by establishing the Bank of Korea and the Industrial Bank of Joseon.

[4] Independence Movements Overseas

Korean nationalist activists who had fled overseas to get away from Japanese military oppression, launched new independence movements. Yi Si-yeong, Yi Dong-nyeong, and Yi Sang-yong set up independence organizations in Manchuria and formed an independence army in the Russian Maritime Territory (Siberia). Independence movements were organized in other places like Shanghai (Sin Gyu-sik), Hawaii (Pak Yong-man and Rhee Syngman), and the mainland U.S. (An Chang-ho), and they were linked to independence movements within Korea. In Manchuria and the Russian Maritime Territory, anti-Japanese movements continued through underground organizations which supported the national independence movement.

[5] The March 1st Movement

In opposition to Japanese military rule, the Korean people announced the Declaration of Korean Independence in Tokyo on February 8, 1919. This

업 · 교통 · 인삼과 담배를 독점하였으며, 항공 · 교통 · 통신시설까지 지배함으로서 민족 자본의 육성을 막았다. 이어 회사령을 허가제로 바꾸어 민족 기업의 해산권을 갖게 되었다. 그리고 한국은행과 조선식산은행을 설치하여 한국 금융을 지배하여 한국의 경제를 장악했다.

[4] 해외 민족 독립 운동의 성장

일제의 무단 정치로 인해 해외로 망명한 애국지사들은 해외에서 독립 운동을 전개하였다. 우선 만주에서 이시영 · 이동녕 · 이상용 등이 독립 운동 단체를 조직하였고, 연해주(시베리아)에서도 이들이 독립군을 창설하였다. 그 외 상하이(신규식) · 하와이(박용만 · 이승만) · 미국(안창호)등 해외에서 독립 운동을 일으켜 국내의 독립운동과 연계하였다. 이때 만주와 연해주에서는 지하조직을 통해 항일운동을 계속하였으며 독립운동의 기지로서 해외 민족독립운동의 산실이 되었다.

announcement was made again in Pagoda Park in Seoul on March 1 of the same year. For the next two months, about two million Koreans joined the March 1st Movement. Over 1,500 demonstrations were staged, and some 7,500 Korean were killed. Another 47,000 were arrested. Notwithstanding, the movement spread to Manchuria, the Russian Maritime Territory, and Hawaii and sparked the nationalist independence movements.

The March 1st Independence Movement was joined by every quarter of Korean society, including 33 nationalist leaders represented by Cheondogyo leader Son Byeong-hee, Christian leader Yi Seung-hun, and Buddhist leader Han Yong-un, religious groups, students, and peasants. The Japanese police and army brutally suppressed the peaceful marchers who called for national independence. Although the March 1st Movement ended in failure, it effectively demonstrated to the world the Korean people's strong desire and determination to win national independence.

Declaration of Korean Independence

We declare that Korea is the nation of independence and the Koewans are the people of liberty. We proclaim it all over the world in witness of the equality of all nations, and we pass it on to our posterity and keep the inherent right of Korean self-respect....

Today what we take an action is Korean national claim for justice, humanity, survival, and prosperity. We earnestly manifest our justifiable mind of nation, even a man to the last, and even to a last second.

[5] 3 · 1운동

일제의 무단정치에 반대하여 1919년 2월 8일 도쿄의 독립 선언 이후 서울 파고다공원에서 독립을 선포하여 3월 1일부터 2개월 동안 전국에서 200 만 명이 독립 만세 운동에 참가하였다. 이 운동은 시위 횟수만도 1,500여회를 넘었고 피살자는 7,500여 명에 달했으며, 47,000여 명이 체포되었다. 그리고 이 운동은 만주 · 연해주 · 하와이 등지로 확산되어 민족 독립운

독립선언서

우리는 이에 우리 조선의 독립국임과 조선인의 자유민임을 선언한다. 이로서 세계만방에 고하여 인류평등의 대의를 밝히며, 이로서 자손만대에 고하여 민족자존의 정당한 권리를 영원히 간직케 하노라(중략)

오늘 우리의 거사는 정의 · 인도와 생존 · 번영을 위한 민족적 요구이니 최후의 일인까지 최후의 일각까지 민족의 정당한 의사를 표시한다.

[Photo] The March 1st Movement

[사진] 3.1 운동

동의 햇불이 되었다.

　3·1독립 만세 운동에는 천도교 대표 손병희, 기독교 대표 이승훈, 불교 대표 한용운을 중심으로 33인의 민족 지도자들은 비롯하여 종교인·학생·농민 등 전국민이 참가하였다. 일본의 경찰과 군대는 평화적으로 시위하면서 민족의 독립을 요구하는 민중들에게 무자비한 탄압을 가했다. 3·1운동은 일제의 탄압으로 실패하였으나, 독립을 염원하는 한국인의 의지를 세계에 과시한 민족운동이었다.

[6] 소위 문화정치의 실시

　3·1운동을 탄압한 일제는 한국인의 반발을 무마하기 위해서 무단 정치에서 소위 문화 정치로 정책을 바꾸었다. 헌병경찰제에서 보통경찰제로 이름을 바꾸었고, 정치 참여와 언론·집회의 제한을 완화하였으나 이것은 어디까지나 표면적인 것이었다. 오히려 내부적으로는 치안유지법을 공포하여 소작·노동쟁의와 민족운동을 탄압하였으며 산미 증식 계획으

[6] What is called Cultural Rule

After suppressing the March 1st Movement, Japan attempted to allay the resentment of the Korean people by shifting from military rule to the so-called "cultural rule." The military police were renamed the ordinary police. Restrictions on participation in politics, the media, and public assemblies were eased. However, these were only superficial gestures. In fact, the Security Maintenance Act was promulgated to suppress tenancy, labor disputes, and nationalist movements; the Rice Production Increase Plan was announced to expropriate rice produced in Korea.

Under the Rice Production Increase Plan (1920~1933), the yield of rice increased, but most of the increase was taken away by Japan in the name of exports. In 1933, over half of all rice harvested in Korea was sent to Japan; the Koreans had to live on millet, sorghum, and beans from Manchuria.

Most farmers were downgraded to tenant farmers. Some in greater poverty ended up becoming wanderers or slash-and-burn farmers to eke out a living. The farmers who stayed on the land defended their rights through tenant farming disputes and joined anti-Japanese movements via means of economic protest.

로 한국의 식량을 약탈하고 실제로 탄압은 가중시켰다.

산미 증식 계획(1920~1933)은 한국 쌀을 증산하고 그 대부분을 수출이라는 이름으로 약탈해갔으며, 1933년도는 전체 생산량의 절반 이상을 일본이 약탈해 감으로써 한국인은 쌀 대신 만주의 조 · 수수 · 콩을 먹고 살았다. 이에 농민들은 소작쟁의를 통해 자신의 권리를 지키며 항일 운동을 전개하였다.

이로서 농민은 거의 몰락하여 소작농이 되었고 생활이 더욱 빈곤화됨으로서 삶을 위해 유민 · 화전민이 되었다. 이에 가난에 시달리던 농민들은 소작쟁의를 통해 경제 투쟁으로 항일운동에 참여하였다.

[7] 일제의 중공업화 정책

토지조사사업으로 토지를 약탈한 일제는 한국을 상품 시장화 정책으로 바꾸기 시작하였다. 동시에 한국을 원료 공급지와 대륙 침략의 병참 기지로 삼기 위해 경공업에서 화학 공업

[7] Japan's Industrial Policy

Once confiscating land through the Land Survey Project, Japan began to treat Korea as a commodity market. At the same time, in order to use Korea as a source of raw materials and a logistics base for its invasion of the continent, Japan shifted the focus of industry in Korea from light industry to chemical industry (heavy industry) and again to the weapons industry to support its wartime economy. Accordingly, Japan shifted the focus of its mining from gold, which was the primary metal of interest in the 1930s, to iron, coal, and tungsten.

Japanese conglomerates such as Mitsui and Mitsubishi controlled the Korean economy, and native Korean industry could not grow. Moreover, Korean laborers were abused, forced to work long hours at less than half the wage of Japanese workers. Just like the farmers who put up resistance to Japan by tenancy disputes, laborers continually staged labor disputes and protested against Japan.

[8] Founding of the Provisional Government

The March 1st Movement was brutally suppressed by Japan, but it led to the establishment of a Provisional Government in Shanghai, China. Ten years after losing its sovereignty, Korea was again able to have its own government, although in exile.

(중공업)으로, 다시 군수 공업을 통해 전시 경제 체제로 전환하였다. 이로써 1930년의 금광 정책에서 벗어나 철 · 석탄 · 중석 채굴이라는 전쟁 수행(군수 물자 조달)의 수단으로 전환 되었다.

이에 미쓰이 · 미쓰비시 등 일본 재벌들이 한국 경제를 지배하여 한국의 민족 산업은 성 장할 수 없었다. 더구나 저임금으로 장시간 혹사당한 한국인의 노동자들은 일본 노동자만큼 의 절반도 받지 못하였다. 이에 소작 쟁의를 통한 농민의 항일 운동처럼 노동자들은 노동 쟁 의를 일으키면서 일본과의 투쟁을 계속하였다.

[8] 대한민국 임시정부의 탄생

3 · 1운동은 일본의 무자비한 탄압으로 국내에서는 민족의 독립을 가져오지는 못했지만, 중국 상하이(프랑스 조계)에 대한민국 임시정부를 탄생시켰다. 이로써 한민족은 국권을 강 탈당한 지 10년 만에 외국에서나마 망명 정부를 갖게 되었다. 이어 국제회의에서는 한국을

The Provisional Government represented Korea at international conferences and led the anti-Japanese movement by promoting the cause of Korean independence to the international community.

The Provisional Government adopted a democratic republic system composed of a legislature (parliament) and the government (executive council). A secret communications system was then established to bring all the various independence forces operating inside and outside Korea under a single command. In 1940, President Kim Gu (1875-1949) and other leaders founded the Korean Liberation Army under the direct control and engaged in combat against the Japanese army in Myanmar, the Philippines, and in China as well. At the outbreak of the Pacific War in 1941, the Korean Liberation Army declared war against Japan and Germany and, as a member of the Allied Forces, took part in battles along the Indian Front.

[9] Armed Struggles for Independence

Since Manchuria was the major base of the armed struggle, fighters for independence were especially active there. Kim Jwa-jin (1889~1929) moved to Manchuria after the March 1st Movement and formed an independence organization named the Northern Route Military Command and cultivated leaders for the independence army. In 1920, along with Yi Cheong-cheon and Yi Beom-seok, Kim Jwa-jin led the independence army and crushed a force of about 3,000 Japanese troops

대표하는 정부의 역할을 하였다. 특히 임시정부는 한민족의 독립과 자주성을 세계여론에 호소하여 한국민의 항일운동을 주도하였다.

임시정부는 국회(의정원)와 정부(국무원)의 이원제 정부로 된 민주공화제를 채택하였다. 그리고 임시정부는 국내외에서 전개 되고 있던 독립운동을 통솔하기 위해 연통 제도라는 비밀 연락 기구를 설치하였다. 1940년부터 김구(1875-1949)주석 등은 임시정부 직속 군대인 광복군(光復軍)을 창설하여 중국 뿐만 아니라 미얀마 · 필리핀 등지에서 일본군과 전투를 벌였다. 광복군은 1941년 태평양전쟁 당시에는 대일 · 대독 선전 포고를 발표하고 연합군의 일원으로 참전하여 인도 전선에까지 출전하였다.

[9] 무장 독립군의 활동

만주가 무장독립운동의 기지였기 때문에 그곳에서 무장독립운동이 적극 추진되었다. 특히 김좌진(金佐鎭, 1889~1929)은 3 · 1운동 이후로 만주로 건너가 북로군정서라는 독립 단체

at the Battle of Cheongsan-ri. He was later assassinated.

Hong Beom-do (1868~1943) organized a force of voluntary fighters in 1907 and fought for independence in Gapsan and Haesan. In 1910, he trained the independence army in Jiandao and became the commander of the Korea Independence Army. In 1920, he defeated the Japanese at the Battle of Bongoh-dong (currently Hunchun), inflicting casualties of over 500 Japanese soldiers. He later moved to Russia to escape Japanese oppression. There, he met Lenin and requested support for Korea's independence movement. Hong Beom-do was forcibly relocated to Kazakhstan in 1937 and died of an illness in Kzyl-Orda. A statue erected in his honor still stands there.

[10] Korean Liberation Army Activities and Japanese Brutality

Among the independence forces organized in Manchuria, the Korea Independence Army led by Hong Beom-do and the Northern Route Military Command by Kim Jwa-jin dealt huge blows to the Japanese army. In order to launch an anti-Japanese protest in full scale, the different independence armies were united and organized into the Korean Liberation Army, which declared war against Japan and Germany in 1941. Under the instructions of Kim Gu (1875~1949), Ji Cheong-cheon (1888~1959) and Yi Beom-seok (1900~1972) even devised a plan to penetrate into Korea as part of an operation to restore the mainland (1945), but it was cancelled after the defeat of Japan.

The Japanese felt threatened by the independence armies' strong resistance and

를 조직하여 독립군 간부를 양성하였다. 1920년 김좌진은 이청천·이범석 등과 함께 북로군 정서의 독립군을 이끌고 청산리싸움(현재 화룡)에서 3,000여명의 일본군을 전멸시켰으나, 자객에 의해서 암살당했다.

또한 홍범도(洪範圖, 1868~1943)는 1907년 의병을 일으켜 갑산·혜산 등지에서 활약하다가 1910년 간도에서 독립군을 양성하고 대한독립군의 사령관이 되었다. 1920년 봉오동 전투(현제 훈춘)에서 일본군 500여명을 살상하는 승리를 거두었다. 그 후 일제의 탄압으로 러시아로 이동한 후 레닌을 만나 독립 운동의 지원을 요청하기까지 하였다. 홍범도는 1937년 카자흐스탄으로 강제 이주된 후 크질오르다에서 병사하였다. 지금도 그곳에 그의 동상이 세워져 있다.

[10] 광복군의 활동과 일본의 만행

만주에서의 독립 운동 중에 홍범도의 대한독립군, 김좌진의 북로군정서는 일본군에 큰

indiscriminately attacked Korean villages in Manchuria where the resistance was based. Thousands of civilians were massacred and hundreds of houses were set on fire (Gyeongsin Disaster). Nonetheless, the resistance by the independent armies in China and Manchuria did not stop and continued until liberation. The Provisional Government founded the Korea Liberation Army and declared war against Japan in 1941, but it was never put into action because Japan had been defeated.

[11] Independence Movement in Korea

The anti-Japanese struggle continued in Korea keeping apace with the independence movements overseas. Some examples of resistance activities include the Independence Demonstration held on the day of King Sunjong's funeral (June 10, 1926) and the Gwangju Student Movement in 1929, where there was a clash between Korean and Japanese students. Meanwhile, with the strong support of the citizenry, a united nationalist organization of both leftists and rightists called Singanhoe was formed in 1927 under the leadership of Yi Sang-jae (1850~1929). The united organization initiated the independence movement by promoting the Korean language, abolishing migration policies, and opposing the self-rule initiative that supported Japanese rule.

타격을 주었다. 그 후 본격적인 항일투쟁을 위해 분열되었던 독립군이 통합되어 광복군으로 창설되었으며, 1941년에는 대일, 대독 선전포고를 발표하였다. 특히, 김구(1875~1949)의 지휘로 지청천(1888~1959), 이범석(1900~1972) 등은 본토수복작전의 일환으로 국내진입작전 (1945)까지 계획하였으나 일본의 패망으로 중단하였다.

독립군 부대들의 강력한 공격으로 식민지 지배 체제에 위협을 느낀 일본은 독립군의 근거지가 되고 있던 만주의 한국인 마을을 무차별 공격하여 수천 명의 민간인을 학살하고 수백호의 민가를 불살라 버렸다(경신참변). 그러나 중국과 만주에서의 독립군의 항전은 끝히지 않고 광복의 그날까지 계속되었다. 임시정부는 대한광복군을 창설하고 1941년에는 대일 선전 포고를 단행하였으나, 일본의 패망으로 실현되지는 못하였다.

[11] 국내에서의 항일 투쟁

해외에서의 독립 운동과 발맞추어 국내에서의 항일 운동도 계속되었다. 1926년에는 6 ·

Numerous women sought to join these pan-national independence movement, and the women-led Geunuhoe was organized. Farmers and laborers also took part in the movement by staging tenancy and labor disputes. The press (Dong-a Ilbo and Chosun Ilbo) strived to eliminate illiteracy and promote the Korean language. At this time, Yun Bong-gil killed Japanese general Shirakawa in Hingkew Park in Shanghai, and Yi Bong-chang attempted to assassinate Japanese Emperor Hirohito.

[Table 4] No. of Tenancy and Labor Disputes

Year	Tenancy disputes		Labor Disputes	
	No. of disputes	No. of participants	No. of disputes	No. of participants
1921	21	2967	36	3403
1923	176	9060	72	6014
1924	164	6929	45	6751
1931	667	10282	205	21180

10만세운동(순종 장례식날 시위 운동), 1929년에는 광주학생운동(한일 양국 학생 충돌)이 일어났다. 한편 국민의 호응에 힘입어 좌·우익의 민족 운동 통합체인 신간회가 이상재(1850~1929)를 중심으로 설립되어(1927) 한국어 보급과 이민정책철폐, 그리고 일제에 협력하는 자치 운동 배격을 통해 항일 운동을 주도하였다.

[표 4] 소작·노동쟁의 발생수

연 대	소작쟁의		노동쟁의	
	건 수	참가인원 수	건 수	참가인원 수
1921	21	2967	36	3403
1923	176	9060	72	6014
1924	164	6929	45	6751
1931	667	10282	205	21180

[12] Annihilation Policy of the Korean People and Nationalist Spirit

In the 1930s, Japan moved to transform Korea into a logistics base for its invasion of China. After the Second Sino-Japanese war in 1937, Japan began to annihilate the Korean national consciousness. By impressing Korean people into service for Japan and expropriating tangible resources, Japan started to annihilate the Koreans' survival and tradition for assimilating them into Japanese culture.

The Japanese first banned the use of the Korean language (Japanese only policy), compelled colonial education, suppressed the media (discontinuation of the Dong-a Ilbo and Chosun Ilbo), and forced the Koreans to assume Japanese names. Then, Japan confiscated grain and metal goods, drafted young Korean men to serve in the army or engage in hard labor, and took away young women to work as "comfort women." More than one million young Korean men underwent painful ordeals on the battlefields or in the mines, and about 200,000 women aged between 14 and 40 were dragged into sexual slavery as "comfort women" for Japanese soldiers.

[13] Preserving Korean Culture

The Japanese government tried to obliterate the Korean national spirit and assimilate the Koreans into Japanese culture by annihilating the Korean national

이어 이러한 거족적인 항일운동에 동참하기 위해 여성 중심의 근우회가 조직되어 항일운동에 참여하였고, 소작·노동 쟁의를 통해 농민·노동자도 거족적인 항일 운동에 합류하였다. 또한 언론(동아·조선일보)을 통한 문맹퇴치와 한글보급운동이 전개되었다. 동시에 윤봉길은 상하이 홍구공원에서 일본군 대장(시라카와)을 살해하였으며, 이봉창은 천황(히로히토)을 저격하였으나 실패하였다.

[12] 민족 말살 정책

일제는 1930년도에 들어서면서 대륙 침략을 위한 전쟁준비체제(병참기지화정책)로 바꾸면서 1937(중일전쟁) 이후에는 민족 말살 정책을 실시하였다. 이 정책은 전쟁 수행을 위한 인적·물적 자원의 징발과 함께 내선일체(內鮮一體)·일선동조론(日鮮同祖論)을 통해 한민족의 생존과 전통을 말살하기 시작하였다.

한민족 말살 정책은 우선 한글 폐지(일본어 강요), 식민지 교육 강요, 언론 탄압(동아·

[Photo] Execution Ground at Seodaemun Prison

Over 40,000 patriots were imprisoned here for independence activities, and about 400 were executed. Among the detainees were Righteous Movement leaders and 33 nationalist leaders. Ryu Gwan-sun, Heo Wi, Yi In-nyeong, and Son Byeong-hee passed away in the prison. There is now an underground cell on the site that was built in memory of Ryu Gwan-sun.

[사진] 서대문형무소에 설치한 사형장

독립운동을 하다가 투옥된 애국지사들의 사형이 집행되던 곳이다. 이곳에 투옥된 자가 4만명, 사형자가 400여명이나 되었고, 의병운동과 33인은 모두 이곳에 투옥되었다. 이곳에서 유관순 · 허위 · 이인녕 · 손병희 등이 돌아가셨으며, 현재 유관순 지하 옥사가 만들어져 있다.

조선일보 폐간) 창씨개명을 강요하였다. 이어 식량공출, 금속기 징발, 청년의 징병, 징용만 아니라 젊은 여성들을 정신대로 끌고 갔다. 특히 젊은이들은 징병 · 징용으로 100만명이 전쟁터나 광산으로 끌려가 갖은 고초를 당했고 20만의 여성(14세~40세)들은 정신대(위안부)로 끌려가 성의 노예가 되었다.

identity and making the Koreans ignorant. The Koreans were eligible for only secondary education or vocational training, and the Korean language and traditions were denied. Some young patriots launched a movement to eliminate illiteracy and build a private university.

Yi Yun-jae and Choi Hyeon-bae organized the Korean Language Society to promote the Korean language. Sin Chae-ho and Park Eun-sik rejected the Colonial Perspective on History and disseminated the Nationalist Perspective on History, which emphasized the identity and legacy of the Korean people. Some, including Park Seung-hee, tried to enlighten the public through contemporary dramas, while Na Un-kyu and Hong Nan-pa upheld the national spirit through music.

[14] Suffering of the Korean People

By ruthless oppression, Japan enslaved the Korean people and put them into the worst situation politically and economically. Their properties were expropriated and they were forced to assimilate into Japanese culture. Some patriots exiled themselves to Manchuria or the Russian Maritime Territory and continued the independence movements from there. Although Korean expatriates in Manchuria were massacred brutally on the pretext of rooting out the independence armies, they laid a foundation to sustain the independence movement against Japan.

In 1937, some 250,000 ethnic Koreans in the Russian Maritime Territory were

[13] 민족 문화의 수호

일제는 한국민의 자주성을 말살하고 식민지 정책에 순응할 우민정책(愚民政策)을 실시하여 우리 민족의 민족정신을 없애고, 일본인으로 동화시키려는 정책을 추진하였다. 따라서 보통 교육이나 실업 교육만 시키고 한국어와 민족의 전통을 말살시켰다. 이에 뜻있는 젊은이들은 문맹퇴치 운동을 전개하였고, 민간 대학 설치 운동을 일으켰다.

특히 이윤재·최현배 등은 조선어학회를 조직하여 한글을 보급시켰고, 일제의 식민지 사관에 대항해서 신채호·박은식 등은 민족의 주체성과 전통을 강조하는 민족사관을 설파하여 민족의 혼을 지키는데 앞장섰다. 그리고 박승희 등은 현대연극을 통해 민중을 계몽하였고 나운규·홍난파는 음악을 통해서 민족의 얼을 내세웠다.

forced to migrate to Kazakhstan and Uzbekistan and other parts of central Asia at the order of Joseph Stalin. The Soviet Union accused the Korean people of being spies for Japan and relocated them to barren lands of the Russian Maritime Territory to develop industry in central Asia. These Koreans, referred to as "Goryeo people," had to cope with an extremely unfavorable environment, language barrier, and various other hardships and challenges, but they have proudly preserved Korean tradition to this day.

[14] 민족의 수난

일제의 무자비한 탄압으로 한국민들은 정치적 경제적으로 최악의 노예상태에 빠지게 되었다. 재산은 모두 약탈당하고, 일본에 동화되는 식민지 정책에 얽매이게 되었다. 이에 뜻있는 사람들이 만주나 연해주로 망명하였으며, 그곳에서 항일 독립운동을 계속하였다. 그러므로 만주의 우리 동포들은 독립군 토벌이라는 구실로 무차별 학살되었으나 항일 운동을 계속하여 독립운동을 이어갈 수 있는 토대를 마련하였다.

연해주의 동포 25만 명은 1937년 스탈린에 의해서 카자흐스탄, 우즈베키스탄 등 중앙아시아로 강제 이주 당했다. 특히 소련은 조선인들이 일본의 첩자라는 구실로 중앙아시아의 산업개발을 위해 불모지에 연해주 거주 한국인들을 이주시켰다. 그러나 조선인들은 불리한 환경과 언어장벽을 뚫고 갖은 수난과 역경을 극복하고 오늘날까지도 고려인으로서 민족의 얼을 당당하게 지켜나가고 있다.

3. Contemporary History
- Liberation of Korean People and Division of Nation

[1] Liberation of Korean People

The attack on Pearl Harbor on December 7, 1941 brought the U.S. into the Pacific War, and the war situation took a dramatic turn. In the Cairo Declaration in November 1943, U.S. President Franklin Delano Roosevelt, British Prime Minister Winston Churchill and Chinese Generalissimo Chiang Kai-shek demanded that Japan surrender and pledged the independence of Korea. This was reaffirmed in July 1945 by the representatives of the allied nations, including the U.S. President Harry Truman, British Prime Minister Clement Attlee, and Soviet Premier Joseph Stalin through the Potsdam Declaration. The Soviet Union entered the war on August 9, 1945 and atomic bombs were dropped on Hiroshima and Nagasaki within days afterwards. On August 15, 1945, Japan finally surrendered to the allied forces and Korea was liberated.

[2] National Division and the Anti-Trust Movement

Although Korea was liberated, the country was divided at the 38th parallel. The

3. 현대사의 전개 – 민족의 광복과 남북의 분단

[1] 민족의 해방

1941년 12월 7일 진주만 공격으로 격화된 태평양 전쟁은 미국의 반격으로 전황이 급변하였다. 1943년 11월 루즈벨트(미)·처칠(영)·장개석(중) 등은 카이로 선언으로 일본의 항복 요구와 한국 독립을 약속하였다. 1945년 7월 포츠담 선언에서 트루만(미)·애틀리(영)·스탈린(소) 등 연합국 대표들은 이를 재확인하였다. 1945년 8월 9일에 소련이 참전하였으며 히로시마(廣島)와 나가사키(長崎)에 원자탄이 투하되자 일본은 전의를 잃고 1945년 8월 15일 연합군에 항복함으로서 한국은 해방되었다.

U.S. and Soviet forces set up military administrations in the South and the North, respectively. At a conference in Moscow, the foreign ministers of the U.S., Great Britain, and Soviet Union adopted a 5-year trusteeship plan for Korea, and the Korean people opposed the idea vehemently.

The U.S. and the Soviet Union organized a Joint Commission to implement the 5-year trusteeship. South Korea opposed the plan, but North Korea was allured by the Soviet Union and approved it, which set the stage for separation of the national land and ideological conflict.

[3] Confrontation between the Left and the Right

The trusteeship by the U.S., Great Britain, and the Soviet Union accelerated the establishment of a unified government, but turmoil continued on the Korean Peninsula due to confrontation between the Left and the Right. With the support of the Soviet Union, Kim Il-sung had already organized the Communist Party and took control of North Korea. In South Korea, an interim government was established by the Right in 1946. This further consolidated the division of nation.

[2] 민족의 분단과 반탁 운동

한국은 해방되었으나 38도를 경계로 미·소가 진군하여 국토가 분단되었고, 미·소 양국은 남·북한에서 각각 군정을 실시하였다. 그러나 모스크바 3상회의(미·영·소)에서 5년간 신탁 통치를 결의하였으므로 한국민은 이를 거족적으로 반대하였다.

그 과정에서 미·소 양국이 5년간 신탁 통치의 실행을 위한 공동위원회를 구성하게 되었다. 이에 남한 측은 반대하였지만 북한은 소련의 사주를 받아 이를 찬성함으로써 국토의 분단과 이념의 갈등으로 민족적 시련이 시작되었다

[3] 좌·우 진영의 대립

미·영·소 3국에 의한 신탁통치안은 통일정부 수립 운동을 촉진시켰지만, 한반도는

[4] Failure of South-North Negotiations

The interim government established in South Korea formed the House of Legislative Council of 90 members (45 privately elected and 45 government appointed). An Jae-hong (1981~1965) was appointed as the chief civil administrator. Then, the government renamed the Interim Government of South Joseon, but the Left-Right collaboration movement fell into a stalemate due to ongoing confrontation and a change in U.S. policy (Truman Doctrine).

In 1948, Kim Gu and Kim Gyu-sik visited Pyeongyang to hold South-North negotiations on the establishment of a unified government, but South-North negotiations on it were used by Kim il-sung (1912-1994) as a means to justify. No progress was made in establishing the unified government. Late in 1949, Kim Gu was assassinated.

[5] Establishment of the Republic of Korea

Political conflict between South and North Korea, the failure of the South-North negotiations, and a setback in the U.S.-Soviet Joint Commission due to an adversarial stance by the Soviet Union led the U.S. to present the issue of Korea's independence to the United Nations in September 1947. Amidst opposition from the Soviet Union, a

좌·우익의 대립으로 혼란이 계속되었다. 김일성은 소련의 지원 하에 이미 공산당을 조직하여 북한을 통제하고 있었으며, 남한은 우익 중심으로 1946년에 과도 정부가 수립되어 남·북 분단은 갈수록 고착되어 갔다.

[4] 남북협상의 실패

남한에서 세워진 과도 정부는 90명의 의원(민선 45명, 관선 45명)으로 입법의원이 설치되어 안재홍(1981~1965)이 민정장관에 취임하였다. 이어 남조선 과도 정부로 바뀌었으나 좌·우계열의 대립과 미국 정책의 변화 (Truman Doctrine)로 좌우합작운동은 난관에 봉착하였다.

이에 김구·김규식 등은 통일정부 수립을 위해 1948년 남북 협상을 위해 평양을 방문하였으나 김일성(1912~1994)은 북한 정권 수립을 정당화 수단으로 이용되었다. 따라서 통일정부 수립에 아무런 방안도 마련되지 못하였고 김구도 1949년에 암살되었다.

[Photo] Establishment of the Republic of Korea
〈Source: The City History Compilation Committee〉

[사진] 대한민국 수립
서울시역사편찬위원회 제공

[5] 대한민국의 수립

　　남·북한의 정치적 갈등과 남북 협상의 실패, 그리고 냉전 당사자인 미·소공동위원회가 소련의 반대로 실패하자 미국은 1947년 9월에 한국 문제를 UN에 상정하였다. 그리고 UN 감시하에 총선거안이 소련의 반대를 물리치고 통과되어 UN감시위원단이 접근할 수 있는 지역인 남한에서만 최초의 민주선거가 실시되었다(1948. 5. 10).

　　이어 제헌의회가 소집되어 헌법을 제정·공포하였으며(7.17), 이승만(1875~1965)을 대통령, 부통령에 이시영(1868~1953)을 선출하였다. 이어 국회의장에 신익회, 대법원장에 김병로가 선출되어 1948년 8월 15일에 정식으로 대한민국(大韓民國)의 수립을 내외에 공포하였다. 그해 12월 제3차 UN총회에서 이승만 정부는 한반도에서 유일한 합법 정부로 승인을 받았다.

proposal for a general election under U.N. supervision was put forth by the U.N. However, the election was held only in South Korea because only South Korea allowed access to the UN commission (May 10, 1948).

The first National Assembly was convened to enact and promulgate the national constitution (July 17). Rhee Syngman (1875~1965) and Yi Si-yeong (1868~1953) were selected as the president and vice president, respectively. Sin Ik-hee was selected as the national assembly speaker and Kim Byeong-no as the chief justice of the Supreme Court. On August 15, 1948, the establishment of the government of the Republic of Korea was announced to the Korean people and to the world. In December of the same year, the Rhee Syngman administration was acknowledged by the Third U.N. General Assembly to be the only lawfully constituted government in Korea.

[6] Establishment of the North Korean Communist Regime

After liberation, backed by the Soviet Union military government, Kim Il-sung seized the political leadership of North Korea. In 1946, radical communist reforms were initiated through land reforms and nationalization of industry. By 1947, over 800,000 North Koreans fled to the South.

The members of the Supreme People's Assembly were elected on August 25, 1948, and the constitution was approved on September 8. The establishment of the

[6] 북한 공산 정권의 수립

해방 이후 북한은 소련군의 지원하에 김일성 빨치산 세력이 정치의 주도권을 잡게되었다. 이들은 1946년 토지 개혁과 산업 국유화를 통해 급진적 공산주의 개혁을 실시함으로써 1947년에는 80만명의 북한 주민이 월남하였다.

이에 북한은 1948년 8월 25일에 최고인민회의대의원 선거와 9월 8일 헌법을 통과시키고, 9월 9일 김일성을 수상으로, 부수상(박헌영, 김책, 홍명희)이 임명되면서 북한에 조선민주주의인민공화국을 선포하였다. 이에 남쪽에는 자본주의 국가, 북한에는 사회주의 국가가 수립되어 남북간 대립이 시작되었다. 이러한 민족 분단은 점차 이데올로기의 갈등으로 정치적 갈등이 심화되어 민족 정체성 확립에 어려움이 따랐다.

Democratic People's Republic of Korea was announced on September 9. Kim Il-sung was the president and Park Heon-yeong, Kim Chaek, and Hong Myeong-hee were appointed as vice presidents. Korea was divided into two parts; South and North which were pitted against each other. South Korea was established as a capitalist state, while North Korea as a socialist regime. The partition of the land gradually escalated into ideological conflict and political confrontation, making it difficult to establish a national identity.

[7] Eve of the Korean War

The newly inaugurated Rhee Syngman administration in South Korea failed to completely eliminate pro-Japanese factions that had been retained under the earlier U.S. military administration. The Farmland Reform Act was not successful and served to increase resentment of the people. Moreover, Rhee Syngman suffered a major defeat in the second National Assembly elections held on May 30, 1950, increasing the political turmoil.

In addition to the political instability, South Korea faced widespread social unrest in various forms led by leftists. Some examples include the Jeju Island Revolt (Apr. 1948), Yeosun Rebellion (Oct. 1948), and Daegu Riot (Nov. 1948). Meanwhile, North Korea had a number of problems prompted by Kim Il-sung's communist dictatorship. He thoroughly swept away the vestiges of Japanese rule, but he needed an external

[7] 6 · 25 전야

새로 수립된 대한민국의 이승만 정부는 과거 미군정하에서 온존되었던 친일세력을 전부 배제하지 못하였고, 토지개혁의 실패에 따른 농지개혁법도 소기의 성과를 거두지 못하여 국민의 불만을 낳고 말았다. 더구나 1950년 5월 30일에 실시한 제2대 국회의원 선거에서 이승만이 참패함으로써 정치적 혼란이 가중되었다.

이러한 와중에서 남한은 정치적 불안정에 더하여 좌익세력의 준동이 이어져 제주도폭동 (1948.4), 여수순천사건(1948.10), 그리고 대구폭동 (1948.11) 등 사회혼란이 계속되었다. 한편 북한도 김일성의 공산당 독재정치로 많은 문제를 안고 있었다. 특히 일제 잔재 청산은 철저했으나 공산당 내부(박헌영)의 권력투쟁을 극복하는 수단으로서 외부로의 분출이 필요하였다. 이에 김일성은 소련(Stalin)과 중국(모택동)의 적극적인 지원으로 남한에 대한 무력 정복을 꾀할 수밖에 없었다.

distraction to overcome power struggles within the Communist Party (Park Heon-yeong). With strong support from the Soviet Union (Stalin) and China (Mao Tse-tung), Kim Il-sung planned an attack on South Korea.

[8] The Korean War

The Cold War between the U.S. and the Soviet Union that emerged after the Second World War became more serious as the confrontation between South and North Korea escalated. With military support from the Soviet Union and China, Kim Il-sung waged a surprise attack on South Korea on June 25, 1950. North Korean forces advanced southward past Seoul and down to the Nakdong River, but they were forced to retreat when U.N. troops and the Korean army counterattacked.

In his recent book titled, "*What Triggered the Korean War?*" Professor Soh Jin-cheol analyzed secret letters exchanged between Stalin, Kim Il-sung, and Mao at that time and determined that they had jointly committed an enormous war crime.

The U.N. forces chased the North Korean army up the Korean Peninsula, liberated Pyeongyang, and moved up to the Amnok River. The war situation changed dramatically with the entry of communist China on North Korea's side. The U.N forces were compelled to retreat southward and the war soon became a stalemate. The Armistice Agreement was signed in 1953, and South Korean and North Korea technically remain at war to this day. During the Korean War, some one million

[8] 6 · 25전쟁

제2차 세계 대전 이후 미 · 소의 냉전은 남북 간의 대립을 격화시켰다. 소련과 중국의 군사적인 지원을 받은 김일성은 1950년 6월 25일 불법 남침하여 남한을 초토화시켰다. 북한군은 서울을 거쳐 낙동강까지 진입하였으나, UN군과 국군의 반격으로 퇴각하였다.

최근에 소진철 교수는 「한국전쟁 어떻게 일어났나」(일본어본에는「朝鮮戰爭の 起源」)에서 당시 스탈린과 김일성, 그리고 모택동 간에 왕래한 비밀문서를 분석하여 3인이 공동 전범(戰犯)임을 밝히고 있다.

연합군은 북한군의 남침을 극복한 후 평양을 해방시키면서 압록강까지 수복하였으나, 중공군의 개입으로 전황은 교착 상태에 빠졌다. 1953년 휴전 성립 후 현재까지 남북은 대치를 계속하고 있다. 이 전쟁으로 한국은 100만 명의 희생자를 냈으며, 산업 시설의 절반이 파괴되었다. 한편 북한은 더 많은 피해를 보았으며, 300만의 북한 동포가 자유를 찾아 월남하였다. 전쟁 포로 37,000여 명 중에서는 북한으로 가기를 거부한 반공 포로 27,000여 명이 석

Koreans died, and half of the capital stock was destroyed. North Korea suffered even more, and about three million North Koreans fled to the South in search of freedom. Out of 37,000 North Korean prisoners of war held, some 27,000 refused to return to North Korea upon their release and decided to stay in South Korea.

Both South and North Korea suffered heavily during the Korean War and the ideological confrontation between the two deepened. Dictatorial governments were established in both Koreas in the process of post-war recovery, and the South-North conflict escalated.

[Photo] A Disconnected Bridge Across the Han Rive

[사진] 한강다리 끊어지는 사진

방되어 자유의 품에 안겼다.

이 전쟁으로 남·북은 막대한 피해를 보았으며 남북 간의 이념적 대립은 더욱 강화되었다. 더구나 남북한 정부는 전후 복구과정에서 독재체제가 성립되었고, 남북의 갈등은 더욱 심해졌다.

[9] 전후의 변화

6·25전쟁은 한국 역사상 미증유의 재난이었다. 경제는 파탄되고, 인구의 격감과 이동으

[9] Post-war Change

The Korean War was an unprecedented tragedy in Korean history. The economy was shattered, and Korean society underwent upheaval due to the sharp decline and dislocation of the population. In South Korea, the Rhee Syngman government stepped up its anti-Communist politics. Agitated by the Russian people's disparagement of Stalin after his death, North Korea in 1968 began to impose on its people an ideology of personality worship called *juche*. North Korea became closed to the outside world to an unprecedented degree, and the dictatorship became further entrenched, which served to heighten the confrontation and tension between the two Koreas yet further.

4. Challenges and Development of the Republic of Korea

[1] Dictatorship of the Rhee Syngman Government

In 1948, the Republic of Korea was established and recognized as the only legally constituted government on the Korean Peninsula. It was the first democratic

로 한국 사회는 큰 변화를 겪어야 했다. 남한에서는 이승만 정부의 반공 정치가 강화되었고, 북한에서는 스탈린 사망 후 소련의 스탈린 격하에 자극되어 1968년 이후 주체사상이라는 개인숭배가 강요되어 미증유의 폐쇄적인 독재정치가 강화되어 남북 간의 대립과 긴장이 고조되었다.

4. 대한민국의 시련과 발전

[1] 이승만 정부의 독재화

대한민국은 1948년에 한반도에서의 유일한 합법정부로 탄생되었고 우리 역사상 최초의 민주정부가 수립되었다. 따라서 정치·경제·사회 등 전반적인 개혁이 요구되었으나 공산게릴라가 준동하여 사회불안이 계속되었다.

government in Korean history. Wide-ranging political, economic, and social reforms were required, but communist guerrillas remained active and social unrest continued.

The Korean War (1950-1953) dealt a huge blow to the Rhee Syngman government. He consolidated his authoritarian rule in the name of "anti-communism" as well as economic reconstruction and pushed forward anti-communist and anti-Japanese policies. Later, Rhee Syngman organized the Liberal Party and attempted to seize life-long power through inappropriate constitutional amendments, in complete disregard of the expectations of the public.

[2] Inappropriate Constitutional Amendments

Incident	Year	Description
Selective amendment of the constitution	1952	Direct election of the president (suppression of opposition parties)
Constitutional amendment by round-off	1954	Abolishment of restrictions on successive terms of presidency
Political turmoil of December 24	1958	Approval of the National Security Act (Detention of opposition party lawmakers)

더구나 이승만 정부는 6.25전쟁(1950-1953)으로 큰 타격을 받았음으로 경제재건은 물론 반공이란 이름으로 독재정치를 강화하여 반공 · 방일의 정책을 밀고 나갔다. 그 후 이승만은 자유당을 조직하고 부적절한 개헌과정을 통해 종신집권제를 기도하여 국민의 기대를 외면 하였다.

[2] 부적절한 개헌과정

명 칭	연 도	내 용
발췌개헌	1952	대통령 직선제(야당탄합)
4사5입	1954	대통령중임제한철폐
24파동	1958	국가보안법통과(야당의원감금)

[3] Changes in Korean Society

The Korean War not only posed political challenges to Korean society; but also brought more serious economic difficulties. Economic aid from the U.S. was a great help in the post-war recovery, which it could not make Korea a self-sufficient industrial economy. However, as light industry producing consumer goods became the mainstay of the Korean economy, Korea slowly managed to lift itself out of poverty.

Korean society underwent dramatic change as a result of the Korean War. Traditional society was dismantled and old values eroded as a result of population dislocation on a massive scale, including an influx of millions of North Koreans and an exodus of Seoul residents to southern regions, and political turmoil.

Western culture flooded into Korea and uprooted many traditional values and customs, and the rise of free democracy disturbed the national consciousness. A mixture of traditional Korean philosophy, vestiges of Japanese colonial rule, and Western culture threw the people's consciousness into confusion. These were considered challenges that inevitably accompanied the process of globalization in Korea.

[4] Challenges of the Republic of Korea

Against the people's wishes, Rhee Syngman increasingly became dictatorial in his

[3] 한국사회의 변화

6.25전쟁은 남한사회에 정치적 시련을 가져왔을 뿐 아니라 경제적 어려움을 가중시켰다. 다만 미국의 경제 원조로 전후 복구에 큰 도움은 되었으나 그러한 지원이 주체적인 산업 발전에는 기여하지 못하였다. 그러나 소비재공업이 주산업으로 자리잡으면서 경제적 궁핍은 점차 벗어날 수는 있었다. 그러나 이러한 과정에서 6.25전쟁으로 한국사회는 큰 변화를 경험하게 되었다. 특히 수백만 북한주민의 월남과 수백만 서울시민의 남쪽피난 등으로 복잡한 인구이동과 정치적 갈등으로 전통사회는 해체됐으며 기존의 가치관이 무너지게 되었다.

특히 홍수처럼 밀려들어온 서구 문화로 전통적인 가치관과 생활풍속이 바뀌게 되었고, 자유민주주의 사상의 전파로 의식의 혼란이 나타나게 되었다. 따라서 한국의 전통사상과 일제의 식민잔재, 그리고 서구식의 풍조가 혼재함으로서 국민의식의 혼돈이 나타나게 되어 한국사회는 큰 변화를 맞게 되었다. 이러한 현상은 한국의 국제화 과정에서 수반되는 시련으로 생각된다.

governance. The sudden deaths of Sin Ik-hee, a strong presidential candidate of an opposition party (Democratic Party) for the 3rd presidential election in 1956, and Cho Byeong-ok, another candidate of an opposition party (Democratic Party) for the 4th presidential election in 1960, served to exacerbate the ongoing political turmoil.

Already in the 3rd presidential and vice presidential election held in 1956, Chang Myeon, an opposition party candidate, was elected as the vice president. In order to assure the election of the ruling party's vice presidential candidate (Yi Gi-bung) in the election on March 15, 1960, the vote was rigged, and public rage reached its peak.

Meanwhile, in North Korea, Kim Il-sung consolidated his dictatorship after the Korean War. He was alarmed at the Russian people's disparagement of Joseph Stalin after his death, and in 1956, Kim Il-sung purged opposition groups such as the Yeonan faction (Kim Du-bong and Kim Mu-jeong) and South Worker's Party faction (Park Heon-yeong) and began to promote the so-called *juche* ideology to build a personality

Kim Il-sung's Dictatorship

In order to consolidate his dictatorship, he purged opposition forces in 1956. He sought to avoid the fate of Joseph Stalin, who had fallen into disrepute after his death. First, he eliminated the Yeonan faction (joined the anti-Japanese movement by organizing Joseon volunteer troops in China) and South Worker's Party faction (initiated the communist party movement in South Korea) and spread out the Cheollima Movement (one is for the whole and the whole is for one) to launch collective innovation movements for creation of a popular hero and lay a foundation of a personality cult.

[4] 대한민국의 시련

이승만의 독재정치가 국민들의 의사와는 반대로 독재화되는 과정에서 1956년 제3대 대통령선거에서 유력한 야당(민주당)후보인 신익희의 돌연한 사망과 1960년 제4대 대통령선거에서 역시 야당(민주당)후보인 조병옥의 급서에 따른 정치적 혼란은 가중되었다.

이미 1956년의 제3대 정부통령선거에서는 야당 후보인 장면이 당선되었기 때문에 1960

김일성의 독재정치

김일성은 개인독재를 확립하고자 반대파를 숙청하였으며 1956년 스탈린격하운동에 자극되어 이를 더욱 강화시켰다. 우선 연안파(중국 섬서성의 연안에서 조선의용군을 만들어 항일운동을 함)와 남노동파(남한에서 공산당운동 추진)를 제거하고 천리마운동(하나는 전체를 위하고 전체는 하나를 위하여)을 통해 대중적 영웅주의를 만드는 집단혁신운동을 전개하여 개인숭배운동에 바탕을 이루었다.

cult around himself. Then, he placed priority on economic development and national defense by focusing on heavy industry and united the people through the Cheollima Movement (economic reconstruction program). These movements heightened the sense of confrontation between the two Koreas.

[5] Revolution of April 19

In 1948, the Republic of Korea was established in the southern part of the Korean Peninsula and the first democratic political system was adopted in Korean history. However, the long-term authoritarian rule by Rhee Syngman led to a serious crisis that climaxed in vote rigging in the election on March 15, 1960.

Public protests denouncing the election fraud spread all over Korea. The demonstration in Masan on March 15 was especially significant as it marked the escalation of the protests against vote rigging into a citizen's uprising against authoritarian rule. Finally, encouraged by a rally by Korea University students on April 18, high school and university students in Seoul participated in an anti-government demonstration on April 19.

The student demonstration on April 19 prompted a group of professors to make a declaration of the state of affairs on April 25. In the end, President Rhee Syngman stepped down and the Liberal Party regime (the First Republic) came to an end. The Revolution of April 19 was a citizen's democratic revolution that challenged dictatorial

년의 선거에서 부통령후보(이기붕)의 당선을 위해 3.15부정선거가 자행되어 국민들의 불만이 극도에 달하게 되었다.

한편 북한에서는 6.25 전쟁 후 김일성의 독재가 강화되어 1956년 소련의 스탈린격화운동에 자극받아 반대파인 연안파(김두봉·김무정)와 남로당계(박헌영)를 숙청하고 개인숭배를 위한 소위 주체사상으로 무장하기 시작하였다. 이어 중공업체제를 중심으로 경제와 국방을 우선하면서 천리마 운동으로 국민을 하나로 묶어 남북의 대립을 조성하였다.

[5] 4.19혁명

1948년에 남한에 대한민국이 수립되어 우리 역사상 최초의 민주정치체제를 이룩할 수 있었다. 그러나 이승만의 장기집권과 독재정치는 1960년 3.15부정선거로 큰 위기를 맞게 되었다.

부정선거를 규탄하는 국민시위가 전국적으로 확산되는 과정에서 3월15일 마산데모를 시작으로 부정선거항의에서 독재정권타도로 바뀌어 갔다. 드디어 4월 18일 고려대학생의 궐기

rule and served as momentum for further progress in Korea's development.

[6] Inauguration of the Chang Myeon Cabinet

The Revolution of April 19 brought down the Rhee Syngman administration (Liberal Party government). Under the caretaker government headed by Heo Jeong, and under the leadership of the Democratic Party, the constitution was amended to adopt the cabinet system and a bicameral legislature. A general election was held on July 29.

The Democratic Party won the election and assumed power, and the cabinet led by Chang Myeon was established. The Second Republic adopted the cabinet system, and Yun Po-sun and Chang Myeon were elected as the President and Prime Minister, respectively. However, within the Democratic Party government, confrontation between the new faction and the old faction caused the old faction break away and set up a new party (New Democratic Party). The yearning for change that boiled over during the Revolution of April 19 and subsequent reforms created greater upheaval in society. These along with the already serious economic hardships hamstrung the Democratic Party in its ability to handle the pending issues.

로부터 4월 19일 서울시내 전 대학과 고등학교 학생까지 반정부시위에 참여하게 되었다.

이러한 4.19혁명은 드디어 4월25일 대학교수단의 시국선언으로 이승만이 하야하고 자유당 정권(제1공화국)을 붕괴되었다. 이 4.19혁명은 독재정치에 도전한 민주시민혁명으로서 대한민국 역사의 새로운 발전에 계기가 되었다.

[6] 장면내각의 출범

4.19혁명으로 이승만 정권(자유당 정부)이 무너지고 허정의 과도정부가 세워져 야당이었던 민주당이 주도하여 내각 책임자와 양원제를 골자로 하는 헌법이 제정되고 7월 29일 총선거가 실시되었다.

이에 민주당이 정권을 잡고 장면내각이 수립되었다. 이로서 성립된 제2공화국은 내각책임제로 대통령(윤보선)·국무총리(장면)가 취임하였다. 그러나 민주당 정부는 신파·구파의 대립으로 구파는 독자적인 정당(신민당)으로 이탈하고 4.19 이후 분출된 욕구와 개혁은

[Photo] Marching Forward
A March by Student Demonstrators of Seoul National University for Justice

[사진] 전진이다
정의를 위한 서울대학교 시위대의 행진

[7] Military Coup d'etat of May 16, 1961

The freedom brought by the April Revolution and subsequent breakup and incompetence of the Democratic Party government only resulted in greater political chaos. On May 16, 1961, General Park Chung-hee (1917-1979) led a military coup d'etat, and public pledges for a revolution were announced. The Supreme Council for National Reconstruction was set up, and a military administration was declared.

The military government (1961-1963) advocated economic security for the people,

사회를 더욱 혼란케 하였으며, 경제적 어려움이 겹쳐 민주당은 이를 극복하는데 한계에 이르게 되었다.

[7] 5.16군사 쿠테타

4.19 이후 분출된 자유의 물결은 민주당 정부의 분열과 무능으로 정치적 혼란만 초래하였다. 이에 1961년 5월16일 박정희(1917-1979)를 중심으로 한 군인 쿠테타가 일어나 혁명공약을 발표하고 국가재건최고회의를 구성하고 군정을 선포하였다.

군정(1961-1963)은 민생안정, 반공, 민족정통성을 내세우고 구 정치인들의 활동금지와 용공세력의 색출, 그리고 폭력배의 검거를 단행하였다. 동시에 농어촌 고리채정리, 부정축재 처리, 국가재건운동, 화폐개혁 등을 시도하면서 국가의 전반적 개편을 시도하였다.

anti-communism, and traditional legitimacy. It also banned the activities of former politicians, tracked down communists, and arrested hooligans. The government simultaneously tried to restructure the nation overall by liquidating high interest debts owed by villagers, disposing of illegally accumulated wealth, and pursuing national reconstruction and currency reform.

[8] Achievements of the Park Chung-hee Government

After two years of military administration (May 1961-Dec. 1963), under the new

[Table 5] Five-Year Economic Development Plans

Plan	Year	Major Accomplishments
1st	1962-1966	Growth of exports and light industry
2nd	1967-1971	Economic self-sufficiency (beginning of heavy & chemical industries)
3rd	1972-1976	Development of heavy & chemical industries (continued export growth)
4th	1977-1981	Growth of heavy & chemical industries (increased efficiency and balance)
5th	1982-1986	Stabilization of heavy & chemical industries (increased efficiency and self-sufficiency)
6th	1987-1991	Improvement of distribution (social equality)

[8] 박정희 정부의 업적

2년간의 군정(1961.5-1963.12)을 끝으로 새 헌법에 의해서 민주공화당의 박정희가 대통령으로 당선되어 제3공화국(1963-1972)이 성립되었다. 박정희정부는 '경제제일주의와 조국의 근대화'를 내세우고 과감한 경제개혁에 박차를 가하였다.

[표 5] 경제개발 5개년 계획

계 획	연 도	내 용
1차	1962-1966	수출주도 · 경공업 육성
2차	1967-1971	경제자립(중화학공업의 시작)
3차	1972-1976	중화학공업 육성(수출증대)
4차	1977-1981	중화학공업 성장(능률 · 균형)
5차	1982-1986	중화학공업 안정(능률 · 자립)
6차	1987-1991	분배개선(사회적 평형)

constitution, Park Chung-hee of the Democratic Republic Party was elected as the president of the Third Republic (1963-1972). The Park Chung-hee government accelerated the bold economic reforms under the "economy supremacy and the Korean modernization" policy.

Through a series of five-year economic development plans, which began in 1962, Korea achieved economic self-sufficiency, overcame societal backwardness, and laid a foundation for a take-off to join the ranks of advanced nations. Then the Fourth Five-year Economic Development was launched. The status of Korea in the international community rose markedly through the normalization of Korean-Japanese diplomatic ties (1965), dispatch of the Korean army to Vietnam (1965), and the ROK-US Agreement (1966).

July 4th South-North Joint Communique

On July 4, 1972, a seven-point joint communique was announced with South Korea and North Korea agreeing to ① achieve national unification independently without foreign interference ② achieve unification by peaceful means ③ promote great national unity, transcending differences in ideology, and ④ promote overall inter-Korean exchange.

The Charter of National Education announced in 1968 was a manifestation of the public's rising collective consciousness for the establishment of national identity. As a result of the Inter-Korean Red Cross Talks (1971) and a visit to Pyeongyang by Lee Hu-Rak (director of the Korean Central Intelligence Agency) and his meeting with Kim Il-sung, the two Koreas announced on July 4th the South-North Joint Communique (1972) and initiated inter-Korean dialogue.

7·4남북공동성명

1972년 7월 4일 남북간에는 ①외세간섭없는 자주통일 ②평화적인 통일방법 실현 ③이념을 초월한 민족단결 도모 ④남북간제반교류 등 7개 항의 공동성명이 발표되었다.

특히 1968년에 발표한 「국민교육헌장」으로 민족 주체성의 확립을 위한 정신적 각성을 보여주었으며 남북적십자회담(1971)과 이후락 정보부장의 방북과 김일성 주석과의 만남 끝에 「7·4남북공동성명」(1972)을 발표하여 남북간의 대화가 열리게 되었다.

특히 1962년부터 추진해오던 경제개발 5개년 계획을 성공적으로 완수함으로서 경제자립을 가하여 후진사회를 극복하고 선진국으로서 도약을 가능케하였다. 이어 제4차 경제개발 5개년 계획을 추진하였고, 한일국교의 정상화(1965)와 월남파병(1965), 그리고 한·미협정(1966)을 통해 한국의 국제지위를 향상시켰다.

[9] Emergence of the Yusin Regime (1972-1979)

Innovative reforms initiated by the Park Chung-hee government, including those for economic self-sufficiency, modernization, and multilateral diplomacy, resulted in rapid development of Korean society. Under the pretext of peaceful national unification and deeply rooting democracy in Korea, President Park attempted to seize power for life. By amending the constitution through various means to allow a president to serve for a third consecutive term and advocating the Yusin (Revitalization Reform) regime, Park Chung-hee became elected as the president of the Fourth Republic.

The Yusin Regime was actually a means for Park Chung-hee to permanently seize the power. It was a setback in the development of democracy in Korea. When the public's opposition and resistance gained greater force, the government completely banned any criticism and opposition.

Opposition to the Yusin Constitution spread, and First Lady Yuk Young-soo was assassinated at a Korean Independence Day ceremony on August 15, 1974. When lifetime rule by Park Chung-hee became evident, the pro-democracy movement intensified. Park Chung-hee was, nevertheless, re-elected as the president in 1978, but he was assassinated by Kim Jae-kyu on October 26, 1979.

[9] 유신체제(維新體制:1972-1979)의 등장

박정희 정부는 경제자립 · 조국의 근대화 · 다원적 외교 등 혁신적인 개혁으로 한국사회는 급속도로 발전되었다. 이에 장기집권의 구실로 조국의 평화적 통일과 한국적 민주주의의 토착화를 내세우면서 3선개헌과 유신체제를 내세워 박정희가 제4공화국의 대통령으로 선출되었다.

그러나 이러한 유신체제는 박정희의 영구집권을 위한 조치였음으로 한국민주주의 발전에 역행하는 사건이었다. 여기서 국민의 반발과 저항이 거세지자 정부는 일체의 비방과 반대를 금지하기에 이르렀다.

유신반대운동이 점차 확대되는 과정에서 1974년 광복절기념행사에서 대통령부인 육영수 여사가 피살되었다. 그러나 대통령의 영구집권이 사실화됨으로서 민주화를 요구하는 시위가 격렬해지는 과정에서 1978년 박정희는 대통령에 당선되었으나 1979년에 김재규에게 저격당해 숨졌다.(10.26사건)

[10] Economic Development of the Republic of Korea

After seizing power by a military coup d'etat, Park Chung-hee was heavily criticized for his military rule, but he effectively oversaw the execution of his economic policies and transformed South Korea from an underdeveloped country into a promising industrialized power. Korea increased its exports by leaps and bounds, developed its heavy and chemical industries, and became a role model for other developing countries. Korea's stature in the international community improved substantially. Despite criticism for dictatorial rule, Park Chung-hee inspired the rise in national power and national spirit of self-reliance in the name of eradicating poverty and increasing economic growth. Foreign capital and technology were introduced to develop industries, which laid a foundation for export-led economic growth. This provided critical opportunities for Korea to escape from poverty and put itself on the path toward becoming an advanced nation.

[11] Miracle on the Han River

The Park Chung-hee government was roundly criticized for the military coup d'etat in its early days and for authoritarian rule later, but its tremendous achievements in economic development and diplomatic policy cannot be denied. The Park Chung-hee

[10] 대한민국의 경제 발전

5·16 쿠테타로 집권한 박정희 정부는 군사정권이라는 비난을 받았지만 경제 정책을 성공적으로 완수함으로써 한국은 후진국에서 벗어나 선진국 대열에 들어서게 되었다. 수출 증대와 중화학 공업을 개발하여 개발도상국의 발전에 모델이 되었으며, 경제적 번영을 바탕으로 국제적 지위가 향상되었다. 박정희 정부는 독재 정치라는 비판 속에서도 빈곤타파와 경제성장이라는 구호 속에서 국력신장과 주체적인 민족정신을 고양시켰다. 특히 외국자본과 기술을 도입하여 공업을 발전시키면서 수출주도의 경제발전을 꾀하여 빈곤타파에 결정적인 계기를 마련하여 선진국 도약의 발판을 마련하였다.

[11] 한강의 기적

박정희 정부는 초기에는 군사 쿠테타, 후기에는 독재정권이라는 비난을 받았으나, 경제

administration (1961-1979) initiated the Fourth Five-Year Economic Development Plan and saw Korea's exports reach US20 billion in 1981, which compares starkly with only US$33 million in 1960. Korea was able to realize world-class efficiency and self-reliance through the growth of its heavy chemical industries. The economic prosperity that Korea achieved in record time is often dubbed the "Miracle on the Han River."

In 1960, the per capita GNP of South Korea was only half of that of North Korea (US$79 vs. US$137). South Korea caught up with North Korea in 1970. By 1978, the per capita GNP of South Korea was nearly twice as high as that of North Korea (US$1406 vs. US$784). Since then, South Korea has continued to grow at a rapid rate, and comparison with North Korea is no longer a useful exercise.

Owing to such economic growth, the Gyeongbu Expressway opened in July 1970 and Seoul Subway Line 1 went into operation in August 1974. Then, in 1977, Korea achieved US$10 billion in annual exports for the first time, raising the pride of the Korean people and allowing Korea to emerge as an economic power.

발전과 적극적인 외교정책에는 큰 업적을 남겼다. 박정희 정권(1961-1979)은 제4차의 경제개발 5개년 계획이 추진되어 수출량이 1960년의 3천3백만불에 불과하였으나 1981년에는 200억불에 이르렀으며 중화학공업의 성장으로 능률과 자립을 기할 수 있었다. 여기서 우리는 '한강의 기적'을 보게 되었다.

그러므로 국민 1인당 GNP가 1960년도에는 남한이 북한의 절반수준(79:137)이었으나 70년도에는 대등하게 되었고, 1978년에는 남한이 북한의 배(1406:784)가 되었다. 그 이후 남한의 경제 발전으로 북한과 비교를 할 수 없게 되었다.

이러한 경제성장에 따라 1970년 7월에는 경부고속도로의 개통, 1974년 8월의 서울 시내 지하철(제1호선)개통, 그리고 1977년 수출 100억$ 달성 등은 한국민의 자존심을 부추기는 계기가 되었으며, 경제대국으로 도약하기에 이르렀다.

[Photo] Gyeongbu Expressway
[사진] 경부고속도로

[12] Realization of the People

Such rapid economic development in Korea was, not surprisingly, attended by some side-effects. Korea's reliance on the U.S. market increased, and the economy had become heavily dependent on the conglomerates. The economic reliance on the conglomerates resulted in great imbalances in development. Most notably, the gap between the urban areas and rural areas widened and the disparity in income distribution became even more extreme.

At this time, the Saemaeul Movement, which called for diligence, self-reliance, and cooperation to improve the situation in rural areas, was extended to urban areas to raise the awareness of the people. This movement increased the momentum for social development in Korea in the 1970s, and it also helped sustain Park Chung-hee's Yusin regime. In addition, in an attempt to establish the national identity, the Park Chung-hee government enacted the Charter of National Education in 1968 and emphasized the importance of education on Korean history to highlight the significance of the people and nation to the Korean people. Despite criticism for the Yusin dictatorship, this allowed Park Chung-Hee to build the self-awareness and confidence of the people and provided a mental foundation for economic development.

[12] 국민의 자각

이러한 남한의 경제발전은 그에 따른 부작용도 있게 마련이다. 특히 미국의 의존 심화, 재벌중심에서 오는 산업불균형, 도시와 농촌의 격차심화, 도시인들의 빈부격차 등 사회문제가 발생하였다.

여기에 낙후된 농촌사회의 환경개선을 위한 '새마을 운동'은 근면·자조·협동을 바탕으로 도시에 까지 확대되어 국민의식 변화를 꾀하였다. 다만 이 운동이 70년대 한국사회발전의 원동력은 되었으나 박정희의 유신체제를 도와준 결과가 되었다.

이와 병행하여 박정희 정부는 민족주체성의 확립을 위한 시도로서 「국민교육헌장」(1968)을 제정한 후, 국사교육을 강조하여 우리 국민에게 민족과 국가의 의미를 부각시켰다. 따라서 유신독재라는 비판 속에서 국민의 자각과 자신감을 불러 일으켜 경제발전의 정신적 바탕이 되었다.

[13] Change in North Korea in the 1960-70s

In the 1960s, when Park Chung-hee was in power in South Korea, Kim Il-sung exercised dictatorial rule over North Korea. Through the Four Major Military Policies, the entire population of North Korea was militarized and all the country was fortified. Moreover, when Stalinism was denounced and a wave of revisionism ran rampant in the Soviet Union and the Cultural Revolution (1966-1968) raged in China, Kim Il-sung tried to make himself an idol to the people through the *juche* ideology, which advocates independence (politics), self-sufficiency (economy), and self-defense (national defense). In the midst of these political changes, North Korea continued to engage in military provocations to communize South Korea and rigorously controlled every aspect of life in North Korea.

In the 1970s, North Korea had already appointed Kim Jong-il, a son of Kim Il-sung, as heir apparent and officialized the lineal succession of power. However, the North Korean economy did not perform well despite the Six-Year Plan (1971-1977) and the Seven-Year Plan (1978-1984), and the economic gap between the two Koreas widened further. Due to increasing economic hardship, many North Koreans defected and lived in difficult conditions in several Asian countries, creating an international problem.

[13] 1960~70년대 북한의 변화

남한에서 강력한 박정희 정부가 수립되었던 1960년대에 북한에서도 김일성 독재가 이룩되어 '4대군사노선'을 통해 전 인민의 무장화와 전 국토의 요새화가 이룩되었다. 더구나 소련의 스탈린 노선이 비판되면서 수정주의가 만연되고, 중국의 문화혁명(1966-1968)이 일어나자 김일성은 자주(정치)·자립(경제)·자위(국방)를 앞세운 '주체노선'으로 김일성 우상화를 이룩하였다. 이러한 북한의 정치변화 속에서 남한의 적화를 위한 무력도발을 계속하면서 북한주민을 철저하게 통제하고 있었다.

1970년대에 북한은 이미 김정일을 김일성의 후계자로 정하고 부자세습제를 공식화하였다. 그러나 북한의 경제는 6개년계획(1971-1977)과 7개년계획(1978-1984)을 추진하였지만 성과를 거두지 못하고 남북간의 경제적 차이만 커지게 되었다. 이러한 경제적 어려움으로 많은 탈북자들이 발생하여 아시아 여러나라에서 비참한 생활을 하고 있어 현재 국제문제가 되고 있다.

[14] Emergence of a Military Government in South Korea and Progress in Democratization

Despite its achievements in economic development, Park Chung-hee's Yusin regime was a constant target of criticism for its authoritarian nature. After he was assassinated in 1979, Choi Kyu-ha was elected president, but a new military government led by Chun Doo-whan soon seized power. The "Spring of Seoul" Movement, set off by the Democratization March in May 1980, led to a pro-democracy civil uprising in Gwangju, but it was crushed by the new military regime, and Chun Doo-whan's military government (1981-1988) was established. During this period, the Fifth Five-Year Economic Development Plan (1982-1986) was implemented. It was designed to bring greater stability, efficiency, and balance, and it placed less emphasis on rapid economic growth.

The Roh Tae-woo government (1988-1993) was founded in 1988. This period witnessed the fall of the Berlin Wall (1989), the breakup of the Eastern Bloc (the dissolution of the USSR), and the end of the Cold War (1989), and it triggered the democracy movement in the economic realm. Korea was not immune to the winds of change. With the successful hosting of the 1988 Summer Olympic Games in Seoul, the international status of South Korea had improved significantly.

The democratization movement had begun to sweep through Korea, spurring professors and middle and high school teachers to take action en masse. The

[14] 남한의 군사정부 출현과 민주화 진전

박정희의 유신체제는 경제발전에도 불구하고 독재라는 모순을 피할 수 없었다. 1979년 박정희가 피살된 후 최규하가 대통령이 되었으나 곧바로 전두환의 신군부가 권력을 장악하였다. 1980년 5월 민주화 대행진으로부터 시작된 '서울의 봄' 운동은 광주민주항쟁으로 이어졌으나 신군부의 무력진압으로 전두환 군사정부(1981-1988)가 탄생하였다. 이 시기에 제5차 경제개발계획(1982-1986)을 통해 안정·능률·균형을 제시하여 성장보다 안정을 추구하였다.

이어 1988년에는 노태우 정부(1988-1993)가 탄생하였다. 그러나 이 시기에 베를린 장벽의 붕괴(1989), 동구의 해체(소련연방해체), 그리고 냉전의 종식(1989)이 계속되면서 경제적으로 민주화운동이 적극화 되어가면서 국내에도 그 영향이 미치게 되었다. 그러나 이때(1988)에 올림픽을 성공적으로 개최하여 한국의 국제적 위상은 크게 높아졌다.

이러한 민주화의 물결은 대학교수 및 중등학교 교사들의 집단적인 움직임으로 나타나 1986년 고려대 교수들로부터 시작된 시국선언문의 발표로 더욱 확대되었다. 이어 대학생들

movement spread further when the faculty of Korea University announced a declaration of the state of affairs in 1986. Then, university student protests for democracy erupted all over Korea. On the political front, a three-party system emerged with the Democratic Liberal Party (a merger of the Democratic Justice Party, Reunification Democratic Party of Kim Young-sam, and Democratic Republican Party of Kim Jong-pil), Democratic Party (a merger of the Peace and Democracy Party of Kim Dae-jung and a faction of the Democratic Party of Lee Ki-taek), and United People's Party (Chung Ju-yung).

Although the Roh Tae-woo government was established through a referendum, it could not escape the shackles of a military government and faced political difficulties as the people demanded democracy and autonomy. Economic growth slowed and civil movements and labor unions gained power as they were backed by opposition groups. In the end, these challenges accelerated the development of democracy in Korea and led to the establishment of the civilian government (Kim Young-sam).

[15] Change in North Korea in the 1980-1990s

In North Korea, the 1980s was a period for consolidating Kim Jong-il's authority. Unlike Kim Il-sung, he did not have any notable achievements. Therefore, many attempts were initiated to idolize him. When Kim Il-sung died in 1994, Kim Jong-il

의 민주 항쟁이 전국적으로 확산되었으며 국내의 정치판도도 민자당(민정당 · 김영삼의 통일민주당과 김종필의 공화당합당)과 민주당(김대중의 평민당과 이기택의 민주당의 잔류파 합당)외에 통일국민당(정주영)의 3당체제로 바뀌었다.

이와 같이 노태우 정부는 국민의 선거에 의한 탄생이지만, 군사정부의 틀을 벗어나지 못하고 국민의 민주화와 자율화 속에서 정치적 어려움을 겪게 되었다. 그러나 이 시기에 경제발전은 둔화되었고 시민운동 · 노동조합운동은 재야운동과 함께 점차 더욱 심화되어갔다. 결국 이러한 시련 속에서 한국의 민주적 발전은 가속화되어 문민정부(김영삼)를 탄생시켰다.

[15] 1980-1990년대의 북한의 변화

1980년대의 북한은 김정일 체제의 공고화하는 시기였다. 김일성과 달리 뚜렷한 업적이 없는 그를 미화하기 위한 여러 가지 노력이 시도되었고, 1994년 김일성 주석의 사망으로 부자세습이 일단락되었다.

assumed power and finalized the linear succession.

In order to overcome chronic economic stagnation and isolation in the international community, the North Korean government appealed to the people through "Supremacy of the Joseon People and Military-First Politics." Instead of making efforts to escape the continuing economic deadlock, North Korea deceived the people with closed nationalism characterized by shutting the eyes and blocking the ears of its people and pursuing a form of politics that had long been discredited throughout the rest of the world. A sharply increasing number of North Koreans defected, and the North Korean government cracked down on defection more severely than ever. North Korea became an "international orphan" and a dictatorial state more closed and oppressive than any other that had ever been seen in the world.

[16] Enhanced International Status of the Republic of Korea

As the Korean Economy developed, Korean companies and technologies made inroads into overseas markets. With the collapse of the Eastern Bloc and the USSR in the late 1980s, Korea established diplomatic ties with Russia, the Czech Republic, and Hungary, further raising its status in the international arena. Korea's international standing ratcheted up and Korea joined the ranks of the advanced nations with the successful hosting of the 1988 Summer Olympic Games and its accession to the WTO and OECD. Korea's exports of automobiles and consumer electronics soared. Korea has

김정일의 북한정부는 만성적인 경제 불황과 국제적 고립을 극복하기위해 '조선민족 제 일주의와 선군정치'로 국민을 호도하고 있다. 계속된 경제적 어려움을 벗어나려는 노력보다 는 국민의 눈과 귀를 막고 폐쇄적인 민족주의로 국제사회와는 시대착오적인 동떨어진 정치 를 계속하여 국민을 속이고 있다. 여기서 탈북자들은 날로 증가되었으며 국민적 단속은 더욱 강화되어 세계에서 '국제적 고아'로서 유례없는 독재국가가 되었다.

[16] 대한민국의 국제적 지위 향상

한국은 경제적 번영을 배경으로 기업과 기술이 해외로 진출하고 있다. 1980년대 말 동구 공산권의 붕괴로 한국은 러시아 · 체코 · 헝가리 등과 국교를 맺게 되면서 국제적 지위가 향 상되었다. 특히 한국은 1988년 서울올림픽의 성공적 개최, WTO와OECD의 가입 등으로 선 진국 대열에 들어서게 되었고, 자동차 · 전자 제품의 수출은 획기적으로 증가하였다. 1997년 에 닥친 IMF의 경제적 시련은 어느 정도 극복되었고, 국민의 정부에서 시도한 민주개혁은 큰

more or less weathered the economic setback brought on by the financial crisis of 1997, IMF. The democratic reforms initiated by the Government of the People (Kim Dae-jung government) bore significant fruit and were continued by the Participatory Government (Roh Moo-hyun government).

Korea continued to pursue economic development throughout the military regimes in the late 1980s (Chun Doo-whan: 1981-1988, Roh Tae-woo: 1988-1993). In 1982, the per capita GNP of South Korea was US$1703 vs. US$735 in North Korea. The gap widened to US$4,040 vs. US$980 in 1988. During the Kim Young-sam administration, South Korea's per capita GNP finally exceeded the US$ 10,000 while North Korea's stagnated at US$957. In 2002, after the financial crisis, South Korea recorded US$ 8900; North Korea had fallen to US$706. Korea has economically performed well by nearly every measure, and its economic success has boosted its international status as well.

[17] Advent of the Civilian Government in the Republic of Korea

The election of President Kim Young-sam in December 1992 heralded the advent of Korea's first civilian government elected by the people since the military coup d'etat in 1961. The civilian government headed by Kim Young-sam overcame the vestiges of the military regimes (Chun Doo-whan and Roh Tae-woo governments) to set democracy in place and launched bold reforms for "change, reform, and progress."

결실을 맺고 있으며, 참여정부에서도 계속되고 있다.

한국의 경제발전은 80년대 말 군사정부시절(전두환:1981-1988, 노태우:1988-1993)에도 꾸준히 계속되어 1982년에는 1인당 GNP가 남북의 차이가 1703:735$ 이였고, 1988년에는 4040:980$ 이었다. 김영삼 정부 시절에 1995년에 드디어 1만$가 넘었으며(북한은 957$), IMF 를 거친 2002년에도 8900$(남한)대 706$(북한)이었다. 이러한 한국의 경제적 성장으로 국제 적 지위도 향상되었다.

[17] 대한민국의 문민정부출현

1992년 12월 김영삼의 대통령 당선은 5.16이후 처음으로 국민의 손으로 뽑은 문민정부의 출현이었다. 이렇게 탄생된 김영삼의 문민정부(1993-1998)는 민주주의 정착을 위해 군사정 부(전두환·노태우 정부)의 잔재를 극복하고 '변화와 개혁 그리고 전진'을 위한 과감한 개 혁을 시도하였다.

203

[Photo] 1988 Seoul Olympic Games
〈Source: Korea Tourism Organization〉

[사진] 88 서울올림픽 개막식
〈사진제공·한국관광공사〉

The civilian government pursued the "creation of a New Korea." It first arrested former presidents Chun Doo-whan and Roh Tae-woo and then sought globalization through the Uruguay Round Agreement (1993), the launch of the WTO (1995), and accession to the OECD (1996). However, all of these efforts ended in a dire economic situation triggered by the financial crisis in late 1997, IMF.

[18] Development of Korean Democracy in the 21st Century
- Advent of the Civilian Government and the Government of the People -

Kim Young-sam's civilian government provided an epoch-making opportunity in the development of democracy in Korea, but experienced a grave ordeal due to the financial crisis. It was the succeeding Kim Dae-jung government, or the Government of the People (1998-2003), that opened a new chapter in Korean history by overcoming the financial crisis and further advancing democracy in the 21st century.

Sweeping reforms for economic restructuring, educational reform, encouragement of basic studies, and legalization of the teachers' union, and inter-Korean reconciliation through the "Sunshine Policy" were important initiatives. The South-North Korean Summit Meeting and the June 15th North-South Joint Declaration (Kim Dae-jung and Kim Jong-il) were followed by a reunion of families separated since the Korean War. However, skepticism over the effectiveness of the Sunshine Policy

그러나 전직 대통령(전두환, 노태우)을 구속하고 세계화를 추진하여 「우루과이라운드 협정」(1993), 「WTO출범」(1995), 「OECD 가입」(1996)등 '신한국 창조'를 모색하였으나, 1997 년 말에 IMF로 경제적 어려움을 맞게 되었다.

[18] 21세기 한국 민주주의의 발전 -문민정부와 국민의 정부 출현-

김영삼의 문민정부는 한국 민주주의 발전에 획기적인 계기가 되었으나 IMF경제위기를 맞아 큰 시련을 겪게 되었다. 그러므로 이어 등장한 김대중 정부(1998-2003)는 '국민의 정 부'로서 외환위기 극복과 민주주의의 발전을 가져온 21세기의 새 역사였다.

특히 경제계의 구조조정, 교육개혁, 기초학문의 장려, 전교조의 합법화 등 개혁정치의 추 진과 햇볕정치의 추진에 따른 남북화해의 대북포용정책 등은 큰 의미가 있었다. 특히 남북정 상회담과 '6.15 남북공동선언문' (김대중과 김정일)이 채택되고 남북이산가족의 상봉이 이어 졌으나, 햇볕정치에 대한 불신이 커지면서 국민의 정부가 추진하는 개혁정치는 큰 성과를 거

increased, and the reforms initiated by the Government of the People failed to achieve significant results. Social movements by laborers and teachers effectively influenced public opinion but also posed a number of problems due to their one-sided political nature and excessive participation in the field.

Main Points of the June 15th North-South Joint Declaration

1. The North and the South agreed to resolve the question of the country's reunification independently by the concerted efforts of the Korean nation responsible for it.
2. The North and the South, recognizing that the low-level federation proposed by the North and the commonwealth system proposed by the South for the reunification of the country are similar, agreed to work together for reunification in this direction in the future.
3. The North and the South agreed to settle humanitarian issues as early as possible, including the exchange of visiting groups of separated families and relatives and the issue of unconverted long-term prisoners, to mark August 15 this year.
4. The North and the South agreed to promote balanced development of the national economy through economic cooperation and build mutual confidence by activating cooperation and exchange in all fields: social, cultural, sports, public health, environmental, and so on.

두지 못했다. 특히 노동자 · 교사들의 사회운동은 국론결정에 긍정적인 면은 있으나, 일방적인 정치적 성향과 지나친 현장에로의 참여로 많은 문제점으로 지적된다.

6.15 남북공동선언문의 주요문자

1. 남과 북은 나라의 통일문제를 그 주인인 우리 민족끼리 서로 힘을 합쳐 자주적으로 해결해 나가기로 하였다.
2. 남과 북은 나라의 통일을 위한 남측의 연합 제안과 북측의 낮은 단계의 연방제안이 서로 공통성이 있다고 인정하고 앞으로 이 방향에서 통일을 지향시켜 나가기로 하였다.
3. 남과 북은 올해 8 · 15에 즈음하여 흩어진 가족, 친척 방문단을 교환하며 비전향 장기수 문제를 해결하는 등 인도적 문제를 조속히 풀어 나가기로 하였다.
4. 남과 북은 경제협력을 통하여 민족경제를 균형적으로 발전시키고 사회, 문화, 체육, 보건, 환경 등 제반 분야의 협력과 교류를 활성화하여 서로의 신뢰를 다져 나가기로 하였다.

[19] Advent of the Participatory Government

The Participatory Government (2003-2008) headed by President Roh Moo-hyun, who was elected in late 2002, upheld Kim Dae-jung's Sunshine Policy and continued progressive reforms. However, this caused conflicts between the conservatives and the progressives and disputes over redress of the past. Although it was not entirely satisfactory, the inter-Korean dialogue continued through the operation of tours to Mt. Geumgang and industrial collaboration at the Gaeseong Industrial Complex in North Korea. For his contribution toward improving South-North Korean relations, Kim Dae-jung won the Nobel Peace Prize, further bolstering the status of Korea.

Sadly, North Korea's nuclear program, diplomatic friction with the United States, the rise of the Right Wing in Japan, rising anti-U.S. sentiment among citizens' groups such as NGOs, and demands for progressive reforms created serious problems for Korean society. In the end, the Participatory Government failed to balance and harmonize the progressives and the conservatives, and the incumbents and the emergents, with the result that the conservative incumbents gained power.

[19] 참여정부의 출현

2002년 말에 실시된 대통령으로 당선된 노무현의 참여정부(2003-2008)는 김대중의 햇볕 정치를 계승하고 진보적인 개혁을 추진하였다. 이에 보수·진보간의 갈등과 과거청산문제에 어려움이 계속되었다. 다만 금강산 관광과 개성공단의 운영으로 미진하나마 남북간의 소통은 계속되었음으로 김대중은 노벨평화상을 수상하여 한국의 위상을 높힌 것은 사실이다.

그러나 북한의 핵문제, 한·미관계의 경직화 그리고 일본의 우익화에 따른 국제정세의 변화에다 NGO등 젊은 시민단체의 반미구호와 진보적 개혁요구가 어우러져 큰 사회문제가 나타났다. 결국 참여정부는 진보와 보수, 기성세대와 신진세력간의 조화와 융합을 상실하여 보수적인 기성세대가 정권을 잡게 되었다.

[20] Establishment of the Lee Myung-bak Government

The progressive nature of policies by Kim Dae-jung (Government of the People) and Roh Moo-hyun (Participatory Government) failed to win support from the incumbent conservative groups, and the one-sided North Korea policy did not gain support from the people. This cleared the way for the election of Lee Myung-bak as the president in the 2007 election.

The Sunshine Policy became a target of criticism and friendly relations with the U.S. were restored, which led to greater conflicts between the progressives and the conservatives. Candle-light demonstrations by citizens' organizations intensified and social unrest continued. Moreover, North Korea's program for nuclearization became an international issue, and tensions between South and North Korea heightened. The sudden death of former President Roh Moo-hyun in 2009 has prolonged the social unrest. However, actions are now being taken to overcome the economic crisis sweeping the entire world and further enhance the international status of Korea.

We have learned that extreme social conflicts only hinder the development and stability of Korean society. It is time for the people to realize that rash actions by citizens' organizations, indecisiveness in government policy, and corruption on the part of lawmakers all militate against social development. Instead of assuming an extreme stance on any issue, we need to behave wisely and promote harmony and forgiveness.

[20] 이명박 정부의 탄생

김대중(국민의 정부)과 노무현(참여 정부)의 진보적 성격은 기성보수세력의 지원을 받지 못하였고 편향적인 대북정책에 대한 국민의 지지를 얻지 못하여 2007년의 선거에서 이명박 정부가 탄생하였다.

이로서 햇볕정책에 대한 비판과 미국과의 우호가 복원되면서 진보 · 보수세력 간의 갈등이 커졌고 시민단체의 촛불시위운동이 격화되어 사회는 큰 혼란이 계속되었다. 더구나 북한의 핵문제가 국제문제화 되면서 남북간의 긴장이 조성되고 있으며 2009년 노무현 전 대통령의 불의의 서거로 사회적 불안이 가시지 않고 있다. 이에 2009년에 밀어닥친 세계적인 경제위기 극복을 위한 노력과 국제적 지위향상을 위한 시책이 보여 지고 있다.

이에 우리는 극단적인 사회갈등이 한국사회의 발전과 안정에 도움이 될 수 없다는 교훈을 얻게 되었다. 따라서 시민단체의 극단적 행동이나 정부의 우유부단의 정책, 그리고 국회의원의 무질서한 행위는 우리 사회 발전에 하등의 도움이 되지 않는다는 사실을 깨달을 때가

[21] Proud Korean Expatriate Community

The Korean people have a proud tradition of overcoming challenges through patience and diligence. Some Koreans migrated to Manchuria and the Russia Maritime Territory to escape Japanese oppression. Yet they started a new lives there, provided a base for the independence movement, and proudly upheld the spirit of the Koreans. Those Koreans who were forced to relocate to Central Asia in 1937 by Joseph Stalin maintained the soul of Koreans by referring to themselves as "Goryeo People."

There are now about seven million overseas ethnic Koreans living all around the world, which is the world's fourth largest contingent of overseas residents from any country. Highly concentrated in the U.S., China (Manchuria), Japan, and Central Asia, the overseas ethnic Koreans had to endure all manner of discrimination and unfavorable environments in foreign lands with different languages and customs and set an example to other ethnic residents.

The Koreans have always had a strong belief in education and a strong work ethic, and they have garnered tremendous respect as residents of their respective countries. They continue to preserve the spirit of the Korean people. Overseas ethnic Koreans have difficulties in balancing their duties as the residents of the countries where they live today and their identity as Koreans. However, no one doubts that they are able to address the situation wisely through their sensible judgement and

되었다. 여기 자신만이 옳다는 그릇된 자세보다 화합과 관용의 지혜가 요구된다.

[21] 당당한 해외 동포들의 세계

우리민족은 끈기와 근면으로 어려운 환경을 이겨낸 자랑스런 전통을 갖고 있다. 일제의 폭정을 피해 만주(간도)와 연해주(러시아)로 이주하여 그곳에서 당당하게 살아났으며 독립 운동의 터전을 마련하면서 당당하게 한국인의 얼을 지켜왔다. 특히 1937년 스탈린에 의해서 강제로 중앙아시아로 끌려간 동포들은 당당한 고려인으로 민족의 혼을 잊지 않고 있다.

현재 700만 명의 해외동포가 전국각지에 살고 있어 세계에서 4번째로 많은 해외교포를 갖고 있다. 특히 미국·중국(만주)·일본·중아시아에 집중되고 있는 우리 동포들은 언어와 종속이 다른 외국에서 온갖 민족차별과 어려운 환경 속에서도 꿋꿋하게 삶을 개척하여 다른 이주민족에게 모범이 되고 있다.

특히 우리 동포들은 높은 교육열과 근면한 성실성으로 그 나라의 공민으로서의 위상은

global mind-set.

Many North Korean defectors today face a great deal of humiliation and ordeals in China (Manchuria) and Southeast Asia. After witnessing their misery, the Association for Overseas Korean Education Development (Chairman Lee Ki-taek) has visited various countries and is striving to make their plight known and devise effective countermeasures to help them. This would also be helpful in understanding the new reality that Korea is becoming a multi-ethnic nation that is already home to over one million foreigners and some 300,000 ethnic Koreans with foreign nationalities.

물론 한민족으로서의 정신을 잃지 않고 있음은 자랑스런 일이라 하겠다. 우리 동포들은 그가 소속된 국가의 공민으로서의 의무와 우리민족 공동체로서 조선족으로서의 정체성(혼)을 조화시키는데 어려움이 있을 것이다. 그러나 지식과 국제 감각을 함께 지닌 우리 동포들은 이 문제를 현명하게 풀어나갈 것으로 믿는다.

최근에 북한의 탈북자들이 중국(만주)과 동남아등지에서 온갖 굴욕과 시련을 겪고 있다. 이러한 처참한 현실을 목도한 (사)해외한민족교육진흥회(이사장 이기택)에서는 각국을 순회하면서 이들의 참상을 직시하고 다각도로 그 대책을 수립하는데 노력을 경주하고 있다. 이러한 사실은 현재 한국에 체류하는 외국인이 100만 명이나 되고 있으며 외국적 동포가 30만이나 되는 다민족국가라는 우리 현실을 이해하는 데에도 큰 도움이 될 것이다.

[Photo] National Flag
[사진] 태극기

About the Republic of Korea

대한민국에 대하여

대한민국전도
0 50 100km
중 국
러시아
일 본
연변조선족자치주
제 주 도
울릉도
독도
인천광역시
대구광역시
울산광역시
부산광역시
124°
126°
128°
130°
34°
36°
38°
40°
42°

National Flag

The national flag of the Republic of Korea is officially known as the *taegeukgi*. It symbolizes the 'yin' and 'yang' concepts of Oriental philosophy.

The *taegeuk* at the center of the flag is divided exactly into halves. In the *taegeuk* pattern, the red on the top represents 'yang,' and the blue on the bottom symbolizes 'yin.' These two forces signify the concept of unyielding will, uniformity, and harmony.

The *taegeuk* is surrounded by four black trigrams, with each representing the sky, earth, fire, and water.

Geography and Climate

The Korean Peninsula is located at the eastern end of Eurasia.

China is located to the north of Korea, and the Yellow Sea is

국기

대한민국 국기의 명칭은 '태극기' 이다. 태극기는 동양철학의 '음' 과 '양' 의 개념을 상징한다.

태극기의 중심에는 태극문양이 정확히 절반으로 나누어져 있다. 태극문양의 빨간색 윗부분은 '양' 을 뜻하고 반대쪽 파란색 밑부분은 '음' 을 형상화한 것이다. 이 두 가지의 힘은 불굴의 의지, 단일성, 조화의 개념을 표현하고 있다.

태극문양은 4괘로 둘러싸여 있다. 각각의 괘는 대자연의 하늘, 땅, 불, 물을 상징한다.

지리와 기후

한반도는 유라시아 대륙의 동쪽에 위치해 있다. 황해를 경계로

214

to the west. Japan is located across the East Sea on the eastern side. About 70% of Korea's territory is mountainous, and Korea has some 3,000 islands along its coastline. South Korea is on the southern part of the Korean Peninsula and is separated from North Korea on the other part by the Demilitarized Zone (DMZ).

Korea belongs to the temperate zone and, therefore, has four distinct seasons. Although spring is brief, it is agreeable and the sunlight is pleasant. Summer is hot and humid, especially during the short rainy season called *jangma* in July. Autumn is the most beautiful season in Korea. Nature is tinged with bright shades of gold and red. Winter is cold and dry, and the snowfall is heavy. Jeju Island to the south of the Korean Peninsula features a sub-tropical climate.

People and Language

Hangeul *Hangeul* is the native alphabet of the Korean language. It consists of 10 vowels and 14 consonants. In 1443,

한국의 북쪽에는 중국이, 동쪽에는 동해를 사이에 두고 일본이 위치해 있다. 영토의 70%는 산으로 덮여 있다. 한반도 해안을 따라 3,000개의 섬이 있다. 한반도의 남쪽에 위치한 남한은 한반도의 북쪽에 위치한 북한과 DMZ(비무장지대)를 경계로 분단되어 있다.

한국은 온화한 기후지역에 속해있기 때문에 사계절이 뚜렷하게 나타난다. 봄은 짧은 편이지만 쾌적하고 햇살이 좋다. 여름은 덥고 습하며 장마철인 7월에 더욱 그러하다. 가을은 가장 아름다운 계절이며 자연은 밝은 황금색과 붉은색으로 물든다. 겨울은 춥고 건조하며 대설이 내린다. 한반도의 남쪽에 위치한 제주도에는 아열대기후의 특징이 나타난다.

사람과 언어

한글 | 한글은 10개의 모음과 14개의 자음으로 이루어져 있는

scholars at the order of King Sejong created a letter system called Hunmin Jeongeum. Before this time, the Koreans had to use Chinese characters for education and communication with each other since they did not have their own alphabet for the Korean language.

Currently, 70 million Koreans in South and North Koreas as well as 7 million Korean expatriates use *hangeul*.

In this book, the Revised Romanization standard adopted by the Korean government in 2000 is used.

Hanbok   *Hanbok* is the traditional Korean costume worn by the Korean people as everyday wear up until 100 years ago, when Western-style garments were introduced to Korea.

The men's garment consists of *jeogori* (shirt) and pants, while the women's dress consists of *jeogori* (blouse) and a skirt. Today, *hanbok* is worn at traditional festivals and celebrations such as weddings.

한국어 고유문자이다. 1443년 세종대왕을 중심으로 학사들이 모여 '훈민정음' 이라는 문자형식을 창제했다. 그 이유는 백성들이 수학하고 학문을 가르치며 서로 교류하는데 고유 문자가 없어 한문을 사용할 수 밖에 없었기 때문이다.

현재 7천 만 명의 남한과 북한의 국민들뿐만 아니라 7백만 명의 재외 한국인들이 한글을 사용하고 있다.

이 책자에는 2000년 대한민국 정부가 채택한 한글의 라틴음역 표기가 사용되었다.

한복 | 한복은 100년 전 한반도에 유럽식 의복이 전해지기 전까지 한국의 국민들이 평상시에 입던 한국의 고유 의복이다.

남자는 저고리(윗도리)와 바지, 여자는 저고리와 치마를 입는다. 현재 한복은 민족 명절이나 결혼과 같은 의식을 행할 때 입는다.

Constitution and Government

The constitution of the Republic of Korea was first enacted on July 17, 1948. The Republic of Korea declared a free, democratic society and underwent political upheaval for the development of democracy. At the center of the democratic society is the National Assembly, which plays a crucial role.

The constitution guarantees fundamental rights and personal liberty, including equality before the law, freedom of residence, the right to vote, the right to hold public office, freedom of religion, freedom of speech and the press, freedom of assembly and association, the right to a healthy and pleasant environment, and the right to pursue happiness.

Under the presidential system, state power is divided among the three branches of government: the legislature, the judiciary, and the administration.

The President is assisted by the State Council and the Prime Minister.

헌법과 국가권력

대한민국의 헌법은 1948년 7월 17일 처음으로 제정되었다. 대한민국은 민주주의 사회 및 자유주의 사회를 천명하고 국회가 중대한 역할을 하는 방향의 민주발전을 위해 정치적 격변을 겪어왔다.

헌법은 법 앞의 평등, 거주지 선택의 자유, 선거권, 공무담임권, 종교, 언론, 출판 및 집회 · 결사의 자유, 환경권, 행복추구권을 포함한 기본권과 국민의 자유를 보장한다.

대통령제에 따라 국가권력은 입법부, 사법부 및 행정부 삼권으로 구성되어 있다. 국무회의 및 총리를 포함한 국회에서 대통령을 보좌한다.

Seoul

Seoul has been the capital city of Korea for about 600 years, since the early Joseon Dynasty. Seoul is a metropolitan city with a population of over 10 million. It is an amazing city where the past and the present coexist.

Royal palaces, forts, and royal tombs, which have preserved Korea's history and legacy for centuries, are located around high-rise observation towers, high-tech industrial complexes, and business centers. Within a 10-minute walk from City Hall are royal palaces, including Gyeongbok Palace, Deoksu Palace, and Changgyeong Palace. Namsan Tower perched on the top of Namsan Mountain is one of the popular tourist attraction. Cheonggye Stream, which was restored in 2005, flows through the heart of Seoul. Insa-dong Street is widely known for art galleries and shops selling traditional handcrafts.

The entire city is surrounded by mountains, which create a beautiful natural environment where the people can get away from the city and enjoy the magnificent landscape.

서울

서울은 조선시대부터 600년 동안 한국의 수도 역할을 하고 있다. 서울은 인구수 1천만 명 이상의 대도시이다. 서울은 과거와 현재가 공존하는 놀라운 도시이다.

수세기 동안의 역사를 보유한 고궁, 성문, 왕의 고분 등이 고층 전망대, 최첨단 산업단지 및 비즈니스 센터 주위에 위치해 있다. 시청 건물에서 도보로 10분 거리에는 경복궁, 덕수궁, 창경궁과 같은 왕궁이 있다. 남산 정상에 있는 N남산타워는 관광명소 중의 하나로 꼽힌다. 2005년 복원된 청계천은 현재 서울의 중심을 흐르고 있다. 인사동 거리는 화랑과 전통 수공예품을 파는 가게로 유명하다.

도시 전체가 산으로 둘러싸여 있어 휴식을 즐기고 빼어난 경관을 감상할 수 있는 아름다운 자연환경을 조성해준다.

Economy

Over the past four decades, the Republic of Korea achieved remarkable economic development, often dubbed the "Miracle of Asia."

The Republic of Korea's high-paced economic growth began with the launch of the First Five-year Economic Development Plan in 1962. From 1962 through 2007, the GDP of the Republic of Korea rose from US$2.3 billion to US$969.9 billion. During the same period, per capita GNP soared from US$87 to US$20,045. In 2007, trade totaled US$728 billion, making the Republic of Korea the world's 11th largest trade power. The Republic of Korea became a member of the OECD (Organisation for Economic Co-operation and Development) in 1996.

The economic development of the Republic of Korea has been a result of strong government support, export-oriented growth, high-tech development, and highly-skilled human resources.

경제

지난 40년 동안 대한민국은 '아시아의 기적'으로 불리며 눈부신 경제발전을 이룩했다.

대한민국의 놀라운 경제성장은 1962년의 제1차 경제개발 5개년 계획이 추진되면서 시작되었다. 1962년에서 2007년까지 한국의 GDP는 23억 달러에서 9,699억 달러까지 성장했고 1인당 GNP는 87달러에서 20,045달러까지 증가했다. 2007년 대한민국은 교역량 7,280억 달러를 달성해 전세계 11위를 차지했다. 대한민국은 1996년 OECD(경제협력개발기구)에 가입했다.

지금까지 대한민국의 경제발전은 강력한 국가적 지원, 수출 지향적 성장전략, 첨단기술 발전, 숙련된 고급인력이 뒷받침해왔다.

또한 대한민국은 전국적으로 보급되어 있는 광역 인터넷과 같은 정보 인프라 기술이 발전된 강국으로 유명하다.

In addition, the Republic of Korea is an IT power well advanced in IT infrastructure technology such as broadband Internet, which is used extensively throughout the nation.

In order to renew itself as a hub for regional business in Northeast Asia, the Republic of Korea continues to improve its business environment.

World Heritage in Korea

Korean history began with the state of Gojoseon, which was founded in 2333 B.C. Over the nearly 5,000 years of its history, Korea created a unique culture based on the rich cultures and traditions of the Asian continent.

So far, eight important historical and natural properties of the Republic of Korea have been inscribed on the World Heritage List (Seokguram Grotto and Bulguksa Temple, Jongmyo Shrine, Haeinsa Temple Janggyeong Panjeon, Changdeokgung Palace Complex, Hwaseong Fortress, Gochang, Hwasun and Ganghwa

대한민국은 동북아시아 지역 비즈니스 발전의 새로운 중심지로 거듭나기 위해 기업환경을 개선시켜 나가고 있다.

한국의 세계문화유산

대한민국의 역사는 기원전 2333년에 건국된 고조선에서 비롯된다. 5000년의 역사 동안 대한민국은 풍부한 대륙의 문화를 통해 고유의 문화를 발전시켜 왔다.

현재까지 8개의 유물이 유네스코의 세계문화유산으로 등재되었다(불국사와 석굴암, 종묘, 해인사장경판전, 창덕궁, 수원화성, 고창, 화순, 강화의 고인돌 유적, 경주역사유적지구, 제주화산섬과 용암동굴).

Dolmen Sites, Gyeongju Historic Areas, and Jeju Volcanic Island and Lava Tubes).

Bulguksa Temple Bulguksa Temple was built in Gyeongju in 774 during the Silla Dynasty. Its architectural style became the prototype for Buddhist temples built later.

Seokguram Grotto Seokguram Grotto is an artificial grotto made from white granite. With the Sakyamuni Buddha statue sitting at the center, 38 Buddha statues stand along the wall of the rotunda. Seokguram Grotto is a masterpiece of architectural style, mathematics, geometry, religion, and art of the Silla Dynasty.

Jongmyo Shrine Jongmyo Shrine houses the ancestral tablets of the kings and queens of the Joseon Dynasty.
Rituals are held on the first Sunday of May each year. Traditional court music and ceremonies performed at the rituals are designated as Intangible Cultural Property No. 1 and No. 56.

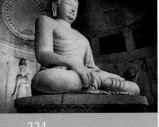

불국사 | 불국사는 774년 신라시대 때 경주에 건축되었다. 불국사의 건축양식은 이후 사찰건축의 토대가 되었다.

석굴암 | 석굴암은 백색의 화강암재를 사용하여 인공으로 석굴을 축조하고 둥근 형태의 내부 공간에는 석가여래불상을 중심으로 38체의 불상을 조각하였다. 석굴암은 건축양식, 수학, 기하학, 종교 및 신라시대의 예술에 대한 지식이 집대성되어 있는 곳이다.

종묘 | 종묘는 조선왕조 역대 왕과 왕비의 신주를 모신 사당이다. 의식은 매년 5월 첫째 일요일에 거행된다. 의식에서 연주되는 기악과 제례는 무형문화재로 등록되었으며 중요무형문화제 제1호와 제56호로 지정되었다.

Haeinsa Temple Janggyeong Panjeon Janggyeong Panjeon is the depository for the Tripitaka Koreana Woodblocks at Haeinsa Temple. Built in 1488, the buildings of Janggyeong Panjeon are completely original: they have never been destroyed by fire or attacks at time of war.

Changdeokgung Palace Changdeokgung Palace is one of five royal palaces located in Seoul. Its layout is not symmetrical or linear; instead, the buildings are laid out in harmony with the surrounding natural topography. Changdeokgung Palace is a prime example of ancient royal palace architecture and landscape gardening with artificial ponds. Trees aged over 300 years and pavilions are in perfect harmony with the surrounding landscape.

Hwaseong Fortress Located in Suwon, Hwaseong Fortress was built by King Jeongjo in memory of his father, who died amid factional strife. It was designed by Jeong Yak-yong, one of major leaders of *silhak* (practical learning).

장경판전 | 장경판전은 해인사의 팔만대장경을 보존하는 보고로서 1488년에 만들어져 이후 화재나 전쟁으로 인해 한 번도 훼손된 적이 없다.

창덕궁 | 서울에 위치한 5개의 왕궁 중의 하나이며 건물배치가 대칭형이나 축 형태가 아니라 주위 자연지형과 조화를 이루도록 건축되어 있다. 창경궁은 고대 왕궁건축과 연못이 있는 조원시설 건축술의 대표적인 실례이다. 300년 된 나무와 여러 개의 정자는 주위 경관과 조화를 이룬다.

수원화성 | 수원화성은 수원에 위치해 있으며 정조대왕이 당쟁에 휘말려 생을 마감한 아버지를 위해 효심의 표시로 축성했다. 화성은 대표적 실학 사상가 중의 한 명인 다산 정약용의 설계를 바탕으로 축조되었다.

Gochang, Hwasun and Ganghwa Dolmen Sites The Gochang, Hwasun and Ganghwa Dolmen Sites were inscribed on the World Heritage List in 2000.

Gyeongju Historic Areas Gyeongju served as the capital of Silla for one thousand years. All of Gyeongju and its vicinity are described as a "museum without walls" because of the huge number of historic monuments and remains concentrated there.

Jeju Volcanic Island and Lava Tubes Jeju Volcanic Island and Lava Tubes cover a land area of 18,846 hectares. Featuring beautiful and extraordinary scenery, Jeju Island is a veritable museum of geological processes.

The Royal Ancestral Ritual in the Jongmyo Shrine and its Music, the Pansori Epic Chant, and Gangneung Danoje Festival are inscribed as World Intangible Heritage. The Hunmin Jeongeum Manuscript (*The Proper Sounds for the Instruction of the People*), *The Annals of the Joseon Dynasty*,

고창, 화순, 강화의 고인돌 유적 | 고창, 화순, 강화의 고인돌 유적도 2000년 유네스코의 세계문화유산으로 등재되었다.

경주 | 경주는 신라시대 천 년 동안 수도의 역할을 해왔다. 경주시 전역과 주변지역은 '벽 없는 박물관' 이라고 불린다. 이 지역에 역사적 기념비와 유물이 집중되어 있기 때문이다.

제주화산섬과 용암동굴 | 제주화산섬과 용암동굴은 18,846 헥타르 지역에 펼쳐져 있다. 아름답고 빼어난 경관을 자랑하는 제주도는 지구의 역사적 발전과정을 잘 보여주고 있다.

이 외에도 유네스코는 조상들에게 제사를 지내는 종묘제례와 제사 동안 연주하는 종묘제례악, 서사시적 음악장르인 판소리, 강릉단오제는 '인류구전 및 무형유산걸작' 으로 선정하였다. 훈민정음

Seungjeongwon Ilgi: the Diaries of the Royal Secretariat, and *Jikjisimcheyojeol* (the oldest extant book printed using movable metal type in 1377) are registered as documentary heritage in the Memory of the World.

The Korean Wave

The Korean Wave is spreading to Asia, Europe, and the U.S. It refers to the popularity of Korean pop culture. One of the most important stars of the Korean Wave is Bae Yong-jun, who gained popularity with his romantic image in *Winter Sonata*. He is a major celebrity welcomed in Japan, China, and many other countries. *Jewel in the Palace*, the most popular TV drama recently aired, caused numerous people to take strong interest in Oriental medicine and royal court cuisine.

The surge of the Korean Wave has helped promote not only Korean popular songs but also Korean cinema. Many Korean artists have won great popularity and fame worldwide through

(백성을 가르치는 바른 소리), 조선왕조실록(조선왕조 연대기), 승정원일기, 직지심체요절(1377년 금속활자로 인쇄된 가장 오래된 책)이 세계기록유산으로 등록되어 있다.

한류 혹은 '한국의 물결'

한류는 아시아, 유럽국가 및 미국에서 확산되고 있으며 한국의 대중문화에 대중들이 관심을 갖는 문화현상이다. 대표 한류스타로는 '겨울연가'에 출연해 로맨틱한 이미지로 대중들에게 다가간 배용준이 있다. 일본, 중국과 여타 국가에서도 환영 받는 스타이다. 최근 가장 인기 있는 드라마인 '대장금'을 통해 사람들이 한의학과 궁중음식에 관심을 갖게 되었다.

한류의 인기는 한국의 대중가요뿐만 아니라 영화산업 활성화에

their creativity and outstanding talent.

Paik Nam-june was widely acclaimed throughout the world as a pioneer in a new genre of artistic expression called video art. Composer Yun I-sang, violinist Chung Kyung-wha, and soprano Jo Sumi are supported and recognized widely all around the world.

Traditional Food

Korean food is known to be very healthy because of its high nutritional value and fermented ingredients. It is recognized for protecting the body from various diseases.

Kimchi is the most representative Korean food and is served as a side-dish at all meals. Enriched with vitamins and minerals, kimchi is made by flavoring salted cabbage with a mix of various seasonings and vegetables.

The most popular dishes among foreigners are *galbi* and

도 기여했다. 많은 한국의 예술인들이 자신의 창작력과 재능을 통해 세계적인 인기와 영광을 누리게 되었다.

백남준은 비디오아트라는 새로운 표현예술 형식의 선구자로서 전세계적으로 명성을 인정받았다. 작곡가 윤이상, 바이올리니스트 정경화, 소프라노 조수미는 전세계적으로 압도적인 지지와 인정을 받고 있다.

전통음식

한국음식은 영양가가 뛰어나고 발효성분이 많아서 건강한 음식이고 여러 가지 질병으로부터 보호해주는 음식으로 인정받고 있다.

김치는 한국의 가장 유명한 음식이다. 김치는 소금에 절여 발효시킨 배추와 여러 가지 채소를 혼합한 것이며 모든 음식에 반찬으로

bulgogi. *Galbi* is beef short ribs grilled on charcoal. *Bulgogi*, also known as "Korean barbecue," is made by marinating thin slices of beef in a sauce primarily made of soy sauce, sesame oil, garlic, and many other seasonings.

Other famous Korean dishes include *bibimbap* (a mixture of rice, vegetables, egg, and chili paste), *doenjang jjigae* (soybean paste stew), *nangmyeon* (cold noodles) and *samgyetang* (ginseng chicken soup).

Sports

According to books on Korean history, the Korean people enjoyed traditional sports such as *taekwondo* or *ssireum* (Korean wrestling). *Taekwondo* originated in Korea and was made an official sport of the Olympic Games for the first time at the 2000 Summer Olympics in Sydney.

The Republic of Korea successfully held the 1988 Summer Olympics in Seoul and the 2002 Korea-Japan World Cup. In

내놓는다. 김치는 비타민과 미네랄이 풍부하다.

외국인들 사이에서 가장 인기가 좋은 음식은 갈비와 불고기이다. 갈비는 숯불 위 석쇠에 구워낸 소 등뼈이다. '한국식 바비큐'라고 불리는 불고기는 고기에 얇게 칼집을 내서 참기름, 마늘 등 여러 가지 양념이 들어간 간장 소스에 재워 요리한다.

이밖에 유명한 한국 요리는 비빔밥(밥, 채소, 계란, 고추장을 섞은 요리), 된장찌개, 냉면, 삼계탕이 있다.

스포츠

역사서에 보면 한국인들은 태권도나 씨름 같은 전통 스포츠를 즐겼다고 나와있다. 한국에서 처음으로 탄생한 태권도는 2000년 시드니에서 개최된 올림픽 경기에서 정식 종목으로 채택되었다.

2002, the Republic of Korea became the first Asian country ever to make the semi-finals at the World Cup, the world's most important soccer tournament.

Today, Korean athletes compete against top-notch players at international competitions in such sports as baseball, golf, archery, shooting, table tennis, sprints, figure skating, and swimming.

한국은 1988년 올림픽 및 2002년 한국과 일본이 공동주최한 월드컵을 성공적으로 진행했다. 한국은 축구경기의 최정상이라 할 수 있는 월드컵에서 2002년 아시아 국가 중 최초로 준결승전에 진출했다.

현재 한국선수들은 야구, 골프, 양궁, 사격, 탁구, 단거리 육상, 피겨스케이팅, 수영과 같은 종목의 국제경기에서 최고의 선수들과 실력을 겨루고 있다.

Shin Hyong Sik

신 형 식

Profile | 경력

- B.A./M.A. Department of History, Seoul National University College of Education
  서울대학교 사범대(역사과)와 동 대학원(사학과) 졸업
- Ph.D, Department of History, Danguk University
  단국대학교 대학원(사학과)에서 문학박사학위 취득
- Professor at Ewha Womans University, Department of History (1981-2003)
  이화여자대학교 사학과 교수 역임(1981-2003)
- Former Member of the National Institute of Korean History and
  the Former Chairman of the Paeksan Society
  국사편찬위원회위원 및 백산학회 회장
- Chairman of the City History Compilation Committee of Seoul
  현재 서울시사편찬위원회 위원장

Publications | 저서

- A Study of Samguk Sagi (Iljogak, 1981)
  〈삼국사기연구〉 (일조각, 1981)
- A New Study of Ancient Korean History (Iljogak, 1984)
  〈한국고대사의 신연구〉 (일조각, 1984)
- The History of Silla (Ewha Womans University Press, 1985)
  〈신라사〉 (이화여대출판부, 1985)
- A Study of Unified Silla (Samjiwon, 1990: Japanese translation published, 1993)
  〈통일신라사연구〉 (삼지원, 1990:일본어 번역출간, 1993)
- The History of Baekje (Ewha Womans University Press, 1992: Japanese translation published, 1994)
  〈백제사〉 (이화여대출판부, 1992:일본어 번역출간, 1994)
- A Comparative Study of the Historical Views of South and North Korea (Sol Publishing, 1994)
  〈남북한 역사관의 비교〉 (솔출판사, 1994)
- An Investigative Survey of Goguryeo Historical Sites in Japan (National Institute of Korean History, 1996)
  〈집안 고구려유적의 조사연구〉 (국사편찬위원회, 1996)
- The History of Ancient Korea (Samyoungsa, 1999: Japanese translation published, 2009)
  〈한국의 고대사〉 (삼영사, 1999:일본어 번역출간, 2009)
- The History of Studies on Korean History (Samyoungsa, 1999)
  〈한국사학사〉 (삼영사, 1999)
- Traditional Korean Culture and Awareness of History (Samjiwon, 2001)
  〈한국전통문화와 역사의식〉 (삼지원, 2001)
- The Silk Road of the Silla People (Paeksan Society Resource Center, 2002)
  〈신라인의 Silk Road〉 (백산자료원, 2002)
- The History of Goguryeo (Ewha Womans University Press, 2003)
  〈고구려사〉 (이화여대출판부, 2003)
- The History of Silla (Juryuseong Publishing Company, 2004)
  〈신라통사〉 (주류성, 2004)
- An Investigative Study on Silla Remains in the Chinese Southeast Coastal Area (Jang Bo-go Society, 2004)
  〈중국동남연해지역 신라유적조사〉 (장보고기념회, 2004)
- Introduction to Korean History (Ewha Womans University Press, 2005)
  〈한국사입문〉 (이화여대출판부, 2005)
- Foreign Relations of Baekje (Juryuseong Publishing Company, 2005)
  〈백제의 대외관계〉 (주류성, 2005)
- New Perception on Ancient Korean History (Juryuseong Publishing Company, 2009)
  〈한국고대사의 새로운 인식〉 (주류성, 2009)